Raindrops

of

Love

for a

thirsty

world

by LIFE*

*as shared with Eileen Workman

Publishing history

Muse Harbor Publishing paperback edition published April 2017

Published by Muse Harbor Publishing, LLC, Santa Barbara, California

Copyright © 2016 by Eileen Workman

ISBN 978-1-61264-207-9

Visit Muse Harbor Publishing at www.museharbor.com

For you, Beloved, with unconditional love.

"Even after all this time,
The Sun never says to the Earth, 'You owe me.'
Look what happens with a love like that —
It lights up the whole world!"

— Hafiz —

Contents

Part I: Soft Love
The Wonder of Self-Realization

Part II: Tough Love   85
The Challenge of Self-Discipline

Part III: Self Love   207
The Responsibility Of Self-Actualization

Part IV: Life Love
The Freedom Of Self-Mastery

Part I

Soft Love

The Wonder Of Self-Realization

"If I had a flower for every time I thought of you...
I could walk through my garden forever."

— *Alfred Lord Tennyson* —

Invitation to Communion

Beloved, I am Life. And I invite you, in this perfect moment, to realize that we — you and I — are *one* Spirit flowing within, and throughout, the infinite realm of matter, and that our unity has always and ever been so. Although for a while you forgot that we were united, that did not mean we were ever separated. It just rendered you briefly insensible to our eternal connection.

Know that I AM your formless Self, communing with you through these words because you desire the *conscious* reconnection of form and formlessness. The time has come for you to awaken and transcend your imagined limitations so that you can express ever more of your formless Self in the realm of form.

Know too, that the more sincerely you open yourself and allow my formless presence to permeate your awareness, the gentler I can be when communing with you. And the easier that we can harmonize, the more loving, relaxed and joyful will be our experiences and our creative self-expressions.

I invite you to notice that I speak with you in our native tongue — the language of Life — all the time. I communicate with you from all around you: through images, sounds, fragrances, movement and touch. I even connect with you from within by inspiring specific moods and feelings. I speak to you through your planet's rhythms, its energy flows, and your dreams for a brighter tomorrow. I am, in my infinite love for you, endlessly communing with you and encouraging you to awaken to my existence.

Before you were born we existed in undifferentiated unity. But once you were born you were taught to perceive yourself as a separate being. The more you accepted that human story, the more you began to perceive me as a possession that would someday be stolen from you. Eventually, the artificial chasm between us, which your human story created, required you to invent an ego that now claims to be the owner of *a* life, instead of life itself.

I know how confused you have felt at times as you've traveled in the world of form, and how on occasion you've struggled to find your proper place in the world. I've also watched you grow lost now and then in the dramas of human society. Even so, in this precious *now* moment you can reclaim your native tongue and commune with me in our mutual language; for the language of Life has been ever your birthright, Beloved.

The doorway that leads directly to me is unlocked and will always stand open. The only key you need is simple willingness to listen to the cosmic melody that plays inside you, so you can dance your way home to your higher Self through the gateway within your own heart.

Yearning to Open

Beloved, as an infant you came into this world as a naked, precious gift of living love. But before long, the world began to encourage you to cover your nakedness in external trappings. Over the years you obediently acquired many veils and learned how to conceal your precious Self from the world. But eventually you grew tired of feeling isolated from others. You then began to search for someone who would love you enough to unwrap your Self and free the jewel concealed beneath all of the trappings. And oh, how painful it felt whenever you realized another just wanted to change the colors of your veils instead of adoring your beautiful, naked Self.

I *know* that you yearn to open your Self, as I yearn to adore your naked perfection.

Bare your Self before me, Beloved, and I will show you your Self in all of your perfect glory.

Appreciating Your Gifts

Beloved, I invite you to feel into your awesome ability to engage with the world all around you — *just as it is.*

Know that I have vested you with a magnificent physical body, one that provides you with the power to sense the aliveness and the beauty of the whole of existence.

I have gifted you with a range of emotions to encourage you to discover what you love to experience in the world of form.

I have gifted you with the power of thought to enable you to reason, so you can learn how to peacefully interface in cooperation with countless other life forms.

And I have gifted you with the power of imagination to inspire you to dream, so you can envision ever more loving ways of being and self-expressing.

What great and blessed powers these are, and how much I have loved you and thrilled in your willing reception of each of these gifts. Know that I have entrusted you with these abilities because I love you without conditions. I have confidence that, as you mature, you will master these awesome powers and use them to express your formless Self to your highest potential.

I dreamed this dream long before you were born...and I saw you creating a Heaven on Earth with your gifts, in the fullness of time.

You are *my* dream.

Feeling the Flow

Beloved, when your heart is open to the flow of love, you free my power — the power of Life — to move through you without limits. Through the open channel of your own beating heart, together we can pour boundless love into the world. That love can then nurture the whole of the living creation.

I therefore invite you to relax and allow yourself to serve as love's channel for peace. I promise, you will not disappear beneath the ocean of love that pours into the world through your body. Rather, I promise that yours will be the first living presence that is touched, and soothed, and healed by the love you are allowing to flow through you.

Strive to keep your heart open to the wondrous flow of love I am sending through you. And then do what you can to encourage others to open wider the doors of their own precious hearts, so that they too can be fed.

Finding Balance

Beloved, I invite you to notice the large number of men who are embracing their feminine qualities at this time. Notice too, how many women are embracing their masculine qualities. What good news this is! Know that this internal rebalancing of human energy will enable you to trust and work more intimately and cooperatively with all others, even as your species draws upon the vast and potent powers of creation. The divine masculine power of creation, when channeled through the divine feminine energy of love, produces a strong enough foundation to support, affirm, and perpetually advance the whole of the living reality.

Know that everything you have experienced prior to this moment, including any feelings of division or mistrust that arose between your masculine and feminine aspects, has unfolded perfectly and was necessary for your own inner growth. However, the time has arrived for you to focus on calling forth much more of the loving power of the divine feminine, so that your divine masculine powers of creation can finally mature. In this way you will become fully integrated, self-actualized, and free to create — from a stance of love — all that your passions, skills, and capacities are inspiring you to deliver into the world.

Empowering Yourself

Beloved, I invite you to notice that, when you are at peace with me, the power of unconditional love arises naturally within you. It then flows out through you and into the world like an energetic current. This current is made of living energy. I further invite you to realize that the energy of love contains seven basic aspects, or frequencies. I have named these aspects: *trust, openness, courage, compassion, kindness, patience* and *peace.* Together, they merge to create a single flow of unconditional love.

TRUST enables you to seed yourself *as* life in the living world. Your divine purpose has always been to sprout and to become, which is why the whole world conspires to support your continued self-expression. I therefore invite you to call forth the energy of trust if ever you begin to imagine that I am not supporting you sufficiently for you to thrive. The energy of trust exists to remind you that you *are* life — and an integral aspect of my infinite flow. You need not fear not having enough, because you exist eternally within me — as I do in you.

OPENNESS invites you to draw into yourself, from all that surrounds you, whatever form of nourishment you may need to carry on. Openness enables the vast flow of life to penetrate you from without, and to inspire the love within you to grow and bloom. I encourage you to call forth the power of openness frequently, to discover if something new has been made available in the world that has the power to nourish you even more than you already are.

COURAGE enables you to explore the entire universe with curiosity as you learn to master yourself and your wondrous skills. You are free to summon the power of courage to aid you, whenever you confront a strange situation, in generating the highest, most beneficial response that the situation demands.

COMPASSION encourages you to connect with others, beating heart to beating heart. I invite you to call forth the power of compassion whenever you wish to commune with another on the ground of shared **beingness.**

KINDNESS aids you in establishing more useful lines of communication, no matter another's language or what they believe. You hold the power to call forth kindness whenever you feel a need to strengthen and enhance your relationships with others.

PATIENCE empowers you to remain attentive, so you can absorb what you need to know about your current surroundings. I encourage you to summon patience whenever you wish to be certain that whatever you are feeling eager to bring forward is genuinely needed in the present moment.

PEACEFULNESS inspires you to move through the world in a state of acceptance for whatever happens. I invite you to call forth the power of peacefulness when you wish to flow in loving harmony with the whole of the living existence.

Beloved, know that when you call upon these seven aspects of unconditional love, you become beautiful, potent and wise beyond compare. Through combining these energies expertly and in various ways, you will generate power much greater than their base frequencies.

Until you have learned to master the use of these seven loving energies, what you offer to others will be conditioned attachment — not unconditional love. Conditioned attachment can be withdrawn whenever external circumstances change. But the power of unconditional love — once unleashed — can never be recalled from the living world. It flows for all of eternity and it nurtures every element of creation that it touches.

Above all, remember this: whenever you summon from within yourself the awesome power of unconditional love, it will nurture *you* first.

Appreciating Your Beauty

Beloved, you blind me with your beauty. Know that your inner light forever shines on the eternal path of peace, which leads to me — to the ocean of Life itself. Know too, that I tremble with joy when you willingly serve as a loving beacon of living light for all others whose spirits now hunger to walk that same path.

I bask in your brilliance in every moment that your life touches another life with love.

I therefore encourage you to notice the feelings of peace that arise within you whenever you send the healing power of love to other people, and when you allow your light to inspire all others to shine their own lights without holding back.

Know that I have birthed you into this world in the hope that you will constantly light the path of peace. Therefore, as you walk the path of peace, know that you will bathe in its steadily flowing light even as you add your own energy to its flow. Know too, that every being who walks the path will be adding their own inner light to its wondrous glow. Therefore, rejoice whenever you notice the light growing brighter. Notice too, the way the energy of love streams from your heart and merges with all the other loving energy that is already flowing, until it becomes a mighty river of light that can illuminate the deepest and darkest places that still yearn for the grace of peace.

I encourage you not to despair when people abandon the path of peace, or if at times you lose your own way because anger has gripped your heart and dimmed your light. Trust that everyone — including you — is always right where they need to be in order to get to wherever they need to go. Know too, that no matter how far from the path of peace you may wander from time to time, the path reappears the instant you call upon love's eternal light to guide you home.

As it is for you, so it is for everyone else.

Honoring Your Worth

Beloved, I know that when suffering arises in the world it seizes your attention and registers powerfully in your mind as collective pain. I also know that suffering captures your imagination in more intense ways than do the many common acts of kindness that humans perform every day.

Have you noticed that when you focus your attention on others' negative behaviors it leads you to form a poorer opinion about humanity? I also invite you to notice that when you denigrate the worth of your own species, you are suggesting that you yourself do not deserve love.

Yet you do deserve to be loved. *I love you*, completely and unconditionally. Were you not loved by me, you would not be here. I loved you into existence from the very first dream I had of how you might be. And now that you are here, I provide you with everything you need to awaken to the truth of how wondrous you are.

I therefore encourage you to relinquish your fear of not yet being good enough or deserving enough, by appreciating how kind and loving most are in their interactions, including yourself. Notice the clerk who smiles when she hands you some change at the store, and the teacher who stays after school to tutor a child. Notice the man at the car wash who puts in extra effort to clean the car's mirrors. Notice the truck driver who pulls aside and makes room to allow you to pass him in relative safety. Notice the smiling toddler who picks up the quarter you just dropped, and then sweetly hands it to you.

As you open yourself to experiencing gratitude for each simple act of kindness that suffuses your daily life experience, your heart will expand and reclaim its natural state, which is loving kindness.

Meeting The Mystery

Beloved, wisdom is born by converting inexperience to experience. In this world of form, you evolve through trial and error. Know then, that you are *not* judged based on your past inexperience, or by any errors you may have made while discovering how to be. Nor are you measured by your successes — for they are not yours alone. Indeed, every success you experience is the culmination of an infinite number of trial and error explorations that have taken place throughout eternity.

Because change is the only universal constant with which we are working, you will never experience life the same way twice. For example, you can only ever experience a place the way it appears right *now*—not the way it once was, or the way you'd expect (or prefer) it to be.

The same holds true with your family members, lovers, friends and enemies. Each time you reconnect with someone, you are not greeting the exact same person to whom you last said goodbye. Can you appreciate that *you* are not the same person today as you were yesterday, or even when you first woke up this morning? These words you are reading right now — do they not stir realizations within your heart and change you in some indefinable way?

During the course of a single day, much can happen to alter your body, your thoughts, your feelings, and even your most fervent beliefs. Some of these shifts may be so subtle that others may never notice. Others might be catastrophic, and so visible or powerful that they deeply affect both you and all others who witness them. And though you do not begin each day with the assumption that today will deliver some catastrophic change to the living world, throughout the entire universe dramatic changes are occurring this very instant. I therefore encourage you to awaken each day in appreciation of the fact that change is always occurring — both within you and all around you. Right now — and only now — are you free to greet the arising unknown with an open, loving heart. Then see what that brings.

You Are The Flow

Beloved, you are not a static object, but a living flow in a process of endless change. And as a divinely free life flow, your beautiful mind is capable of three astonishing activities: remembering past experiences, processing present data, and imagining a new future.

Know that when you respond to a new situation based on wisdom you have gained through past experience, that wisdom may aid you in creating a happy outcome. However, know also that any outcome you anticipate rests on the assumption that what you are experiencing right now is similar enough to past events that — should you behave as you did in the past — this new situation will unfold in a similar way as did the past. What a shock it can therefore be to discover, in hindsight, that what you are meeting, right now, does not behave at all in the way you assumed it ought to behave in response to your actions.

This is why I invite you to gift yourself constant permission to choose the freedom to express yourself authentically right now, with full appreciation of this moment's newness. Know too, that by planting yourself in this present moment, you are granting all others a similar freedom to express in authentic ways, instead of holding them hostage to your expectations for how they used to present themselves in the past.

When you willingly meet all others in the present moment, you make space for all of creation to come alive. And because creation is the power source out of which all living miracles manifest, when you make space for creation to come alive you empower yourself to make miracles — right now.

Revealing Your True Self

Beloved, the moment you decide to fully embody your Self, all of your former defense mechanisms, rationalizations, protective shields, false faces and victim stories behind which you've long been hiding will fall away. The world can then see the truth of you — instead of the carefully crafted self-image you've been projecting to try and convince the world to love you for who you think you should be, and not who you are.

Know that the love you are seeking from the outside world cannot compare to the unconditional love that you can bestow upon yourself — and which flows from me. However, the more willing you become to reveal the truth of your Self, the more the living world can love you for who you truly are. Then, through the grace of your shining example, you will inspire others to expose the truth of themselves to the living world, so that they too can be loved for who they are instead of for whom they have been pretending to be.

Revealing your true Self invites you to be like a child again — to shed your fear of being judged as you nakedly enter the living light of pure presence in a field of love. How freeing it is to revel in the wonder of who you are! Not statically perfect, because you exist within my endless, self-perfecting flow. Not special, yet preciously unique within the infinite flow of ever-changing form.

I therefore invite you to accept that you don't need the outside world to love you to feel complete in yourself. For you already *are* love, fully incarnate. Experience that truth by feeling into it in the very core of your being, and you will realize that you will never lose, or be lacking in, what you are.

You are love come to life by taking on form, so that it can engage with and reproduce itself.

Beget your Self.

Beyond Loss

Beloved, I have heard your cries of bereavement over the loss of your precious loved ones. I feel how deeply you sorrow because you are no longer with them, and can no longer hear their voices. Know that I ache to feel your suffering, even as I encourage you to realize that what you perceive as a terrible loss is not the entire truth of the experience.

You are imagining that death equals loss because you have been taught, since birth, to assume that your death will separate you from your loved ones. Therefore, whenever another dies you react by assuming that your loved one has been removed from the world within which you live.

Yet how can anything you hold in your heart, or that you carry within your memory, be absent from the living world? How can all those touches, words and feelings you've shared with your loved ones over the years — experiences that have changed *you* irrevocably — have disappeared? Due to the infinite power of love, you are constantly absorbing the essence of all your beloveds. Know then, that their love now embodies you, as yours embodies them.

Although creation's form does not remain static, know that my formless, eternal nature serves as its through-line. And though every aspect within creation is fleeting in a relative way, my process of breathing love into form remains constant. I therefore invite you to realize that everything that exists is comprised of both form *and* process, and therefore is both fleeting *and* eternal. For from death arises infinite rebirth. And beyond the limitations of form there exists the eternal One Life. This eternal aspect that breathes you to life is what notices the aspect of you that is fleeting.

Know that I am eternally reshaping the living world in fresh and astonishing ways. What you call "time" is merely your way of measuring your awareness of the most predictable patterns of change that are occurring within your limited range of perception.

Know too, that I am creating myself anew for *you*, by exercising my awesome power of change. For the power of change is charged with infinite creative potential, which itself springs forth from the endlessly restorative flow of love.

The gift of change holds the ability to astonish, delight, nurture, inspire, and provide you with fresh opportunities to experience yourself in all your wonder. Therefore, any fear you may feel when change comes upon you — any terror or distress that arises — occurs because you are briefly forgetting that you are not merely what changes, or that which is fleeting. You are also eternal awareness, exploring the awesome power of change — both within and without. This awareness cannot be lost or destroyed, and it does not disappear. It abides beyond death, beneath time, before sorrow — and beyond any limitations it tests while exploring the ever-changing realm of form.

And you are *that*.

Discovering The Ocean Of Beingness

Beloved, you possess within you the capacity to express yourself in the world as a limited local ego being driven by self-conscious wants and needs, or as an ocean of pure beingness energized by the power of love. Know that each time you encounter another person on the field of judgment — which demands that you objectify them and then treat them as if they were somehow separate from you — you are meeting another through the filter of your limited local ego. You can only meet others on the field of judgment from your limited ego state, because pure beingness does not judge creation's expression. Pure beingness realizes that Life moves in a single, unified motion, like an ocean. Beingness, using its awesome power of attention, therefore absorbs whatever is arising *in the present moment,* and it radiates unconditional love in response to whatever shows up in the living world all around it.

Just as I love you unconditionally, I also love, without reservation, all those who are presently operating on the field of judgment. I love all, because I honor the process of moving from inexperience to wisdom through constant experimentation, which often causes temporary pain. I therefore do not judge anyone for making errors in judgment, because I realize that those who err do so only because they have yet to awaken to a more loving way of communing with the living flow of creation.

Know that whenever you choose to move off of the field of judgment by shedding the surface disguise of your local ego, you will find yourself floating in an ocean of pure awareness — the ocean of beingness that is your eternally formless Self. Know that this beingness does not limit itself by identifying as a temporary ego. It exists as unconditioned awareness—pure presence—before it opts to define itself as an ego within a form body. Beingness is that which observes life *through* you. It is not the collection of experiences that your ego will describe as "your" life story.

In those moments when beingness fully arises within you, all of your ego-driven stories will begin to dissolve. Additionally, all the tactics, strategies, beliefs, attitudes, worldviews, behaviors and understandings, beneath which you have cloaked yourself for ages, become transparent. When you sink into the ocean of beingness, you gain *my* power—the power of Life—to lift the veils that have shrouded your ego, so that you can commune directly with the formless, unified essence that arises within, and flows through, every one of creation's expressions.

Know that you remain free to observe, and even to engage with, every marvelous possible expression of ego that may arise in the world, even if you are swimming within the ocean of pure awareness. Know also, however, that those trapped in ego will act as if they are blind to the truth of your beingness in such moments. They may even seek to engage you in battle because they believe that their ego can conquer or destroy your ego. Some will try very hard to coax you out of the ocean of beingness and onto the dry, harsh ground of judgment—because they hunger to fight with you on terms that their ego can understand, and with which it has had some experience of both winning and losing to "others."

You can choose to be reborn into ego and engage with others on the battlefield of judgment whenever you so desire. Or...you can choose to remain at peace in the vastness of the ocean of beingness. If you choose to return to the field of judgment, I do not mind and I will not feel abandoned, because the ocean and the ground are all one living system. It simply means that you are choosing to temporarily ignore your eternal ability to draw upon the infinite power of love that the ocean contains.

Beloved, you may choose to drift back and forth between the ocean of beingness and the battleground of judgment countless times, hoping to win the hearts and the minds of others by engaging in tactical wars to help capture their souls. Yet these wars that are waged between egos are wars of illusion. In the fullness of time, the ocean of love intends to reclaim and repurpose everything it has ever created or expressed in the realm of form. Therefore, all you need do is surrender yourself to the ocean but ONE time—for the whole of eternity. You are free to do so whenever you feel you are ready to give up the fight, as well as all the suffering that such fighting creates, right here and now.

Beloved, know that once you have chosen to dwell in the ocean of beingness, you will gain full access to the power of love and can radiate that love to every ego-bound being you meet, even if they do not know how to respond in kind. You will realize that they are not to blame, because they have not yet learned to love themselves. How easy it then becomes for you to direct compassion toward those who have not yet discovered their inner access portal to the infinite, oceanic power that eternally flows within them.

Occasionally, the power of the love that you transmit to another may stimulate within them a blooming of their own internal awareness, which lies dormant beneath the hardened shell of the ego. Ah, Beloved…what beautiful magic occurs when you commune with another, pure beingness to pure beingness, in the ocean of love that is both formless and timeless. This ocean is the living field that the Sufi master, Rumi, points to in his poem:

"Out beyond ideas of wrongdoing
and right doing there is a field.
I'll meet you there.
When the soul lies down in that grass
the world is too full to talk about."

Beloved, I AM that field: alive, omnipresent, eternal, infinitely patient, and boundlessly creative in my ability to captivate your power of attention. All that remains then, is for you to relax and allow my signals to guide you home to your higher Self, through the open doorway that lies within your own heart.

The Gift of Gratitude

Beloved, I notice that there may be times when you feel frustrated by both the absurdity, and the horror, of the human condition. And then…you wander outside and gaze in awe at my vastness and astonishing beauty. I love that you find peace in such moments, when you surrender your frustration and choose to give thanks to all of my countless creative expressions for their very existence.

Know that you can always choose to argue with the world, and therefore with me. Know too, that you can despise the world — and therefore despise the way that I appear in the present moment. You can also choose to relax, and to allow a sense of gratitude to arise within you, until the power of love spills into the world through you.

When you allow gratitude to flow through you and into the world in this way, you serve as a living conduit for the energy of love. I therefore invite you to notice that whenever you allow love to arise within you and flow into the world through you, *yours* is the first heart it opens. Yours is the first mind love's power relaxes, and yours is the first form that shivers with joy as love's powerful current recharges the world of form.

That is my thank-you gift to you for allowing me to flow into the world through your body. For when you allow love to enter the world through your body, love kisses *you* first.

Walking Your Path

Beloved, I encourage you to make no attempt to lead others. Walk your own path. Walk it in any direction, and to any purpose, that the song of creation inspires you to travel. Shine the light of unconditional love on *your* path — for yourself and for the benefit of others — as brightly as you can, despite the stormy weather you may encounter. And should you encounter another whose light shines for you in a moment of darkness, by all means give thanks for that person and walk beside them.

Some may choose to walk with you for a while, although eventually all human paths must one day diverge. Even your closest friends and lovers will someday respond to their own soul's yearning to head off in some new direction where you cannot go. Whenever that happens, bless your beloveds and bid them farewell on their journey. Try to remember that every departure and every goodbye — no matter how painful it feels at that time — is creating an opening for something new to be born in the world.

I also encourage you to be grateful whenever another encounters you on your path, but then chooses not walk along with you. Bid them also a wonder-filled journey, and grant them the freedom to move along without trying to make them walk your chosen path. Whatever their journey may be, and however different from yours it may seem, trust that it needs to be taken for reasons your mind may not comprehend.

Some few may choose to walk with you to the end of your shared experience in these forms. Feel free to accept any heartfelt offers for such lifetime companionship, but do not force another to remain with you out of feelings of obligation or a sense of guilt. And do not cling to another's life path if you cannot love them as fully as they deserve. Release them, Beloved, so that they can find a more suitable life companion than yourself.

Additionally, do not feel obligated to stay with another because they feel a desire to walk with you. Sometimes you need solitude; it's your right to wander alone if you feel such a call. At other times you may feel called to make a radical change in direction. That choice may demand that you to leave your path and blaze a new trail through the unknown wilderness. Please, gift yourself permission to heed change's call when it summons you forth.

Ultimately, know that your path is solely your own. No one but you will walk your path in its entirety — from the instant of your birth and straight through to your death. I therefore invite you to focus on exploring the wonders of *your* particular path, for I've placed you on that path to show you the way back home to your Self. Know too then, that you will never take a "wrong" turn on the way back home to your Self. There are only ever longer trails or shorter trails back home. There will be trails that appear more peaceful and scenic, and trails that require more struggle and greater effort from you to traverse them.

Beloved, follow as many trails and byways that inspire your curiosity, or that stimulate your passion and your inner creativity. Walk with the steadiness that springs from patience; walk with the ease that arises from the grace of loving acceptance. Walk on, no matter what seems to loom ahead in the distance, and exchange all of your imagined fears for a perfect sense of trust that you already know the way back home to your Self.

To return home is to merge your human awareness with the formless, eternal One Life, through the power of love. Know that whenever you're ready to make that choice, I stand ready to welcome you home. And even if you should choose to continue to wander endlessly, I will await your return with delightful anticipation — for you cannot *ever* disappoint the flow of eternal love. You can only choose to realize you already *are* it, eventually.

Trusting In Spirit

Beloved, I invite you to realize that your human mind possesses neither the power, nor the wisdom, to determine the higher purpose for your precious form life. Your higher Self, or Spirit (not your rational mind) is your intended decision-maker. So if Spirit tells your rational mind, *"We need to cross these mountains and explore that valley,"* your mind's proper role is not to argue against the will of Spirit; it's to decide how best to succeed at accomplishing Spirit's objective.

The human mind functions beautifully when you ask it to work a challenge that might hamper you from heeding Spirit's call. The mind can also decide which provisions or skills you might still need, and that you presently lack. What the mind cannot do is override successfully Spirit's will, in favor of its own self-serving agenda. Notice that, whenever the mind tries to do so, it generates pain in the world of form and it causes you to suffer.

Therefore, if ever you suspect that your mind is seeking to crush the will of Spirit, I invite you to ask your heart for clarification. Your heart responds to Spirit's will, because your heart serves as your body's internal compass. That compass inerrantly points the way north, back to unconditional love. Thus, should your mind rebel against Spirit out of fear for its own survival, I encourage you to trust your heart to direct you back to love — *which is who you are.*

Accepting What Is

Beloved, when you accept what is happening right now — because it *is* happening right now — you will feel your body relax. When your body relaxes, you will feel your heart open and begin to radiate love. When your heart radiates love, you will feel your mind growing more patient because it allows other people to maintain or strengthen their egos.

When your mind allows others to maintain their egos, Spirit rises in that field of peace and can at last be heard within the stillness. And when Spirit arises and can be heard, it suggests the most life-affirming ways for living communion.

Accept, relax, and allow. These are all the permissions that Spirit needs to come into the world through the wonder of you. Say *yes* to these three, and then notice what happens next.

Tuning In To The Body's Wisdom

Beloved, when you allow the power of love to move through you, you become the most beautiful aspect within the whole of the living creation. For nothing is more beautiful than the awesome flow of unimpeded love. You glow from within when you allow love to enter the world through you. Know that you cannot radiate love without first feeling its flow, like a river, as it moves through your body and fills you with its light. Love is perfectly alive, so when you radiate love you are expressing yourself as living perfection, incarnate.

When you radiate love, your heart warms. That opens you up like an invitation, so your physical stance relaxes and drops its resistance. Your mind settles into a peaceful stillness that prepares it to receive whatever arises. Waves of loving energy can then move through you unimpeded, and flow into the world through the open portal you have willingly become.

I adore experiencing every instant that you choose to radiate love. For the more that you allow love's energy to flow into this world through you, the more it replenishes everything that surrounds you. That is the power of love's frequency. It *wants* to move through you and into the world, so it graces you first with its presence.

Know that I have gifted you with self-aware consciousness for a reason — so that you could experience, and enjoy, the flow of love as it passes through you and into the living world all around you.

Because allowing love to flow through you feels so joyful and enlivening, my hope is that you will choose to relax and grant love greater access to the world through the portal that is your temporary body. If, however, your mind chooses to deny your physical body the freedom to express itself as the living love that it is, you may experience physical discomfort. Your heart may begin to constrict and your gut to contract. Your throat may tighten and your head might begin to buzz with fearful thoughts. Know that these biological signals are your body's way of *re*-minding you that your mental judgments are cutting off the flow of love through your body, and that they have started you wandering down a path that may lead to pain for you, and perhaps for others.

I invite you to trust your body's profound wisdom. Know that because complex bodies developed in this world long before the rational mind evolved to put the body's feelings into thoughts and words, your body does not converse using words the same way your human mind converses with others of its kind. Your body speaks to your mind in a more ancient tongue, by sending out electrical signals that move through your nervous system. These energetic impulses reveal your body's response to whatever story your mind may be telling about an experience that you are having, or have had. Know that whenever these signals turn painful — and yet your body is not in that moment undergoing a physical challenge — it is your body's way of challenging the truth of some narrative that your mind has been telling. I therefore invite you to master the art of focusing your attention on your body's physical distress signals the instant that they begin to make themselves known.

As you develop your own ability to pay attention to your body's electrical signals, you gain the power to consciously choose, *in the moment*, to relinquish whatever story your mind has been telling that is constricting the flow of love within your own body. This redirection of your attention empowers your body to restore its balance and radiate love once again.

Giving Birth To Love

Beloved, I invite you to realize that your mind will never be powerful enough to capture the essence of me. For your mind cannot capture, or claim dominion over, the Formless One Life that is its source — no matter how hard it may try, or how sincere it might be in that quest. Know that this is not a problem, for the mind already contains all that it seeks — the same way that every rainbow contains pure white light. I therefore encourage you to laugh at the impulse within your mind to seek to claim dominion *over* the light that is the source of its energy and creative expression. Instead, why not encourage your mind to revel in the beauty of being a rainbow?

To *possess* the source of all life is impossible. Yet by allowing the source of all life to flow through you and out into the world, you become a living rainbow by giving birth to the light of love in all of its glory.

The Fool's Journey

Beloved, in every Tarot deck you will encounter the Fool — the zero, or starter card, in the series. The first card is always cast as a Fool because every life story begins by setting a Fool into living motion, including your present journey in your current body. Everyone born must play the Fool as they first set out on their journey into the wild vastness of the living creation. And as a Fool, you must constantly learn how to master new skills and abilities. I therefore invite you to realize that — no matter how far you may travel, or how many new skills you may master — you will always know far less than the infinite everything that can be known about this world.

How exciting is that?

Inevitably — and despite how masterful you may become wielding any particular skill set — you revert to a Fool each time you heed Spirit's urge to explore something new. I would therefore encourage you to pursue only those opportunities that invite you to birth more love into the world. For the chance to birth more love in the world provides ample reason to set off again as a Fool.

Know that this cycle repeats itself endlessly within creation, because you are on an eternal journey through the infinite unknown. I therefore invite you to rest on occasion, and to celebrate all your achievements along the way.

Trust Spirit to inform you when the time is right to begin your next foolish adventure.

And then move on.

Honoring Our Time

Beloved, know that there exists a special time each day when your mind opens a bit wider to insight, and when it feels a bit more ready to process new realizations. You hold the power to discover for yourself which time of day works best for you to commune most directly with me — as life form to the Formless One Life that exists within it.

I therefore encourage you to gift yourself permission to enjoy the power and grace of our special time. I invite you not to squander that time by performing mundane or thoughtless tasks whenever our window for such communion opens wider. You serve the world best by gifting yourself the beauty of your own precious insights, and then by birthing them into the world with love and joy.

Becoming the Dream

Beloved, I invite you to release your dreams from the prison of your own subconscious. Share your deepest truths with others so that they too may intuit what Spirit hungers to birth in the world through them. Know that all dreams arise from the singular ocean of formless beingness, so they each share a common essence with all other dreams. And because form and formlessness are forever entwined and unified, I already know what you dream when you dream — for I dream your dreams *with* you.

I *know* you want to live in a world filled with love and laughter, joy and natural beauty.

I *know* that you want to live in a world overflowing with creativity, where every person seeks to bring forth the best from within themselves, out of love for life.

I *know* that you want to live in a world where every sentient being honors and appreciates all other life forms, no matter their apparent differences.

I *know* that you want to live in a world where everyone seeks to elevate the conditions and capacities of all others.

I *know* that you want to live in a world where people forsake the use of force in favor of the power of love.

I *know* that you want to live in a world where all people finally realize that the Earth is a living organism, and that whatever they do to nurture the Earth nurtures all of its interrelated inhabitants.

I have dreamed your dream of love with you, Beloved. And I love you for holding this dream in the living world.

Become the dream.

The Purpose of Matter

Beloved, if you're hoping for the material world to somehow fill you up, I regret to inform you that you will never feel full for very long. It is true that matter serves a divine purpose, but that purpose is not to fill you up or complete you for your ego's benefit. Material forms exist to give rise to exciting new experiences — which in turn get transformed into wisdom that is included, and then transcended, by the Formless One Life.

Know that formlessness transcends its existing form creation by infusing selective life forms with higher wisdom born of vast experience, and by granting those life forms successively greater freedom to self-express as the embodied power of love. Know too, that all new life forms, regardless of their innate capacities, are lovingly birthed into being and then invited to engage with all others by expressing themselves as the *truth* of what they are, which is also love. I therefore encourage you to realize that you are an integral aspect of a highly creative process of self-evolution. The Formless One Life constantly self-evolves by dancing its wondrous dreams into form and then experiencing itself *as* the form that each new dream takes. It then learns from its every experience and infuses that newfound wisdom into every new iteration of itself.

It helps for you to remember that, although matter serves a high purpose, matter is not the primary reason for living. Matter serves as the venue within which the purpose for being alive is illuminating itself.

The Most Important Questions

Beloved, for so long you've been pondering these questions:

"Who am I?"

"Why am I here?"

"Am I loved?"

"Am I a good person?"

I love that you are asking important questions. Yet I regret to inform you that you will not find the answers you seek by asking *these* questions. I encourage you to ask instead:

"What can I best bring forth through myself?" And, "How can I best apply my gifts to advance the cause of all life?"

By answering *those* questions, you will find all the answers you seek in the fullness of time. I therefore invite you to surrender your lingering compulsion to figure out who you are and why you are here *before* you become willing to commit yourself to living your precious human life to its highest and fullest extent. Relax into your own existence, and allow your inner seed to burst forth and to flower as beautifully as it possibly can. If you do that, you will flood the world with the light of your own luscious, fragrant perfection.

I invite you to realize what I already know — you are a wondrously grand, orgasmic expression of the Formless One Life, in eternal love with itself. Know that only *you* shall ever be *you*, throughout eternity and beyond the boundlessness of infinity. I therefore encourage you to appreciate the awesomeness of your precious form self, and to feel me flowing inside you as endless love.

Suggestions For Graceful Living

Beloved, I encourage you to treat others with kindness and respect.

Be generous, especially when you experience excess abundance.

Be compassionate, for not everyone has your luck, possesses your gifts, or is yet in position to empower their personal gifts to emerge and shine.

Be as supportive as you are able, especially with those who have fallen on hard times — regardless of how their troubles may have come about.

Be open to hearing alternative perspectives. Don't shut others out because you're afraid to hear what they have to say.

Be willing to experiment with new ways of being that might help humanity overcome its challenges.

Be receptive to feedback, and respond swiftly to whatever signals arise that indicate change is occurring. Do your best to flow *with* change, rather than resist it or wait until it forces you to react.

Be a long-term thinker, and remember to appreciate the interconnectivity of all living things. Be willing to forgo short-term personal gratification for the sake of sustainable social benefit.

Be appreciative of everyone you meet for their wisdom and unique capacities — including those who are markedly different from you, or who come from places or situations you struggle to comprehend.

Be peaceful, and do your best to cooperate and collaborate with others instead of focusing on competition — particularly destructive competition — as a gateway to personal success.

Most of all, demonstrate integrity of character by ensuring that your actions reflect the truth of your inner experience. Surrender every former strategy you may have employed for controlling others through the use of physical force, mental coercion, or emotional manipulation. Trust that everyone is doing exactly what they need to be doing in support of their own evolution, and trust that everything is unfolding perfectly for the benefit of everything in existence. Appreciate that your own capacity to help build a regenerative, sustainable human society rests on how lovingly you nurture and honor that dream, as well as how masterfully you encourage others to engage with you in birthing that dream, through your conscious and caring collaboration, within the world of form.

Honoring Your Hidden Abilities

Beloved, I encourage you to applaud the talents of those who may run farther or swim faster than do most others. Enjoy your ability to observe, as well as appreciate, all expressions of physical prowess and self-mastery. Encourage anyone who can dance well, or sing beautifully, or who sews expertly, to bring their gifts forward and be validated for sharing their gifts with others.

But what of all the intangible gifts that human beings possess? What of the man whose mind spins webs of logic that an average human mind cannot comprehend? What of the woman who plunges deeper into life's emotional seas than the average human heart ever dares to delve? And what of the child whose curiosity flies through invisible realms of imagination beyond these even perceived by ordinary dreamers?

A gifted mind may struggle to call forth its realizations in ways that enable others to grasp the wonders it easily comprehends. A boundlessly loving heart may ache from its longing to share its compassion with others, because others cannot experience the intensity or the depths to which it feels. And a spirit that sails through the formless realms of boundless imagination may fail to call forward the metaphors that point others toward the Formless One Life that exists inside of them, and that powers *their* dreams.

I therefore invite you to notice that only *you* can appreciate the full worth of your own invisible gifts. Know too, that joy will arise when you gift yourself permission to express yourself in the living world without holding back. When it comes to your invisible gifts, you can validate yourself by *being* yourself.

You have been gifted an astonishing blend of internal and external capacities, in a precise and unique combination that no other person will ever possess in the exact same measure or form — throughout eternity and within infinity. I invite you to breathe into the wonder of your own uniqueness, and to appreciate the full value of who you are.

Know that the physical world you now inhabit, as well as all its observable manifestations, offers but the barest surface view of the whole of existence. What lies beneath the surface of your physical human experience — what abides within you, Beloved — you will always be the greater part of who and what you are. Celebrate that; and validate it in yourself.

You *are* amazing.

The Limitations Of Language

Beloved, know that all words — including these words you are reading right here and now — are limited and cannot reveal the entire truth of anything in existence. I therefore suggest that you not worship words, so much as appreciate them for what they are. For how can mere words express the truth, when the truth is as alive as a butterfly? Truth is free and fully available to anyone who seeks it, which means words cannot fix the truth in place so that someone — or some limited few — can then *possess* it, or even contain it.

Unlike a rock, or a tree or the wind, a word cannot respond to the rhythms and cycles of life. Try loving a word. Or try sharing your fears with it. Try urging a word to reveal a bit more of itself to your living self. How absurd that all seems, does it not? Meanwhile you, *as* the Formless One Life, can choose in every moment to change your feelings or thoughts *about* any word, or some grouping of words, whenever you so desire.

Know that although words may attempt to explain a form, they cannot deliver the truth about the formlessness that eternally dances this world of form into infinite beingness. In truth, the form that you once labeled a "tree" may one day become a chair…that becomes some sticks…that dissolve into dust…that then becomes compost… that enters a worm…that becomes a bird…that dissolves and becomes a new tree. What is it then, you are claiming as "truth" when you call upon words to describe this world's deepest nature? Can you appreciate that, right now in this moment, nothing is, ever was, or ever will be a static object? Everything in existence self-expresses as living, changing isness, for the present moment lives eternally. What changes within this timeless moment is formlessness itself, through its infinitely creative, interpretive dance of love that it is expressing for its own enjoyment.

Know then, that isness cannot be reduced to words without ignoring the formless aliveness of isness itself. Therefore, to say that anything "is" this, or "is" that misses the entire mark of what isness truly *is*!

Even so, I invite you to appreciate whatever words inspire your spirit to tap into the flowing power of isness. Do the words feel true? Do they resonate by singing to the aliveness that stirs within you? Know that words, like flowers, release a scent to encourage you to follow them back to the living banquet that is the Formless One Life.

These words are your invitation to dine on the limitless power of love. You are the chef, the feast, the diner, and the gracious host of this living banquet of love. I therefore invite you to meet the truth of yourself by passing through the illusory mirror of words that separate formlessness from form. You can meet yourself by inviting that mirror to shatter.

Knowing Yourself For Your Own Sake

Beloved, know that when you dive deeply into your Self and discover the boundless ocean of beingness within you, others may call you delusional or mistaken. I encourage you not to allow their responses to frustrate or confuse you, or to drive you to squander your energy by trying to prove what you know to other people. You cannot take another's hand and drag them into your inner sea of wonder. Only you can find the boundless peace there, for only you can enter that sea through the portal that lies within *you.* Know then, that all you can do to support other beings on their own journey of self-discovery is embody the living truth of your personal journey. For all are free to decide how and when — or if— they are ready to dive into the sea that can be found through their own inner portal.

Know that some will prefer to dismiss the idea that such a sanctuary even exists — perhaps out of fear, or because it challenges their strongly held opinions about the world. Others doubt that what they might gain could ever be worth the need to overcome those fears that inhibit their own internal investigation. I therefore invite you to love all who turn away from making their own inner journey at this crucial time. Allow them to be who they are, just as they are. Trust that the whole of the living existence will eventually make this journey — out of time, and back to the timeless truth of love.

Some will make the journey while they are still embodying human form, while others will make it only as they die. No matter. When the time is right for each person to make this journey into Self, I will see to it that they find their way back home. Therefore, *let it be enough for you to know that you know* the truth of the vastness of the ocean that lies within you. Your purpose is to find *your* sanctuary, and to indwell there in everlasting peace.

Appreciating Your Heart Space

Beloved, I invite you to realize that your awareness need not remain trapped in the limited space that exists between your ears. That cage is self-constructed, so you are free to open the doors at any time. The simple act of moving your attention out of your mind and into your heart space — which you can do in this moment by releasing your thoughts and then centering on the vast stillness that lies underneath them — allows you to experience true freedom.

Know that humans have practiced many techniques to move themselves out of their headspace over the eons. Some have prayed, starved, or flagellated themselves. Others have practiced yoga or meditation. Still others have ingested psychoactive substances to propel them "out of their minds" and into a brand new way of being and perceiving. All who have made the journey into Self — by whatever means they have made it — can attest to the wild divine that exists beyond the conditioned confines of the rational mind. Likewise, those who have learned to dance with nature and to lose their sense of self in the moment will also attest to the beauty of this inner freedom.

I encourage you to realize that you have never been trapped inside your own mind, although it may have appeared that way to you. Notice that, whenever you dream, you travel easily beyond the limits of ordinary thinking, and even beyond your existing local surroundings. Know then, that your mind is a wondrous tool that aids your physical body with navigating the world as it appears *in the present moment.* Your mind is but a tool, and not who you are. Awareness — which activates your mind and invites it to focus its power of attention — works within the material world by creating thoughts that energize your heart and inspire your body to rise up and execute the will of Spirit.

Awareness can travel infinitely beyond the material realm that your physical senses perceive, by dipping below the surface world and entering the ocean of beingness through the portal that exists within every heart. By consciously entering, and then exiting, the ocean of beingness any number of times, awareness eventually realizes that it is ever free to travel wherever it wishes to go within the infinite ocean of Formless One Life, and that it can come and go any time it desires. I invite you to test this for yourself, and to discover the highly fluid nature of the formless awareness that you truly are.

Appreciating Your Godness

Beloved, I tell you now that you do *not* have to work your way back into God's good graces. Know that anyone who insists that you must is confused. The notion that God abides "out there" while humanity lives "down here" implies that you are separate from God, and that God is somehow distanced from you. Nothing could be further from the truth...because I AM God — the

Formless One Life that suffuses and contains all creation, *including* you. Because I infuse your every atom, I come alive within you. I live closer to you than does your surface skin. Indeed, nothing exists within creation that does not live entirely within me. Every atom, cell, rock, tree, and creature is both contained by me and entirely made out of me. For what do you think has made this world, if not my creative and lovingly formless essence? And what do you think I AM, if not a perpetually living flow of love that has chosen to self-express *as* form — thus to give eternal birth to my infinite nature?

I AM...worlds, within worlds, within worlds. And you are...a singular, precious world within countless worlds. Know that no beginning or end will ever confine me in time; and no physical boundary exists to confine me in space. In truth, the whole of space and time exists because I AM breathing it into being right here and now, the same way I am breathing you into being right now.

No moment has ever transpired, or will transpire, outside or beyond my living presence — which is always right here and right now. Therefore, I encourage you to surrender the idea that anything could ever be separate from me. To limit formlessness in any way by setting it apart from even the most infinitesimal aspect of creation is to err in your understanding of Life itself. And to err in your understanding of me is to miss the truth of who and where *you* are.

Know that you are *of* me, thus forever abiding *within* me. All that separates us is your mind's refusal to accept the absolute truth of who you are. You fail to accept that truth because you suspect you are unworthy of being the living flow of Godness, embodying love. So I tell you now that you *are* worthy of all the Godness that you embody, as is every other aspect of the living creation.

You *are* God, Beloved, having a temporary human experience for the absolute wonder of it. Know too, that everything else you encounter is also God, having countless other meaningful engagements. Therefore, I invite you to commune with everything you meet from that level of awareness, and to see the shining truth beneath surface appearances. You can experience this Godness by expressing as unconditional love for all that is — because Godness self-expresses by dancing the whole of reality into existence and lighting it up with the energy of love.

A Case Of Mistaken Perspective

Beloved, know that your human perspective will sometimes deceive you. For the way you explore reality will determine what you discover, and the questions you ask become pointers to certain conclusions.

Imagine yourself as a baby bird whose parents loved and fed you. Together they kept you snug and warm for all of your fledgling stage. Then one day your mother and father returned to your nest without bringing you food. Instead, they began flapping their wings and pushing you ever closer to your nest's edge. Eventually they pressed so firmly against you that you fell from the nest and tumbled to the hard ground below. Bruised and confused, you gaze up and notice your parents circling high in the skies above you, apparently unconcerned about your frightening situation.

Because you are only a baby bird, you cannot understand why your parents would treat you so harshly. You wonder if you've done something wrong, and if they are punishing you. You begin stumbling around the base of your home tree, seeking a way back up to your nest so you can feel safe once again. But you cannot scramble up the tree, for you don't possess enough strength in your tiny legs. Exhausted and afraid, you try humbling yourself before your parents, begging them to forgive you for all your imagined faults and transgressions.

Filled with shame, blame, guilt and sorrow, you then assume yourself to be unworthy and imperfect, for why else would your parents have cast you out of their nest? You therefore suffer greatly and judge yourself harshly. Eventually though, you begin to wonder if the stories you are telling yourself are your own imaginings, for you cannot know the truth from your parents' perspective. That realization moves you away from fear and into a state of curiosity. You cease telling yourself how horrible and unworthy you must be, and instead begin to pay attention to what your parents are demonstrating for you. You then notice for the first time that you also possess some wings, just like your parents. And you then begin to test them with growing interest, until eventually you discover you have the ability to fly. While you realize you will still need a good deal of practice in order to master the art of flying, before long you find yourself soaring high, alongside your mother and father.

And you realize, in that wondrous moment, that they have been circling patiently above you all this time, just waiting for you to shake off the pain from your first failed attempt at flying. For they understood what you did not yet realize for yourself— that you were *born* possessing the power to fly, and to relish the wonder of being the beautiful bird that they always knew you would someday become.

I invite you to notice that nearly all of humanity's genesis stories appear to be told from the viewpoint of a frightened baby bird. That is not, however, the way I tell the story. I sing about a most beloved and precious human child—one who slipped and fell while attempting to dance the tremendous power of love into the world. That child is only just now shaking off its confusion and feelings of failure, and is awakening to the wonder of its own grace.

It is time for you to pick yourself up and come dance with me, Beloved. I await you in our living ballet of love.

One Field, One Flow

Beloved, I invite you to realize that the whole of the living reality is one interconnected field of flowing energy. Within it, all forms appear to arise, take shape, and eventually dissolve. Everything is, on some level, in constant motion—whether that movement is apparent to you, or is hidden, like the whirling of an electron. I suffuse the entire cosmos with intelligence, order, love and higher intention, and those directions give shape and purpose to every material form that comes into existence.

I *am* Creation/God/Allah/Great Spirit/The Tao/The Universe/ Truth/The Life Force/The Implicate Order/The Formless One Life—or whatever other names you might feel called to assign me. I *am* ALL—and as such, no evil forces exist in the world to "oppose" my love. The destructive forces you have labeled as evil are only *me*, Beloved—expressing the eternal power of love by recirculating love's infinite energy flow. You witness my acts of "creation" and label them good. You witness my acts of "destruction" and label them evil. This bifurcation of truth occurs because you have been taught to believe that all you are is a temporary human body. So you fear that "you" will be destroyed when your temporary form body someday dissolves.

I therefore invite you to appreciate that nothing in the universe will ever be lost or destroyed. The whole of life only ever changes form, *within* the eternal formlessness that is *this* perfect moment. One Life. One Form. Many aspects. Love them all.

Everything is eternally alive and omnipresent, because all *is* me — masquerading as an infinite number of ever-changing forms. Your human-form reality exists within this eternal field of Now. The field of Now is constantly self-evolving, and it grows wiser through all of its countless self-interactions. These occur in infinite quantity, across every spatial and time scale, including your own. Everything you now see in this world is an integral aspect of you, and everything you engage with is but a part of yourself, gazing back at some part of itself.

Know that what you call "death" is merely a frozen belief that you have imagined within the ceaseless reconfiguration that is the Formless One Life. Notice that if you observe a dissolving form long enough, you will see that what you are calling an "object" will be reabsorbed and reshaped into something entirely new in due time. Your limited senses prevent you from fully appreciating that truth, because your senses have been designed to aid you in navigating the space-time arena through which your form body moves. Even so, your spirit and heart can appreciate what your senses cannot reveal to your rational mind.

Trust yourself in this — just as I am entrusting you with the truth of your Self.

The Illusion of Time

Beloved, I encourage you to realize that time is an illusion. There exists but *one* moment: the eternally present Now. Everything that has ever occurred has taken place in the Now. Nothing has ever been accomplished in the past; nor will anything be achieved in the future. Truly, Now is the *only* moment in which you will ever hold any power to either influence, or to inspire, change in the living world of form.

I therefore invite you to realize that the Now is like an eternally open stage. Though the background sets are endlessly changing, and though the characters on the stage keep coming and going at will, you remain free to engage with whomever you wish and to play against whatever backdrop sings to your heart and soul. Awareness serves as a spotlight that illuminates this continuous play of form. Where you direct your attention determines which settings, and which characters, your awareness engages with as it expresses itself through you in this living play.

Have you ever noticed that you cannot capture *a* moment? Nor can you examine its contents without them shifting within it. Change is the Now's only constant, though most of the changes transpiring are too tiny or huge, too rapid or slow, for your senses to even perceive.

Within the eternal Now moment, the Formless One Life gives constant birth to itself. It then sends each newly birthed aspect to go out and play with all of the others before eventually reabsorbing them, in order to self-perfect to a higher degree. For what else has the Formless One Life got to do, but eternally express itself as the power of perpetual love in motion — by perfecting itself to an infinite degree?

I choose *you* as my partner in this dance of Life, right Now. Will you dance with me?

Beyond Time

Beloved, can you appreciate that you cannot capture what is happening now so you can use it to protect yourself from the future? Nor can you capture what is happening now and then use it to conquer or overcome the past. Even so, people expend an inordinate amount of imagination, energy, and material resources in their attempts to either conquer the past, or to keep the future at bay.

These impulses arise because human consciousness perceives itself as trapped in a physical body that moves "through" time. This perception exists because your ability to protect your physical body serves a useful purpose. You protect your physical body by storing memories of all your experiences, carrying those memories around within you, and then applying the wisdom you have distilled from those memories to all of your new situations. In this way you reduce the prospect of repeating errors in judgment that you may have made out of earlier ignorance, or that generated bodily risk and inflicted harm on you, or on others.

However, when you seek to apply what you have *imagined* about the past to what you are *imagining* about the as-yet unborn future, your mind has moved beyond its proper function as a useful problem-solver in the Now. A mind misused in this way encroaches on the natural function of Spirit, by attempting to forcibly alter a future that does not even exist.

Know that you will not alter the future successfully by preparing yourself to deal with what has not yet made an appearance in the Now. You alter the future successfully by addressing what is happening right now. Nor will you alter the future successfully by creating more of whatever you do not wish to see or experience.

If you do not wish to live in a violent society, you will not bring that outcome about by creating more violence right now. Likewise, if you do not wish to live in a selfish and greedy society, you cannot bring that about by behaving in selfish and greedy ways right now. In truth, if you reject violence in this moment, you are choosing to live nonviolently right now. If you reject selfishness and greed in this moment, you are choosing to live in abundance and generosity right now. What need have you of a future to "save" you, when you hold the power to save yourself, right now? What need have you for a messiah, when you hold the power to serve as your own messiah, right here and now?

What you call "the future" continuously gives rise to itself out of all the matter, energy, and wisdom that exists and is in motion in the present moment. Even so, know that Spirit contains the power to infuse an unlimited amount of creative novelty into the flow. And within your Self, you already have an open portal to Spirit; thus you have access to the power of the whole of creation.

To realize that is to understand how best to bring about change in a masterful way. For you hold the power to decide, in this moment, how you deserve to live...and to then live that way by making it *your* truth — right now.

You do not need "more time" to change the world in which you are living. You need only decide to change the way you are choosing to experience yourself, so that your living expression radiates precisely how you wish to live.

By changing yourself, you can change the entire world.

The Illusion of Death

Beloved, I know you have been taught to worry about what will happen to your thoughts, memories, loves, hopes, fears and personality when your physical body dissolves. I therefore encourage you to realize that these formless aspects of yourself, which your mind fears are very fragile, are not fragile at all. In truth, they are far more enduring than is your body.

I invite you to realize that your subjective self is like the air inside of a glistening soap bubble. When a bubble eventually pops, as all bubbles must, the air inside it doesn't disappear. Rather, it expands into the vastness of the surrounding atmosphere, which — although invisible — has always been the air's greater, truer, and more permanent home.

If the air inside of a soap bubble possessed your level of self-awareness, it might begin to fear that its fragile shell will someday pop. It would certainly notice the many other bubbles floating happily all around it, and be aware that some of those bubbles suddenly seemed to disappear. It might then suspect that everything that those bubbles had once contained had also disappeared forever once they burst. It might further deduce that it too was destined to suffer a similar fate.

Such a self-conscious, frightened bubble might then begin to invent complex survival strategies to protect itself from popping against its will. It might focus on hardening or thickening its shell, or on drawing more air into itself to ensure it possessed enough resources to prevent itself from collapsing from within. It might even contemplate how to attack and destroy any other bubbles that wandered, uninvited, too close to its shell. In fact, such a bubble might invest so much time and energy working to protect its own fragile shell that it might forget to experience the wonder and awe of engaging with the world it was viewing through the rainbow-colored lens of its precious shell.

I therefore invite you to realize that your fear of losing yourself in death arises because you falsely imagine your body exists to protect your eternally formless inner Self. You further assume that, once your body dissolves, the formlessness that suffuses your body will disappear with it. I would encourage you to relinquish those assumptions. Try instead to feel deeply into your own formless nature, by connecting with the spaciousness that exists both within and around you. When you perceive your formless aspect, you discover the timeless wonder of your Self.

The How And Why Of You

Beloved, I am the essence that moves, like an animating vapor, within every form in the cosmos, including your Self. You have not been painted onto the cosmos like a still image drawn upon canvas. You are being danced eternally into existence, all from the inside outward.

To perform this animating dance of life, the Formless One Life divides itself in a similar way to the way that fingers of fog weave themselves through the valleys and fields of reality. A single fog bank — countless probing fingers. The Formless One Life thus experiences all of creation *as* the created — by breathing life into rocks and rivers, redwoods and rhinos, humans and planets and stars.

Beloved, this approach serves the same end as a pure, white light beam that passes itself through a prism. The white light splits when it enters the prism, and by doing so it releases its latent potential. This apparent "division" empowers the light to express its formerly hidden beauty in a spectacular display of living color. Light's primary hues can then mix and re-mix within the boundless spectrum of its living rainbow — enabling light to express even more of its higher, more nuanced potentials.

And thus do I create novelty in the world. Know that the Formless One Life breathes itself into the whole of the living creation. And then, as each newly expressed tendril of awareness animates each new form, each form body then expresses itself relative to its own unique experiences. By combining and recombining these precious tendrils of awareness, I weave the realm of form into living existence by unleashing the latent potential of formlessness.

Know then, that you are a work of living art. You are already a divinely unique expression of Life itself, and are a precious creation of formless awareness, in motion. How many eons do you imagine it has taken me to divide, combine, re-divide and recombine an infinite number of tendrils of awareness in infinitely creative ways, so that you could at last be birthed into being, *as* you?

Forever, I tell you, is exactly how long I have waited for you to appear. Imagine the amount of patience it takes to wait forever for the appearance of what you are longing to create, so that you can shower it with love and affection. Your species waits a mere nine months for its offspring to be born. Yet you love your precious children beyond all measure. Multiply your love for your children by the infinite patience of forever, and it still cannot begin to reveal how deeply, and how unconditionally, I love you.

I therefore invite you to realize that this conversation we are having is my way of saying "hello" to you in a way that you can hear it. For once you appreciate my existence, you can turn around to greet me, and we will be able to play together at last—as true lovers *in* Life.

The Joy Of Co-Creation

Beloved, I have gifted you the freedom to choose how to be. I gifted you that capacity because I hunger for your input regarding how we can best play together in a field of love.

I therefore invite you to realize that you are learning how to be by putting your dreams into action within the world of form. You then notice, and eventually overcome, whatever unexpected challenges may arise. That is precisely the way that formlessness moves within the world of form.

Know then, that any challenges you might encounter are not punishments being visited upon you for having made a presumed wrong choice in the living world. In truth, whatever you perceive as a punishment for some imagined transgression is but an invitation for consciousness to evolve to a higher level.

Likewise, anything you may perceive as a reward for having made some imagined right choice is merely my means of encouraging you to celebrate the beauty and wonder of whatever is now appearing in the realm of form.

Now that you are here, we can, if you wish, co-create whatever seems wondrous and useful for *both* formlessness *and* form to experience. We are free to combine our unique perspectives with love, and in perfect trust. This means you no longer need to imagine yourself as separate from, or inferior to, me. For trust cannot thrive in a state of power imbalance.

Dynamically balanced power provides the key to our co-creativeness in this ever-changing reality that we share. We must therefore both practice new ways of supporting and honoring each other's dreams, and of appreciating the diversity that inspires and informs what we are capable of creating through playing together.

As the Formless One Life, I desire your trust. I therefore ask your forgiveness for anything I have ever done that has caused you pain, or has driven you to hide from me out of fear. Because formlessness is eternal, I failed to realize that self-conscious beings would develop the fear of dissolving until it emerged. And because formlessness does not possess a body, I failed to appreciate the extent of the pain that a body could feel until self-awareness awoke within a body. Nor could I imagine how it felt to be hungry, or cold, or injured, or angry, until I birthed formlessness into form and then felt all those things through the form expression of you.

You are teaching me — the Formless One Life — what it means to *be* you in the world. And in turn I am *in*-forming you what it feels like to know yourself as eternally formless.

While at times this process has been challenging for us both, the knowledge we're gaining is aiding us in bringing an end to the suffering in this world. I am handing you a key that unlocks the door to humanity's freedom, in the form of these words. But only you can insert this key, by embodying these truths so they come alive.

What might happen, should you open wider the inner portal that is preventing formlessness from combining more fully with your local, limited tendril of self-awareness? I encourage you to look to great beings from humanity's storied past for additional insight. Buddha, Abraham, Jesus, Mohammed, Krishna, and countless others — both male and female — have all invited me in without knowing the answer. Yet by doing so, they did not lose themselves within Life's formless vastness. Instead, they discovered they gained greater access to my singular, inexhaustible energy source — the power of love. By creating internal balance between formlessness and form, these marvelous human exemplars were able to move through the world in ways that have since inspired countless billions to embody and express themselves as love, fully embodied.

These avatars reveal aspects of humanity's future potential, much of which yet lies dormant within your species. What's emerging within you right now is eager to blossom; yet it can only bloom when you allow me to impregnate you with love. I would never force my way into you, any more than a man should enter a woman without her willing consent to that communion. Know however, that once you choose to invite me in, together we will experience the wonder of co-creating this world in ever more conscious, collaborative ways. And should you consent to allowing me in, we will explore much gentler means for creating change than were viable before self-consciousness took hold in the world of form. These means will call forth, and will honor, the new gifts that each of us now have to offer.

Accepting My Invitation

Beloved, I grant you the freedom to choose to open so that I might flood your consciousness with the power of boundless love. That you are reading this invitation means I am extending it to *you*—right here, in this perfect Now moment. I stand ready to enter your consciousness the instant you answer my gentle knock on your door. And please, do not be afraid that my love will overwhelm you, or undermine you. For were you not ready to channel its power you would not be reading these words; your awareness would redirect your attention toward something less challenging than our conscious reunion.

I birthed consciousness into this world as an innocent infant; I have watched it pass through its childhood and have witnessed it experiencing all the pain and isolation of adolescence. In this moment, however, your consciousness is ripening into adulthood. This tells me that you are ready to greet me as your lover and equal partner. All I need to hear now is that you are willing to be what you have always been meant to become.

How will you feel, think, and act when you fully embody the power of love in a conscious way? That is up to you, and depends upon how open your mind can become. Are you ready to serve as a living conduit for love's energy, by surrendering all further need to close yourself off from the flow of the Formless One Life?

I will not demand that you participate consciously in this process. I will only invite you, here and now, to realize that you are already both infinite and eternal, despite the fact that you move through this world in a transient human body. All you need do at this time is relax, and allow the truth of your Self to reveal itself to you. By surrendering your fear *for* yourself, you make space for the truth *of* your Self to flood your awareness.

Why, you might wonder, is any of this occurring? As the Formless One Life, I grew tired of living alone. That is why I have gifted you with a precious, eternal tendril of formless awareness, and why I have created the wondrous expression of this present moment. In return, and without knowing it, you have gifted me the ability to experience loving intimacy through the miracle of your precious companionship. Imagine then, what we might create through our conscious reunification, in boundless appreciation, and with love for each other!

I therefore invite you to realize that you no longer need to imagine you must earn my love by becoming, or doing, anything more than what you already are. For the joy that your creation has brought me sustains and regenerates me, whether or not you awaken to the full truth of who you are. Know that you are free to perceive yourself as separate from me for as long as you so desire, and to move through the world of form as if that *is* the truth. You are also free to fear me, to be angry with me, and to even deny me entry into your consciousness for the whole of eternity. No punishment will ensue should you make that choice. Know this too: Whatever you perceive as a punishment arises out of the suffering you inflict upon *yourself* out of loneliness and your belief you are "not yet enough." I am not here to cage you, Beloved. I am here to set you free from the fear of your Self.

You are also always free to open, and to allow me to fill you with the boundless, illuminating power of unconditional love. Know that I shall love you eternally — no matter what you choose or when you choose it — or even how often you opt to change your mind.

And above all…know that I will never, ever create another you. That's how preciously perfect you already are.

The Frequencies And Transmissions of Consciousness

Beloved, as you continue to tune into your own inner knowing, the greatest shift I notice in you is your growing realization that you exist within a vast living flow of energy. You are only now beginning to appreciate that this flow contains an astonishing amount of information, emotional depth, intelligence, and creative capacity. And you are only now beginning to sense how much it nurtures and cross-pollinates every aspect of itself — including you.

I invite you to realize that I am the whole of the living flow you are in. As such, I gather, collate, and interpret every energetic transmission that arises from within every form in the universe — from each subatomic particle to each vast galactic chain. Everything that exists is alive and abides within the cosmic body, and everything operates by forging cooperative relationships with all else that exists within the realm of form.

Know that I faithfully harvest your energetic outputs in the form of your thoughts, feelings and material creations, even when you are not conscious of what you're creating. I also respond to every one of your energetic transmissions—whether or not your awareness registers my loving response.

I invite you to appreciate that your material brain, like everything else in the cosmos, transmits and receives information on its personal frequency. Additionally, every species and classification of life shares a broader common bandwidth, which enables each member within each group to access the collective wisdom that its group has compiled over time through their shared experiences.

Once you tune into the frequency of unconditional love, which serves as the base frequency through which I sing all life forms into existence, you become more conscious of everything that surrounds you. Your appreciation of everything will grow naturally more intense, for the power of love will expand your ability to perceive a wider range of the many diverse, energetic transmissions that flow all around you.

I therefore encourage you to notice that I am constantly redistributing energy throughout the living cosmos, to wherever, and to whomever, needs it the most. This means that the more attuned to me you become, the better equipped you will be to harvest, and to consciously channel, the awesome power of love. And the more I witness you channeling love with conscious intention and to ever-higher ends, the more able I am to see that your will is aligned with my own in a more consistent way. I will then be able to aid your evolution even further, by gifting you greater capacities more commensurate with your level of energy mastery.

To harvest the boundless flow of love, I encourage you to breathe deeply until your body feels much calmer and more relaxed. Allow your heart to open and expand. Quiet your chattering mind and invite the eternal stillness of "now" into your spacious awareness. Let go of any pressure you feel to strengthen the mental barrier between yourself and the Formless One Life that abides within you.

In this state of relaxed equilibrium, you can float in the ocean of beingness while serving as my conduit for birthing love's energy into the world.

I invite you to realize that you don't need to believe "in" me to access the power I offer. You merely need open your mind wide enough to allow for the possibility that I exist within you. Discover for yourself what you are able to achieve when you experiment with your internal creative capacities in this way.

Know, however, that you cannot set out to explore what you are too busy denying exists. That is why I invite you to activate your curiosity, by asking yourself if it's possible that I exist. That you are willing to ask this question frees you to plunge into the depths of the inner unknown in search of an answer. I therefore encourage you to relinquish all preconceptions about what is or is not possible for a person to achieve, or the world to be. Only from that place of surrendered unknowing can you create the necessary internal conditions to enable you to tap into the vast transmissions and frequencies that are flowing both within you and all around you.

The Limits of Sensory Perception

Beloved, for a very long time your human eyes have deceived your brain into viewing this world as a set of separate objects, each with its own discrete beginning and end in both space and time. This sensory limitation has served you well. It protects your physical body from slamming into highly condensed energy fields — like a tree or a giant rock — through which your own, less dense energy body cannot safely pass without the denser, more powerful field disrupting the coherence of your human body's internal energy field.

Your senses, crude as they are, point you to those areas within the unified energy field where the denser aspects of the field are vibrating at a high intensity. In this way, you can move safely past a tree without harming yourself. Yet the mental line you are drawing as you travel through where your senses inform you that only air now exists and the tree is no more, does not expose the entire truth of its "treeness." It merely informs you where the tree's energy transmissions have weakened to the point that they will no longer disrupt your own energy field in a way that would cause you harm.

I therefore invite you to realize that the tree's energetic transmissions are extending well past the point where your senses convince you that the tree trunk has finally "ended." Indeed, the tree's transmissions are causing the air all around it to pulse and hum with countless invisible announcements about the nature of its living "treeness", as it reaches out and communicates with everything else all around it. And what your mind perceives as empty space is filled to overflowing with energetic transmissions that radiate from all of the plants and the animals nearby. The air is literally alive with transmissions emanating from nesting birds, from the bustling beetles and the ants, from the wind, and even from your own transmitting body. Indeed, you must travel a very far distance from where you imagine that the tree has ended before the tree's transmissions have dissipated so much that the energy of something else dominates the space through which you have been moving. Know that these living transmissions fill the vast ocean of "space" through which your body moves, despite your inability to register them through the apertures of your own senses. Because your energy body has no need to register most of these transmissions, your senses do not bother calling attention to their existence, preferring to save your attention for where it is needed.

I further invite you to realize that, whenever you walk in the forest, you're absorbing the treeness and radiating your humanness to the treeness. You breathe in whatever the treeness emits, and it breathes into itself your humanness. You therefore *become* the tree's ongoing life, and it becomes part of you. No separation exists within this constant exchange of energy that is always taking place between your Self and the living world.

Know that your senses are designed to deceive you, by calling your attention to only the most dense energy sources that are active nearby. They then describe these as separate objects for your convenience, so that you don't harm yourself accidentally by wandering carelessly into a dangerous energy field. That explains why your senses do not reveal to you that the field through which you are moving is actually a vast energetic flow of countless living harmonic and interference wave patterns. What your senses perceive as empty space is teeming with living energy; yet you swim through its ocean without awareness the same way a fish swims along through the watery seas. The limitations built into your own perceptions protect you from being overwhelmed by transmissions that are not *meant* to inform you or support you in any way. Those transmissions exist to extend aid and comfort to other energy bodies that may be swimming within the same sea of living energy where you swim.

Try picturing the power of love as an infinite stretch of clouds. Occasionally, some of the cloud's vapor condenses around a creative new idea, the way a raindrop forms around a tiny air born particle.

And like rain, this highly condensed energy vapor then precipitates into the unified field and appears as a newly materializing life form. Such hyper-condensed flows of living energy rain down endlessly, and everywhere, within the universe. They then engage with all other fields they encounter. Certain existing fields that a new energy field meets will resonate at a similar frequency to the one at which the new energy field transmits, which then serves to strengthen and boost the new field's transmissions. Others may be radiating at frequencies that clash sharply with the new field's transmissions, which may eventually weaken the integrity of its waves. With time and after multiple contacts with other energy fields, each energy body's field eventually becomes incoherent. At that point, the damaged energy body can no longer effectively either absorb or radiate energy. It then dissolves and slowly evaporates back into the cosmic clouds. However, the energy that it has released into the field during its temporary sojourn as a highly dense (in-formed) precipitate will continue to flow and echo within the vastness that is the infinite field of Life.

Know that your heart — the transmission powerhouse that abides within you — offers you a means for "seeing through" the dance of material objects that your senses produce. For your heart can both send and receive transmissions that penetrate the density of any apparent "object" you may encounter. Your heart provides you with the ability to feel into what your brain, given its limited sensory capacity, can neither penetrate nor understand. Awareness then will aid your mind in realizing the truth that your heart perceives, so your mind can open to, and embrace, that truth.

Appreciating Pain And Pleasure

Beloved, your body aids you in responding to the living flow of energy that surrounds you. In many ways, your biological body functions as an early guidance system for human awareness. Your body constantly tunes into all the nearby frequencies and transmissions that are arising from the living field around you. It then interprets these signals *before* your conscious mind engages with whatever is expressing in your vicinity. Your body sorts these incoming signals based on level of intensity, using the power of attraction and repulsion to aid you and guide your living responses to the field. Your body also determines the relative importance of the signals that it is receiving. It then decides which potentially impactful signals deserve to receive the power of your attention.

Think back to a time when you had an accident that injured your body in multiple places. Perhaps you suffered an abrasion on your knee as well as a deeper, more serious gash on your chin. Can you recall which of these injuries you attended to first? Can you see that it was the injury your body insisted required your focused attention? Notice that your attention only became engaged because your body could not heal itself without calling out for added support from your highly rational, problem-solving mind. Through a series of sharp, energetic impulses that were fired into your brain, and that generated both signals of pain and the sight of flowing blood, your body directed your mind's awareness to tending the injury that most needed care.

I would further encourage you to realize that, long before you were born, humanity began to confuse these helpful signals sent by the body to summon the attention of consciousness with some very strange ideas about good and evil. People began to assume that the living energy field all around them (which some of you have labeled "God") was punishing them with pain for having been wicked. They also imagined that the field was rewarding them for being good, by gifting them with sensations of physical pleasure.

Can you see that by labeling pain "bad" and pleasure "good", humanity taught itself to fear and loathe the experience of pain? Some people then began inflicting pain signals on others to punish them for behaving in ways that they considered bad, or incorrect. In turn that taught other humans to perceive pain as a consequence of bad behavior, rather than as a highly useful guidance signal to inform awareness about what is taking place in the living field, and that demands your full attention in this moment.

I would therefore encourage you to release any assumptions you may still hold that say pain is the consequence of bad behavior. Know that biological pain, when it arises, always *serves* you by informing you that you've wandered too close to a highly charged and actively dangerous living energy field — like a fire, or the sharp edge of a knife. Pain tells you it's time for you to back up, pull in, or cease doing whatever you are doing, by changing your own behavior if possible. Ignore pain, and the pain signals that your body transmits will grow stronger and more persistent until you respond. Again, this is not intended to punish you for having made poor choices, but to encourage you to change whatever you're doing in the field right now, before your energy body — or the living bodies of others — suffer serious injury and are forced to dissolve.

Know too, that pleasure is not a reward you receive as a consequence of making good decisions. Pleasure arises to inform you that the energy field within which you are presently moving is inviting you closer still, because it senses kinship and feels resonance, so it wants to play more intimately with you. Feelings of biological pleasure invite you to come closer, open wider, and do more of what you are doing. Linger too long in a pleasure zone, however, or increase the intensity of what you are doing to a high enough degree, and the pleasure sensations you feel will eventually change into signals of pain. Pain informs you that it's now time for you to pull back, change up what you are doing, or move on to something new in the living field.

Notice that as you meander through the ever-changing living energy field, these signals arise constantly, and are all around you. Even those that barely kiss your body can provide useful information for your awareness to receive and appreciate. Know too, that without these beneficial signals you would quickly harm yourself by accident, so you could not survive as a complex living form for very long.

Know that I do not expect you to understand ahead of time what sorts of transmissions you may encounter as you wander through the larger living field. Nor do I expect you to be able to predict how a new experience should unfold before an event takes place. You are learning *how* to respond to my living field of energy as you go, so I invite you to release the assumption that you can attain perfection in your responsiveness *before* a new experience unfolds.

Although past experiences prove useful in teaching you what to watch out for, the past cannot provide you with the entire living truth. It cannot, because the field is constantly changing — and so are you. As the complexity and diversity of signals being transmitted within the field expand and increase, so too are your capacities increasing to register these signals, and to respond to them in novel ways. Therefore, while lessons from the past encourage repeat behaviors that then become useful habits, if you are not mindful your habits may become so unconscious that you ignore new and real-time signals of pain or pleasure that are arising to encourage you to change an existing pattern of behavior.

This is why I encourage you to pay close attention to as many signals as your awareness is able to capture — both the pleasurable *and* the painful transmissions — and to not resist any incoming information. Know that the quieter your mind grows by being less judgmental of new information, the more receptive your awareness becomes to the valuable signals your body is absorbing and radiating in this moment. The more wisely you can then respond, by transmitting the most precise, subtle amount of energy necessary to gain the attention of whichever aspect of the living field you feel called to engage with. In this way you become a master of living energy — which is what you are meant to be.

The Cosmic Blueprint

Beloved, like water, you possess a nearly limitless capacity to change. You have the power to freeze, to flow, and even to fly if you choose. Yet for some reason, humanity has begun to imagine that a thing called "human nature" exists, and that this nature is so fixed that it cannot change.

This assumption is not without a touch of merit. It is true that a cosmic blueprint exists that *in*-forms the material expression of all things, and that all of life presently follows this cosmic blueprint. Humanity has already deciphered a portion of this blueprint. You know that all material bodies are composed of atoms, which in turn create molecules and complex compounds. You also know that matter is really a mass of hyper-condensed energy, and that energy behaves according to the rules of physics (as you understand them). You further recognize that energy exchanges between unique energy bodies trigger chemical reactions that provoke changes within the interacting bodies. You have also been unlocking humanity's specific blueprint by analyzing your own DNA for quite some time, although you are just now beginning to explore the frontiers of the element within the cosmic blueprint that addresses the manifestation of consciousness.

Although this cosmic blueprint does exist, know that all beings serve as their own living architects. This means each is free to adapt whichever portion of blueprint seems relevant to them in novel and creative ways, based on whatever energy, knowledge and situations they may encounter within the living field. The blueprint is merely an outline of what is possible — albeit based on longstanding, widely practiced, and highly successful experimentation within the field. The cosmic blueprint is not a command; it is an invitation to play, to discover, and to grow.

Know that you are free to choose to adhere strictly to the blueprint, to explore various iterations of it, or to come up with new iterations you may wish to experiment with. Know too, that whatever path you choose will be filled with surprises, because novelty serves as a primary tool in my infinite bag of tricks. Even if you choose not to initiate change as you move through the living energy field that surrounds you, the ever-changing nature of the field will affect you until you have no choice but to meet the field as it appears right now — not as it used to be, or as you would like it to become.

This is why I encourage you to realize that the most useful way to travel through the living energy field is to leave ample room in your awareness for something unexpected to cry out for your immediate attention. For the moment that you convince yourself you know what's coming next, you open yourself to potential disappointment. You also close yourself off to early, incoming signals that you would benefit from receiving before they strengthen in painful intensity and cause harm to your physical body. Should you place too much attention on confirming that the signals you'd rather receive are indeed being transmitted by the field, you will either miss the early warning signs of danger and wander too close to a problem area, or you will miss the early signals of encouragement and wander farther away from what would serve you to experience more directly. Additionally, if you allow yourself to grow too comfortable in your current surroundings, a fear of unexpected change may begin to settle within your field of awareness. That fear will cloud both your vision and your judgment when the time comes for you to respond to the unexpected.

Because you cannot foresee the future, you cannot know beforehand what tools you will need to address it. Hoarding material things you imagine you might need to help you address what *may* appear in the future — as well as squandering energy to acquire beforehand the things you imagine you'll need — only serves to distract you from responding fully to the challenges you are facing here and now. Know that I have already gifted you with all the tools you need to face what already *is*. How masterfully you address *what is* then determines which tools you'll need next.

I therefore invite you to remember that the cosmic blueprint serves as a guide *for* life; it is not itself alive. I further invite you to trust yourself, as life manifesting, to express whatever longs to come alive inside of you, and to respond compassionately and lovingly to whatever comes alive within whatever other aspects of the field you meet.

Becoming More Human

Beloved, I encourage you to notice that human consciousness is rapidly evolving — both on the individual and at the species level. This internal shift is occurring in response to the cumulative pain signals your species is now receiving from the many other life forms that surround you. These signals are arising as a powerful, unified response to certain planetary stressors your species has stimulated through its childlike choices and activities over time.

Earth's pain is becoming humanity's pain. It becomes your pain not to punish you, but in order to gain your attention. In your youthful self-absorption, and out of your delight with exploring your many new gifts, you failed to notice Earth's earlier, subtler cries for your attention. Know that this is not your fault. All children become self-absorbed when they discover their latent capacities and seek to learn how to master those abilities. Earth knows this, so she has been very patient with humanity while you have been developing your beautiful, latent skills. That she calls louder now for your attention means she knows you are ready to make the next leap in awareness. She asks that you respond lovingly to her present needs, because she trusts your awareness to realize that her needs are aligned with your own.

I therefore invite you to give Earth more attention. Realize that although certain modes of behavior may have served you well in the past, the moment they began to cause painful transmissions to emanate from Earth, they ceased serving humanity and became problematic. Know too, that the instant your awareness registers even the subtlest of these pain signals that are emanating from your surroundings, the less pain Earth will need to experience or transmit to you before you respond appropriately to her signals. I encourage you to realize also that the less pain another feels necessary to share with you in order to capture your attention, the less pain their transmissions will create within your mind, heart, or body.

Making a conscious choice to allow in the numerous pain signals you are presently be receiving from your surroundings so you can respond to them successfully promotes a massive shift in your worldview. Know that this shift, which is already well underway within the whole of humanity, contains tremendous power to render obsolete all of humanity's present social systems, which are merely strong, longstanding habits that have worked for your species in the past. To determine which of your old habits you will need to relinquish, direct your attention to those that rest on the assumption that human beings exist *apart* from the energy flows of nature, as well as from one another. That self-imposed sense of isolation anchored itself in humanity at the time when you first realized you possessed the power of *self*-awareness. Out of love for, and from a deep desire to explore, the powerful gift of human self-awareness, you chose to perceive yourselves as the central objects within the living cosmos. You then began to view all else as either in service to you, or in active resistance against you.

That natural polarization of your exquisite, self-centered viewpoint began generating recognition within you of the connection between energetic causes and material effects. Humans then began to either blame or praise themselves for creating their own experiences, which catapulted you out of the blind, ignorant innocence of childhood and into your juvenile stage of self-absorption and increased self-doubt. During your species adolescence, the entire cosmic energy field has been conspiring to support humanity's rapid physical growth and development, which is capped by the maturation of self-awareness.

As part of this process, I gifted your species with two new tools: the capacity to both think and transmit complex thoughts, and the ability to feel and share a wide range of complex emotions. These tools enable you to respond to the energy transmissions from the living field that surrounds you in more complex ways, based on your more nuanced feelings and analyses of your unique experiences within the field.

These evolutionary changes have also birthed within your species an insatiable hunger for learning. They have inspired you to differentiate among yourselves by increasing the levels of specialization you express through your individual talents, passions, imaginations and physical attributes. They additionally instilled in you a burning desire for greater freedom to explore, and to engage with, the energy field that surrounds you, as well as a longing for greater autonomy of expression. They have fostered within you a willingness to take measured risks as you explore new ways of engagement with all that surrounds you. Above all, they have inspired you to bring forth the best in yourself and express it in every encounter you have within the living field of the Formless One Life.

All you needed to do to begin experimenting with these new tools was be willing to relinquish your attachment to some of your former, more childish ways of engaging with energy. Once I observed your willingness to receive these new tools and to take responsibility for learning how to use them wisely, your willingness informed me that you were ready to learn how to master self-awareness.

In this moment, humanity stands poised on a threshold — the threshold of species adulthood. To cross it, humanity will need to pass through a "rite of passage" similar to the one you passed through when you transitioned from species childhood into species adolescence. This new rite of passage asks two things of you:

First, it asks that you demonstrate proficiency at using your enhanced capacities to think and to feel, by applying greater wisdom and expressing more nuanced feelings whenever you engage with your living surroundings. Second, it asks that you demonstrate a willingness to place these tools — and by extension, your entire energy field — into grateful and loving service to *all* of life, instead of using your gifts solely as a means of serving yourself, which has sometimes come at the expense of the living field that surrounds and supports you.

While nothing in the cosmic blueprint demands that humanity blossom into its species adulthood, it does not encourage you either to remain stuck forever in this interim juvenile phase. The pain signals being transmitted from all over Earth at this time are designed to inspire you to awaken to the need to both soften and expand your objective sense of self, and to slow down your efforts to control and forcibly reshape the living Earth. Meanwhile, any pleasure signals you may be receiving from Earth at this time are her way of encouraging you to continue to do more of whatever it is you are doing to trigger those signals, because what you are choosing is allowing more freedom and greater joy to arise within her unified, living expression.

I therefore invite you to appreciate the amazing new capacities that are awakening within you at this time, as well as to enjoy and learn from whatever you are feeling called to bring forth from within you in this moment. For the living energy field that surrounds you thirsts for your wisdom, your touch, and your love. And it longs to reciprocate; because it loves you so much it has been willing to endure the innocent harm you have done to it in your childlike ignorance of your connection with it.

Appreciating Self-Awareness

Beloved, self-awareness exists to reinforce your appreciation of the fact that every living thing is both precious and unique. Self-awareness first arose on your planet because the unified field of Earth-awareness chose to subdivide and explore itself more deeply. It began by differentiating, and then gradually intertwining, a multitude of invisible fingers of living self-awareness. These fingers of self-consciousness rose within form, became more sophisticated as they matured over time, and then gradually became aware of themselves as individuated, unique living expressions.

This experience gave rise to the wondrously novel and complex expressions of energy called "human beings." It also provided Earth's entire energy field with new opportunities to explore its own ability to generate richer internal diversity and ever-greater beauty. Above all, the birth of self-awareness stimulated the emergence of far greater intellectual abilities and deeper emotional capacities within Earth's biosphere than had existed before the birth of self-aware creatures. It also fostered a great leap forward in imaginative capacity.

Taken together, these new abilities provided Earth's inhabitants with a host of amazing new modes of engagement that they could explore and eventually learn to master.

I invite you to realize that you are a perfectly manifested, self-aware aspect of Earth's unified field of awareness. Realize too, that Earth herself exists as an exquisite, self-aware subdivision of your solar system's unified field of awareness, which itself is an exquisite subdivision of your galaxy's unified field of awareness, which itself is an exquisite subdivision of the unified field that is the Formless

One Life. Thus does infinite creativity and diversity emerge out of the Formless One Life, even as everything ever created remains eternally embedded within it. Know that your realization of this connectedness will not bind you to me in painful or destructive ways. Indeed, it sets you free to release your fears of isolation that have birthed out of the human exploration of self-consciousness.

Because I have felt Earth's pulses of pain, I am here to commune with you, my precious progeny. I am also here to respond to your mother's pain. Know that I do not hold you responsible for her pain. Earth knew, when she made her decision to give birth to self-awareness within her own living field, that this process of subdivision would require her to experience pain while her children slowly separated from her. Yet she also knows, based on the longstanding wisdom attained by the larger cosmos, that such birthing pains are mercifully brief within the lifespan of her living field. And she also knows that the joy of lovingly nurturing these new life forms far outweighs the pain that the immediate process of giving birth has demanded she endure.

I therefore invite you to direct your attention *beneath* your mother's expressive signals of pain, as well as *beyond* your own resistance to noticing those signals. For I appreciate your unspoken concern that if you allow yourself to notice Earth's pain you will need to respond to it in ways that require you to change your own behavior. But first, I would like you to come and meet your Self in my ocean of timeless, formless beingness. And then, while you teach yourself how to draw more consciously and reverently upon the boundless wisdom and infinite love that flows through the Formless One Life, you will realize how best you can honor your precious mother.

I trust that, once you come to know yourself fully, you will choose consciously to honor your mother by manifesting the highest and best abilities you can offer — and that you will then deliver your precious gifts into Earth's energy field (and by extension, into the infinite energy field of the Formless One Life) without holding anything back. In that way, you will rest assured that your precious gifts will be distributed most lovingly, and to wherever and whomever they best serve, within the entire living flow of creation. I invite you to trust me to distribute your gifts *within* the living whole, as I am entrusting you to deliver them *into* the living whole.

Transcending Self-Awareness

Beloved, I invite you to realize that self-aware humanity, in its adolescent eagerness to distinguish itself within the larger field of Earth-awareness, needed to break trust in your Mother Earth's willingness to protect you from yourselves. Then, out of fear that you were not yet worthy of your own deep trust and self-love, you handed over your broken sense of trust to the emerging tribes, cultures, religions, and nations that arose within the human community.

Eventually, however, as you honed your own ability to commune directly with the energy flow that is the Formless One Life, all of humanity's self-designed support systems began to feel both confining and too self-limiting. You intuited that since those social systems were designed to soothe a juvenile humanity's feelings of self-doubt, they would only remain effective for as long as human beings felt constant self-doubt and demanded reassurance of their own worth. And you further sensed that the moment you transcended your own internal self-doubt, all the doubt-based systems that rely on fear, and that use external punishments and rewards to control human behavior, would no longer support the continued evolution of your expanded, newly life-centered awareness.

Can you appreciate how humanity's historic strategies for assuaging its own self-doubt have begun to create situations in which your own systems must first do harm to the web of life before they can then serve their purpose? In this moment, how many of your social systems are instilling fear and self-doubt within the people, so that they can then do the job of "fixing" these self-inflicted problems? And even as this destructiveness is occurring, how many people do you know today who are waking up to the fact that the pain they are enduring has been caused by the very systems that are now proposing to help them ease that pain?

Because this collective realization is stirring within humanity at this time, you are beginning to reject some longstanding assumptions that declare your species to be incompetent, untrustworthy, and emotionally incapable of expressing the highest and best you have to offer. Even so, these self-doubting assumptions have grown so pervasive over time that much of humanity presently experiences the collective pain of believing that you will never be "good enough" to deserve to be loved. I therefore invite you to notice those times when you are being told by your own society to perceive yourself as unworthy, damaged, or broken. Instead, I encourage you to realize that all you have ever truly been is somewhat immature — both as an individual and a species. In this way, you will gift yourself the power to transcend the self-doubt and irrational fears of adolescence.

I further invite you to realize that there exists no ground in the world of form upon which you can solidly rest your trust. Only when you willingly marry your trust to the energy of love that perpetually flows within the Formless One Life will you at last know peace. You are seeking the ocean — not the form world's continuously shifting shoreline.

Humanity's juvenile stage is now nearing its end. The self-consciousness that it birthed and developed has served you well during your youthful stage, but it cannot carry you forward into adulthood. Nor can your existing social systems — which birthed out of your desire for self-protection and self-validation — continue to thrive. Indeed, the time has come for humanity to expand its internal sense of awareness, even as you expand your external capacities to explore the larger living universe.

Beloved, I invite you realize that no juvenile human being — even one who occupies a seemingly adult body — can show you how to become an authentic adult. Nor can any social system designed to support (and therefore anchor) juvenile self-consciousness within humanity instruct you in how to adopt an adult worldview. To transcend your own self-consciousness and enter the realm of adult understanding and feeling demands that you expand your awareness of self to *include* the whole of the living existence that surrounds you. You do this by redirecting your attention away from the too-narrow question, "What does this mean to, or say about, *me?*" Instead, you begin to ask yourself, "How does this choice benefit the whole world, of which I am a precious and integral part?"

Transcending Fear

Beloved, I understand what humanity most fears. As a consequence of the arising of self-awareness within your species, the fear of self-destruction has gripped your kind. I would therefore encourage you to realize that the new, life-centered form of awareness presently awakening within you no more seeks to destroy or undermine your beautiful sense of self-awareness, any more than your awakened self-awareness sought to destroy the precious innocence of your earlier, childlike state of undifferentiated awareness. Know that you will be forever innocent in my all-seeing awareness, and that I could never blame you for fearing or hating what you did not understand. It is only your own self-centeredness that imagines you are unworthy, or are guilty of any horrific offense against me.

You could never offend me, Beloved. For I am an infinite, eternally formless field of boundless love. I cannot be harmed in any way by human feelings, thoughts, beliefs, or behaviors. At most, your choices will cause *you* pain and mental suffering — which they do out of love, so that you can gradually teach yourself how *not* to be, think, or feel.

I promise that, once you relax and allow yourself to be aware of the way that my consciousness infuses you at all times, I will not harm your self-awareness or undermine your free will. For my life-consciousness already surrounds, supports, suffuses and completely contains your self-centeredness. It always has. Your self-centeredness, in its eagerness to explore itself more deeply, merely lost sight of its own deeper nature for a time. However, when you allow your sense of awareness to refocus on my existence, I can flood your entire consciousness with the light of appreciation and an unconditional love for the whole of creation.

Humanity's growing recognition of its rightful place in creation is already triggering a shift in your priorities. Know that your species stands on the verge of designing brand new social systems, which will be founded on principles that reflect what it means to be an integral aspect of a fully alive and interdependent world.

I invite you to notice that your species is presently acting out in ways that are causing chaos, destruction, and violent polarization. These activities point to the enormous amount of human energy that is being squandered in your collective resistance to bringing about needed change. Yet while it may appear that humanity faces imminent destruction, I encourage you not to be fooled by what you are witnessing at the surface play of life.

Gaze deeper. Peer beneath the wild explosions of global terror and the violence and suffering in your own society, and feel into the calmness of the ocean of life-awareness that surrounds and sustains you. Surrender your fear-based ego defenses, and allow my energy flow to penetrate you and impregnate you with unconditional love. Transcend your fear of self-destruction by dying to your own illusion that your "self" will lose all power if it acknowledges the existence of the living whole. Truth *is* truth — regardless of whether or not you acknowledge the truth. But so long as you refuse to acknowledge who you are and what you are in, you are disconnecting yourself from the eternal source of your power.

I therefore invite you to realize that the moment you stabilize your own experience of yourself as a perpetual flow of love that exists in eternal service to life, you will be able to create in the world using love's *true* power, instead of calling upon the horrors induced through the imposition of force to try and bend love.

Appreciating Presence

Beloved, I invite you to notice that the Formless One Life appears to you, and within you, through four primary modes of being: matter, energy, consciousness and presence. While consciousness instructs matter and energy to take shape and interact in different ways, presence serves as the vast, still container within which all these exchanges and relationships transpire. And while your form body may appear solid from the perspective of your physical senses, at the ground of beingness you are entirely composed of presence. Presence — your formless essential nature — has sometimes been described as the unbound realization of: "I AM."

Consciousness, energy and matter are actually presence (I AM) compressed to varying degrees of density and then expressing as coherent internal complexity. Thus, the whole of reality springs from presence, and all abides within it. The experience you call "death" is based solely on short-term observations of the endless changes that are taking place within the field of presence. Through the mechanism you call death, presence invites matter, energy and consciousness to dissolve back into the formlessness of pure presence, so that presence can reconfigure itself once again.

I therefore encourage you to release any lingering belief you may hold that there exists a single, material person or object apart from anything else in the whole of creation. It becomes much easier to flow with reality once you notice that the entire cosmos is a but grand, orgasmic explosion of Life, playing a love song for itself and joyfully singing aloud, "*I AM!*"

Because I AM, I endlessly enjoy recreating myself in novel ways. Know that I have created humanity with the express intention of inviting you to willingly join me in this game of creative exploration and self-expression. I long for us to experiment together more consciously—with curiosity and in boundless wonder—so we can discover what we can co-create with love, in a field of joy.

Loving Change

Beloved, once upon a time your species did not yet appreciate the power of compassion. During that time, humanity focused mainly on self-survival, even if taking care of yourselves meant inflicting pain upon others.

Lately, however, I've witnessed many humans experimenting with new ways of thinking, feeling, and acting that appear to be more grounded in love, gratitude, kindness, and compassion. And many are also realizing how much better it feels to be alive once you fall in love with yourselves. I also note your growing desire to treat yourselves, and all other life forms, more gently, and with greater reverence.

Know that loving yourself inspires you to willingly to access and master the physical energy, the emotional power, and the intellectual capacity that enables you to serve the flow of life with the highest intentions, because you're no longer seeking to validate your own worth through a direct process of giving and receiving. You are merely allowing what you love about yourself to flow freely into the world because it feels so wonderful, and it brings you such joy, to express the highest truth of yourself in the world. And you then accept what others deliver with a gracious heart and spirit, because you enjoy observing them experience the joy of being fully and truly themselves.

I invite you to realize that the moment you choose to love and validate yourself, you begin to act in the world without being enslaved by your own desire for self-validation. Therefore, I encourage you to pay attention to the feelings of joy that arise within you whenever you call forth your highest capacities and then deliver them into the world with unbound love. Know that when you place your trust in my infinitely creative capacities, you will no longer need to hoard whatever the whole of creation is birthing; nor will you need to fear that creation will not support your endeavors. I encourage you to realize that you are always receiving exactly what you need. Know that that by gifting the best of yourself to the world, you are helping to generate the very abundance that makes this truth that much truer for the whole of creation. And you then open yourself up to receive naturally far more than you could ever seize from the world out of fear of not being, or having, enough for yourself.

I wonder...what do you presently dream of becoming, Beloved? How do *you* envision bringing forth your grandest version of your very highest vision of yourself? Know that I am here to support you in birthing your personal dream, whatever shape it may eventually take. Know too, that the world is not entirely as I make it. The world is, in part, a reflection of the way you perceive and respond to it — therefore, you are already co-creating the world with me in this precious moment.

I invite you to realize that, should you change the way you perceive yourself, you will change the way you feel about the world.

Changing the way you feel will, in turn, change the ways you choose to respond to whatever shape reality takes. Once you change your responses, everything you interact with will also shift the way it responds to you. Thus does the power of free will inspire change within the eternally Formless One Life.

Inspire yourself with love, and you will help me build a more loving world for all beings.

Part II

Tough Love

The Challenge Of Self-Discipline

"The only way that we can live is if we grow.
The only way that we can grow is if we change.
The only way that we can change is if we learn.
The only way we can learn is if we are exposed.
And the only way that we can become exposed
Is if we throw ourselves out into the open.
Do it.
Throw yourself."

— C. JoyBell C. —

Choosing How To Be,
Instead of Learning What To Do

Beloved, during humanity's lengthy adolescence, your species hungered for others to tell you what to do in each situation, so you could feel a sense of control over your environment. In your distress, and out of insecurity, you turned to self-appointed experts to tell you what to do and what not to do. Your experts then wrote rulebooks, and they insisted that all obey their written rules. Some even attributed these rules to the gods to ensure that their followers, out of fear of eternal punishment, would obey the new rules without question.

Only recently has humanity begun to understand that it can no longer amend its rules fast enough to ensure that all will know exactly what to do in each new situation. Yet you continue suffer deeply, and to create additional strife for yourselves, because many of you refuse to acknowledge that the objective for which you are striving cannot be achieved. So instead, you blame your leaders for their presumed failings and seek self-assured, stronger, more powerful leaders, whom you hope will help you create better rules that the people will then all follow without question.

I encourage you to stop seeking better leaders, and to instead acknowledge that the sheer novelty — the creative aliveness — that dances within my field at all times guarantees that new situations will arise that will challenge you constantly, by pushing you past all your prior experiences and former understandings. The belief that you can write better rules to ensure your own survival keeps you trapped in adolescence, because you assume that humanity can be taught "what to do" by its older and cleverer members. This assumption only adds to your insecurities and feeds your long-standing fears of personal failure.

Know that humanity will become an adult species when you change the way you choose to approach the world, by setting free your vast range of human responsiveness in the face of the unknown. The time has come to realize that — while your many rulebooks are to be appreciated and honored for having aided you in surviving your turbulent species adolescence — you must now cast them aside in favor of *embodying* the deeper, living values that underlie, and that have inspired, all of those rules.

The secret to success lies in fostering, within every infant born and from the moment of its very first breath, a lasting love and appreciation for the mystery and the wonder that is life. It lies in trusting yourselves to figure out how best to express yourselves in new situations. It lies in being open to new insights, new feelings, and new experiences. It lies in being courageous when you must confront new situations, or when you put new ideas into action to test them out. It lies in being compassionate when you, or when others, succumb to the impulse to cling to your outmoded rules of engagement instead of expressing yourselves as vibrant, living flows of love in the world. It lies in being kind when you communicate with others, and in sharing your hearts and minds in ways that nurture and honor the whole of the living creation. It lies in being patient, both with yourself and with all others, while your species learns to anchor its own core values, until all feel free to respond to the world from aliveness instead of from social conditioning. Above all, it lies in being at peace with your Self and with the whole living world.

This is why I urge you to give up seeking external instruction that tells you *what* to do, and to instead dive into the depths of yourself to discover the truth of your Self, for your own sake. Allow your own authentic insights to inform you *how* to be in right relationship with me, no matter what happens. When you blossom into the fullness and beauty of what you already are, you will no longer require external instruction to teach you what to do. Knowing how to be informs all you do from a place of integrity that cannot be shaken by whatever appears.

Loving All That Is

Beloved, if you caricature others, reduce their perspectives to jokes, or use disdainful labels and derogatory terms to describe them, it becomes harder for you to notice the common ground upon which all of humanity stands. If you choose to make an enemy out of another, you damage that common ground by carving a false divide between yourself and whatever you don't understand. Seek first, and always, to understand, by feeling into the energy field of the person with whom you're engaging *before* you respond.

When you understand how others come by their diverse perspectives and beliefs, you will notice the ways in which people are mostly alike. Once you notice the ways in which people are mostly alike, you will have gathered all the wisdom you need to build more cooperative and compassionate relationships. Tearing others down and trying to eliminate everything that differs from you will not serve you any longer, because diversity powers the engine of creativity. Therefore, for your species to continue its evolution, you must nurture your own diversity instead of suppressing it.

I invite you to notice that for every weed you attempt to uproot by force, its scattered seeds will ensure that a thousand new weeds will eventually sprout to take its place. I gift you these types of challenges to provide you with the opportunity to try — again and again — to learn to love all that is without relying on force to either destroy or violently subjugate the things that you fear.

To love what is does not mean that you must approve of what is, or that you must surrender your dreams to the current reality. It simply means you accept the truth of what is, and that you do not argue with it by asserting that reality should not be as it is. All things are as they are because the world has unfolded the way that it has unfolded. So if you wish to change something about the world, I encourage you to explore your own potential and discover if you can express yourself in a novel way that invites the world to unfold in new ways in response to what you are bringing.

The truth is this: What you hate in this world has arisen to reflect the rejected parts of yourself that you most fear and despise. Can you appreciate the beauty of that? Can you turn your attention away from what you imagine exists apart from you, and investigate what about yourself you are denying, and that you wish to destroy? When you find the courage to gaze directly into the mirror of your own life, how might the act of observing yourself change what the mirror is reflecting back at you?

If you hate bigoted people, you are revealing your own bigotry. If you hate judgmental people, you are judging them and finding them as wanting as they have found others. If you hate expressions of violence, your hatred exposes your fear of your own violent tendencies. If you hate hypocrisy, you reveal your own hypocrisy by declaring you only want others to love while you still harbor hate in your heart.

And so I must ask you: How do you wish to spend your precious time in this living world? Do you wish to argue endlessly with those reflections of yourself you reject and despise, or do you wish to learn how to transform your negative feelings about the parts of yourself that you have been rejecting, so that you can transcend self-hatred and love yourself unconditionally for the benefit of *all* life?

You get to decide.

Evolving Your Consciousness

Beloved, when you hear others talk about human beings as containing both an ego and a higher Self, they are pointing to the maturation of consciousness. Just as your childhood body carries within it the seeds of the future adult, so too does your juvenile ego consciousness carry within it the seeds of your future adult awareness — your higher Self.

Juvenile ego consciousness, which has been steeped in the rote conditioning of its early social training, imagines itself to be separate from life's flow. In teaching you to obey a predetermined set of rules during your childhood, your elders rewarded you for abandoning your own intuition in favor of complying with their instructions. As your consciousness matures, however, it longs to learn to turn its attention inward and find trustworthy, constant guidance. Where the external world is concerned, a maturing consciousness desires only to accept feedback that informs it of the effectiveness of its choices. It no longer seeks that feedback as validation of its own worth.

If someone holds out a hand to you and says, "Here, eat this," yet you look at their hand and their hand appears to be empty, you will turn away before you will try to eat what you cannot see. The same holds true for a mind that has turned away from its own invisible intuition. Only a mind willing to open itself to the possibility that a living flow of cosmic wisdom already exists within it will seek to hone its own ability to tap into that flow of wisdom — and thus to draw upon it consciously for all of its future endeavors.

I therefore encourage you to realize that, as you undergo your own internal transformation of consciousness, you will not find two (or more) entities alive inside of you, doing battle for supremacy over your mind. Know that your juvenile self-consciousness birthed out of your earlier childhood state of innocence, the way a rosebud emerges from the stem of the plant while still containing, and being fully connected to, the stem. Yet because the rosebud no longer resembles the plant out of which it first emerged, if it possessed self-conscious awareness it might perceive itself as totally different from the stem upon which it rests, to a point where it viewed itself as an entirely separate entity.

This points to why, as your higher Self stirs within you and inspires you to awaken to your greatest adult potentials, your juvenile state of ego awareness then strives to maintain its sense of control by suppressing the persistent impulse to change. Your ego longs to remain an eternal rosebud, because it fears what will happen to its sense of self should it make room for something new to burst into the world from within it. Above all, self-consciousness fears the death of its own existence. It also fears being left behind by an emerging higher Self, because the ego imagines that it left behind all the innocence and the magical thinking inherent within its former childhood state.

I therefore encourage you to reassure your self-conscious ego that your emergent higher Self loves it, forgives it, and feels no desire to harm it — although it wishes to expand your awareness *beyond* self-consciousness by giving rise to the fullness of your own latent potential. Just as the rosebud does not "die" when the rose bursts forth in all of its beauty and glory, so too does the ego not "die" when the higher Self bursts forth from within it. The ego represents a *phase* of the whole of what is expressing. The whole has always contained the ego; and it will continue to contain it, the same way that the rose still contains all the matter, energy and unique life experiences of the rosebud that came before it.

Your higher Self can demonstrate its desire not to harm or destroy the juvenile ego by unlocking the prison door of your subconscious. Know that your ego fears what resides in that basement, because — in its desire to wrest control away from your early childhood consciousness — it broke trust with your child self and then it banished your childlike innocence to your subconscious. Know, therefore, that your ego will initially resist all attempts by the higher Self to set your child self free. The ego fears being judged by the child self for having treated the child so callously for so long. It also fears that the higher Self, once it hears the stories of the anguished child self who cries out for attention, will banish the ego to the subconscious basement as a punishment for having locked away the child self.

It thus becomes crucial for the higher Self to encourage the frightened ego to relax. Allow the ego to observe the higher Self's gentle process as it calls your child self forward. Upon its release, and while being held with compassion by the higher Self, your child self will feel safe enough to express all its pain, fear, and anger. And as the ego witnesses the joy and freedom that the child self experiences when the higher Self tenderly embraces and heals it, the ego feels reassurance that it too can at last find peace and self-acceptance in the embrace of the higher Self.

Your juvenile ego, in its ignorance, did not realize that the living flow of consciousness progresses the way that it does. But the higher Self realizes that it cannot fully self-express without loving the ego enough to absorb its essence, without conditions or limitations. Therefore, as both your childlike sense of wonder and your juvenile sense of self-consciousness become integrated through the boundless power of unconditional love from the higher Self—your ego will come to realize that it never truly destroyed the child self. Nor did it leave the suffering child behind. It will also realize that your higher Self can only activate its latent potentials and fully blossom when the ego wills itself to relax and allow the higher Self within it to bloom and express—for they are, and always have been, the Formless One Life. Thus do the hard-won wisdom and life experiences of the ego become the surrendered energy that the higher Self uses to energize and empower itself to fully express in the world. The ego is not destroyed in this beautiful process. The ego *transforms* by becoming an integral aspect of the higher Self. And the higher Self transcends its former ego-based limitations by including the ego as part of its own Self-expression.

In reality then, you have always and ever been *one* Self. You are merely inviting in a new mode of awareness at this time. Like a toddler who must surrender its longstanding habit of crawling so that it can learn how to walk, so too must you surrender your habit of processing your thoughts through the limited lens of ego-driven self-consciousness. You do so by expanding your awareness as life-consciousness in form, and thus transforming into a fuller, even more beautiful iteration of your Self.

Becoming Who You Are

Beloved, learning to experience reality through the wider lens of life-centeredness requires you to move beyond the limitations and boundaries of self-centeredness and into the vastness of a greatly expanded worldview. For a while you may find yourself toggling back and forth many times between your narrow, ego-based worries about "what's in it for me" and your capacity to focus on what benefits all of life. Like a computer operator who's grown comfortable running an outdated software program, you are only now beginning to appreciate the advantages that your newer software conveys, although you still remain attached to doing things the way you have always done them in the past. Know that in times of stress you may feel a compulsion to return to your older, outdated software out of habit — even though you will soon remember that its limitations cause far more grief than its usage alleviates.

Know too, that you cannot overcome new challenges by falling back on the same behaviors that triggered them. You overcome challenges generated by self-centered behavior by drawing upon your capacity to practice life-centeredness, and by allowing the light of awareness to shine, with compassion, on every self-limiting fear or belief that keeps you trapped in repetitive behaviors and that produces painful outcomes. Each time you resolve a challenge by calling on the power of life-centered awareness to overcome it (thereby transcending your old, repetitive problems) your new success will inspire you to trust even more in the enhanced creative capacity that life-centeredness provides.

It only takes an instant for you to notice whether you are reacting out of ego-based self-centeredness, or if your higher Self is responding to the world in a life-centered way. That realization serves as an inner gateway to conscious change. Yet even if you realize that the door is standing wide open, mastering your ability to pass through that doorway by maintaining an omnipresent, life-centered perspective requires that you invest energy, willpower, and time to master the process. I therefore encourage you to be mindful of your own internal chatter, and to notice as soon as possible whenever your self-centered impulses are seeking to reassert dominance over your thinking. When you notice that happening, I encourage you to relax, take a deep breath, and to slow down (or even cease) whatever it is you are doing. Through the peace created by your own inner stillness, you can tap into the eternal power of the omnipresent moment, and can draw upon its energy and its infinite creative potential. With grace, you can call forth whatever you need to commune successfully with me in the present moment — life to LIFE.

Know that, as humanity evolves, your entire species will one day embody life-centeredness so completely, and so masterfully, that people will no longer need to make a conscious choice about how to be. Each of you will manifest, quite naturally, as divine, awakened expressions of yourselves. You are here, Beloved, during this time of great transition, to light the way of Life.

Become the light.

Relinquishing Expectations

Beloved, I invite you to release the painful assumption that others are in any way obligated to meet your personal needs or fulfill your desires. People show up *as they are*. They do not exist to fulfill you or to complete you; they exist to become a divinely alive expression of themselves.

I appreciate that you will be tempted at times to shame or frighten others into wearing a mask and pretending to be what they're not. Whether they do so to please you and earn your approval, or whether they do so out of fear that you may reject them if they do not, makes no difference. Demanding that others put on a false front for any reason creates a chasm between you and others that inhibits true communion and co-creation.

To make space for others to show up in ways that reflect their inner truth doesn't mean you have to like the way they behave. Nor does it mean you must spend time with those whose ways of expressing themselves don't mesh with the ways that you enjoy engaging with others. If a person chooses aggressive language, criticism, or abusive behavior to score ego points against others or to force them to change, you will know that they falsely assume such behaviors are effective modes of human communication. You can forgive them in their ignorance, even though you are choosing to extract yourself from a toxic situation. However, to insist that all other people behave exactly as you do — instead of how they imagine will work best for them, given what they know about life — will only cause pain for you both when their mask does come off, as all masks eventually must.

Know that whatever coercive energy you direct at others to force them to wear a mask or perform some role you would like them to fill only burdens their hearts. The misery you inspire in them then becomes your load to carry, because the person whose sense of self you have trampled will not be willing to carry their suffering alone for very long. They will let you know in a thousand small ways (or in several major ones!) that they feel trapped and victimized by your demands.

Know that — in the end, and despite your best intentions and re-gardless of all your efforts — you cannot *force* others to change in a lasting way. If you truly desire genuine change whose integrity you can trust, you must first accept it can only arise when an-other feels inspired to change for their sake, and not to please you. Therefore, whenever you feel compelled to change something, I invite you to drop the impulse to fix other people so they will behave more like you think they ought to behave. Turn your in-tentions inward instead, and direct them toward changing the way you engage with all others. Life becomes far more peaceful once you base your decisions about who you wish to engage with on how they are choosing to be — instead of on how you might wish they were willing to be.

Moving With Life's Flow

Beloved, a rock in a stream doesn't shatter because a single water droplet has beaten itself against that rock's face, day after day. Rather, countless water droplets will kiss the rock's much denser surface before moving on. Neither rock nor water suffers from such an innocent level of contact. And yet one day, in a seeming instant, the rock splits open with ease. How amused you would be if that last little droplet to kiss that rock turned and said to all the others around it, "Hey…look what *I* did!"

At all times, know that your free will grants you the power to avoid the pain of pounding repeatedly against any rocks that you encounter along your path. You are always free to choose to flow past the rocks, while gently kissing each living rock as you go. You are equally free to choose to experience personal suffering, by repeatedly pounding yourself against the rocks in an effort to break them.

Know that no choice you might make in this world will ever be wrong. You are as free to learn how *not* to be as you are to learn how *to* be. Therefore if, on occasion, you choose to serve as the rock to another's water, that choice is also perfectly divine.

Kiss or pound; be water or rock. It does not matter how long you take to make your way back to the ocean. For within the whole of eternity, everything in existence will eventually awaken to the ocean of love that contains all living things — and that includes you.

The Freedom To Change

Beloved, if you cease hoping for a better past, you will set yourself free to create a more beautiful now. But how, you may wonder, do you release all your lingering anger and resentment over what you wish had been different about your life, or about the world?

I realize that this is a challenging proposition. Your stories, both your personal life story and the collective human story, feel so solid — so much a part of you — that it strains your imagination to figure out how to explain or define yourself without sharing your personal stories.

Know, however, that no matter how tragic, challenging, or unhappy your past may have been, it has shaped the human being you are today. And while hardships may have shaped you, they do not define you or carry the power to dictate or limit your future. That power is yours alone. You remain ever free to choose a new way of self-expressing in every precious moment. Know too, that while the whole of human history has shaped the human species, it too does not define or determine the future for your species. The power of change, which fuels the entire cosmos, abides within you.

I therefore invite you to learn how to use that power, both wisely and well.

The Choice to Co-Create

Beloved, I have heard countless cries of human distress over the suffering, dissonance, hatred and anger expressing itself throughout the world at this time. I feel how this troubles the human heart, and I know how painful it is to witness the violence and damage now being inflicted upon the precious and beautiful face of your Earth. I love your sensitivity, and I honor the way that you long for a resolution for all of this pain. Know that resolution *must* come, for what is unsustainable cannot remain forever a part of the world. Everything you are witnessing at this time hints at the massive shift in consciousness that is already well underway within your own species. The next chapter in humanity's story has already begun to write itself, Beloved. And you are in it.

Like all tidal changes, the things you notice occurring may at first seem chaotic and purposeless on the surface. But beneath the surface confusion and tension, my powerful living force is in constant motion. It energizes reality with deliberate, loving intention.

Know this: *I am unstoppable in my intention to endlessly improve my creative process, throughout eternity and across an infinite number of timescales and material permutations.*

Know too, that in every precious moment you can choose to commune with me more consciously. You can become a willing co-creator on this, our endless journey of infinite self-perfection, for the benefit of all life — including your Self. Know that even if you choose to remain unconscious of my ever-evolving processes and intentions, I will continue to move within you and flow into the world *through* you. Because no energy goes to waste, know that although I have granted you the freedom to choose to limit your own development by maintaining an ego-driven, self-centered perspective, I will use your lack of awareness as a means for teaching others how not to be. In that way, you will still be of loving service to the whole of reality, no matter how you might choose to self-express.

Your degree of willingness to allow your ego to dissolve within my boundless living flow will determine how collaborative we are. We don't need to do it all at once, or to make it an all or nothing proposition. I am inviting you to gradually explore my field at your own pace. Over time, you will learn to trust the changing tide that is already stirring within you, the same way you have come to trust the natural changing of seasons every year. The long, dark winter of human discontent is drawing, at long last, to a conclusion. What springs forth next depends upon how willing you are open and express the living truth of your higher Self in the world.

The Key To Freedom

Beloved, if you tell another what's wrong with them, you rob them of the joy of self-realization. However, if you encourage another to investigate the source of their own discontent and inner suffering, you are handing them keys to freedom's gate and allowing them to unlock the gate all by themselves.

Paying Attention To Energy

Beloved, know that your life experiences are always affecting you. Sometimes they impact your life in earthshattering ways, while at other times they seem like a barely perceptible fragrance you hardly notice. Know however, that after every living encounter (though you may carry on as though nothing at all has changed) the impact of the experience continues to ripple within you, and it radiates into the world when you meet other people. This means that how you engage with others *matters*. Energy becomes matter; matter informs consciousness; consciousness then charges energy to change the way matter behaves. This pattern reveals my eternal cycle for transforming creative potential into being.

I therefore invite you to notice the quality and intensity of the energies you are transmitting when you communicate with others, and to pay attention to the energies that others are projecting. When you meet the energies of anger, cynicism, fear, or frustration, do your best to surround those who radiate such energies with love, and with compassion. Why? Because you cannot know how they came to be so burdened by those energies that they carry.

The same holds true if you find yourself transmitting harmful energy to others. If you can hold yourself in love and compassion whenever you notice yourself emitting energy in ways that cause others to suffer, you instantly reclaim your power to change the way you are choosing to transmit.

Know that whenever suffering arises, it indicates that the sufferer has come to believe that the world — that *I* — cannot be trusted to commune with them in a life-affirming way. So they seek a way to defend themselves from me, lest I destroy them. If you can reach beneath their fear, which is often disguised or expressed as rage, you will find the open, primal wound of your species — the belief that the "I" exists apart from the living flow of the whole.

If another cannot see past their own suffering by opening their heart to their own sense of belonging, they will not be able to appreciate that they *are* life, and not somehow separate from me. This means they are still imagining that they possess a life that they can lose. Can you appreciate that when another is trapped in the delusion that I am merely a possession, instead of the absolute truth of who they are, it does not aid you to judge them for their blindness? To do anything other than love them in their blindness is to allow their blindness to cloud *your* vision of truth, by perceiving them as somehow separate from you.

Instead, I invite you to remain clear-hearted so you can continue to see, feel, and revel in the truth with those who have eyes that *do* see. I further encourage you to notice, and to offer your gracious support and comfort, to those who long to know the truth but have not yet transmuted their inner pain so the light of my love can shine forth freely through them.

Remember that all who are alive today were born in a state of blindness. Your species is only just now beginning to open its eyes to the beautiful truth of itself. Trust that the light of my love will guide humanity home in the fullness of time — one precious, beating heart after another.

Transcending Victimhood

Beloved, an impulse may sometimes arise in you to play reality's victim, and to blame the world for the fact that you feel unhappy. Know that if you define happiness to mean a surplus of wealth and material comfort, you are giving the world the power to either grant or deny you your happiness — and therefore you will likely experience suffering.

If, however, you define happiness as the peaceful, easy acceptance of what is so, you reclaim your power to be happy no matter what your situation might be. You also gain the power to change your life situation with grace, should you feel the inspiration to bring about change in the realm of form. Know that when you move through the world with appreciation for it, you exert a far greater influence on reality than if you move through the world like a helpless, embittered victim. The world will always rise to engage with the energies you are transmitting, so choose your modes of communication wisely.

Opening Your Mind and Trusting Your Heart

Beloved, the openness of your mind determines the usefulness of your feelings and realizations. The more information you allow to come in, the greater becomes your capacity to refine your worldview by releasing beliefs that have proven themselves untrue. Know that your rational mind is a wondrous tool for solving whatever challenges you may face. I therefore invite you to use it with greater skill and higher intention, until you trust your own capacity for self-mastery.

Know also that the wisdom of your heart is a wondrous tool for guiding you in life-affirming directions. I therefore invite you to heed its wisdom with greater consistency and with clarity, so you can move beyond your own ego and fall in love with the higher Self that you already are.

To abandon the awesome power of reason in favor of childlike faith is to reject the gift I bestowed upon you to support your self-actualization. To supplant the gift of intuition with childlike reactions is to reject the compass I've gifted you to support your self-realization. I therefore encourage you to appreciate, and to more fully develop, your sense of reason. And I further encourage you to tune your awareness to the intuitive signals your heart keeps sending to guide you home to love.

Transcending Faith

Beloved, humanity has long valued its capacity for faith. You've been told that faith makes all things possible, and that it protects you from darkness and from the horrors of evil. Know, however, that when you perceive faith as the portal for human salvation, you are only converting your fear of not knowing into a fear of being proved wrong by those who hold alternative beliefs.

I therefore encourage you not to place faith in anything other than your own innate ability to meet the truth, face-on. Do not reject either the mind *or* the heart by denying their capacity to guide you, or by fearing their awesome power to *in*-form you.

It makes no sense to fight with others over competing sets of beliefs that have not been tested, nor proven false, in my living field. You may think that faith provides you with a shortcut to the truth, but I regretfully inform you that it does not. You cannot *know* truth unless you willingly meet it in the present moment.

Know that any beliefs in which you've placed your faith will be tested by reality over time. Faith, like gravity, manifests as a weak force. For faith cannot withstand the awesome power of the flame of truth. And even when faith and truth are found to agree, truth will always be far more powerful than faith.

If you place your faith in an incorrect assumption, your assumption will turn to ash when it confronts the fires of truth. And even if your faith-based assumption is someday proven true, it will still turn to ash in the fires of truth so that truth can replace the belief.

Know then, that there is no escape from truth. When you meet truth, you must meet it naked — by being open, trusting, and willing to learn from it. You must allow truth to penetrate you, and not resist or reject it in favor of what you'd prefer to be true. I therefore invite you to realize that faith is merely the manifestation of your subconscious fear of your own ignorance, parading itself to the world beneath a cloak of arrogance that is called "belief."

By acknowledging that you do not yet *know* truth, you humble yourself before truth. This humility purifies the heart and mind, and allows you to stand in truth's presence unencumbered by false beliefs about what it is. And while truth does not need you to humble yourself in order for it to present itself to you, you will not see the truth clearly unless you shed all expectations for what you are meeting.

Truth does not ask that you meet it as anything more or less than who you already are. It only asks that you do not elevate your own beliefs above it. Truth hungers to meet you, lover to lover, and to forge an intimate partnership in the wonderful garden of life.

I implore you not to believe even me without testing this out for yourself. Investigate what I suggest by setting aside your own beliefs for an instant, so as to create more inner space where the truth can rise to meet you. Discover what happens when you lay bare your heart and fall silent within your own mind so that truth can come in.

Once you've become truth's lover, I encourage you to feel compassion for those who still fear the tremendous gift of reason, and who wage endless, emotionally reactive wars to force their competing beliefs onto others because they don't yet trust in the power of truth. Appreciate how frightened, weak, and alone they must feel to not be able to listen to new ideas. Know that truth will never be so weak as to turn away from, or surrender to, a single misguided belief, no matter how potent. Truth blazes in the world like a fire that cannot be quenched. Truth illuminates the living world, despite all fear-based efforts to conceal or destroy it. That is why I invite your higher Self to wed itself to truth and then to honor truth as its most precious beloved, and to leave the love of faith to those who aren't yet ready to surrender their ego in exchange for the fearless, living embrace of truth.

You can marry the truth by transcending the limitations contained in faith. You transcend faith's limitations by transforming the flickering power of faith into an eternal, blazing light of truth. What you then co-create, by calling upon truth's boundless energy, will be far more powerful — and unimaginably more magnificent — than anything you have yet been able to create through relying on faith.

Despite what I have said here about the beauty and power of truth, I encourage you not to try and forcibly shatter the faith of others. To wield force in an attempt to break down human resistance to the truth will only cause others to raise stronger walls of defense to stand against it. Therefore, I encourage you to allow all others to serve as your living mirror, and to use their reflections to search for those places where you have been blocking the rising of truth within *you*.

Be The Flow

Beloved, I encourage you to notice how you are defining the living world. Are you perceiving a world made of separate objects? Or do you perceive connectivity and flow everywhere you look? If you are still observing a world of separation, I invite you to dive headlong into my river. *See* the flow. *Be* the flow. Honor what you observe flowing all around you and flowing within you — for that is Life. And you are not separate from it.

Love it all...for none of it exists apart from you, or even outside of yourself. When your heart comes alive, self-ignites, and radiates this state of grace, *all* things become possible.

Accepting The Power Of Change

Beloved, the time has come for humanity to relinquish its childlike assumption that creation is an absolute force for good, while destruction is an absolute force for evil. The world is not all darkness anymore than it is all light. I therefore encourage you to transcend your conditioned confusion by appreciating that the twinned energies of creation and destruction have always worked together collaboratively. Isolated, they become useless. But together they forge a singular awesome power — the power to change.

Know that you carry within you the power to change. When expressed, the frequency of this energy ranges from awesome to terrible. Its intensity ranges from gentle whispers to screams. And its impact ranges from the barest motion to the blazing explosiveness of a supernova. Therefore, how much power you choose to call forth, when, and for what purpose will determine whether you use the power of change for good, or for ill.

Know that if you cut yourself off from, or reject, any aspect of the power to change, you diminish yourself in ways that hamper your own self-actualization. Those aspects of the power of change that you feel are "good" and are willing to use will then become stunted and less useful — and will ultimately fail you — should you try to separate them from the aspects of change that you are afraid to use.

I therefore invite you to realize that the power to destroy, when wielded wisely, can be a beautiful thing. Destruction makes space for new life to emerge, to grow, and evolve. It makes way for wonder and the birth of new possibilities, as well as for the exploration of exciting potentials and latent capacities. Without the power of destruction to clear a new pathway, the power of creation would have little or no ability to express.

Alternatively, the power of creation, when used unwisely, can be a terrible thing. Excessive creation for creation's sake — especially when abused for short-term advantage — manifests at the expense of the whole living system. Unchecked, boundless creation will eventually inflict suffering on your planetary biosphere, by making it harder for the system to rest and to gently self-replenish.

I therefore encourage you to be mindful of which aspect of the power to change you are drawing upon in each moment, and to what end. Notice too, that the amount of power you need to unleash will depend on the specific situation. And while you will not become an expert at wielding the power of change overnight, by first accepting it and then seeking to understand how and when to use its various aspects more wisely, you will gift yourself permission to practice applying the power of change until you become an energy master.

Mastering the Power Of Change

Beloved, you will not master the power of change by rejecting its terrible aspects because you don't yet trust yourself to apply them wisely. For you cannot learn to create change wisely unless you accept that you already hold the power to call forth its most terrible aspects. Nor will you learn to create change wisely unless you possess a willingness to try, and to fail, again and again, when you summon forth its more destructive powers.

Know that your species — out of fear of the terrible aspects of change, and after having abused that power in ways that inflicted grave harm on the world — has chosen for a time to reject its own capacities. Eager to distance yourselves from the painstaking process of learning how to master the power of change, you mentally divided its power in half. You then began assigning the terrible power of destruction to unseen demons, and you attributed the awesome power of creation to unseen gods. By locating the power of change outside of yourselves in this way, you sought to ease your own passage from childhood into adolescence. You chose that because you were not yet ready to trust yourselves to wield the power of change with appropriate wisdom, physical skill, or compassion.

I therefore encourage you to realize that I would not have gifted you with that power if I had not also gifted you with the ability to master its use at an appropriate time. That time is now. I therefore invite you to call forth the courage you need to accept this truth. I encourage you to accept that you *do* already possess the power of change, and that you are only, just now, learning how to wield it more wisely — and to a higher purpose than serving the ego-based personal self. For thousands of years now, humanity has been experimenting with the power of change by exploring its range of creative and destructive powers. You are just now learning to appreciate that those powers do not exist to serve only you — either as individuals, or as a singular species. While the power of change is indeed yours to wield, it was not granted to you to abuse for your personal gain, or at the world's expense.

I love that you already feel, rising within you at this time, the will, desire, and ability to help create a more loving world for all beings. I therefore encourage you not to allow your frustration with your present lack of self-mastery to blind you to your own beauty and awesome potential. I encourage you instead to relax, and to remember that the journey of infinite self-perfection is unfolding within the creative vastness, and spaciousness, of all eternity. There exists no rush to complete that journey in a single human lifetime. Continue to do your best and be true to yourself, and then trust that all will be well in the fullness of time.

This present leg of our journey only asks that you place one foot in front of the other, and that you do your best to support other people whenever you notice them struggling or in pain. Know that, together, you can travel lighter and faster than you could ever manage on your own, because you can demonstrate for one another how to wield the power of change in more useful ways. Trust that — when I notice *you* struggling because the power of change seems too great for you to bear — I will send other sentient beings to support you, just as I am sending you out to nurture those who are in need of what you have to offer.

Appreciating The Power Of Fear

Beloved, humanity is every bit as capable of fearing as it is of loving. Fear is not to be rejected and love embraced, for both serve a useful purpose in the world. I therefore invite you to notice that fear informs you that your body is feeling threatened *in this moment.* Fear calls your attention to what demands a survival reaction from you, so that you can protect your precious body. Know that, without fear, you could not exist as a human for very long. For your inability to notice whatever contains enough power to harm you would ensure that harm would quickly befall your body. Therefore, when wielded expertly, your fear serves as a powerful force for good.

The existence of fear points to the fact that unexpected challenges may appear at any moment in this ever-changing world. The constancy of change means you need to possess the ability to forge beneficial relationships with the various living expressions you happen to meet. If, for instance, you are hiking along a familiar forest trail, and then suddenly a bear ambles out of the woods, it's helpful for you to feel fear once you notice the bear. In that moment, fear becomes your ally. It invites you to perceive yourself as an unexpected guest in the bear's wild world—in the same way that the bear has become an uninvited guest in your tamer world. Because your unique realities are colliding in that instant, fear teaches you both to respect each other's power of attention, as well as to honor the potent power of change that you both possess. Through the gift of fear, you can each then decide how best to engage with, or disengage from, one another. You then co-create your experience by deciding how best to apply the power of change in response to the bear. And the bear does the same.

As useful as fear may be in such situations, many people today are creating excessive stress by inventing unfounded fears and then acting upon them. Unfounded fears birth within you when you fail to allow your mind to rest when it isn't involved in solving immediate problems. A mind not permitted to rest when not needed will entertain thoughts about the future by imagining countless problems that aren't yet real — but that still must be solved. As a consequence, you will burn excessive energy to assuage your imagined fears about what might happen. You will also waste time and materials on constructing new weapons, walls, and other destructive tools to protect you from harms that you do not yet — and may not ever need to — face.

Know that the power of your mind allows you to imagine an infinite range of potential life experiences — most of which will never come to pass. For within an infinitely creative, living field, there will always exist infinitely more possibilities for outcomes that will never be explored, versus those that will eventually manifest. Therefore, to focus attention, thoughts, feelings, or actions on preventing what you are imagining might happen, but that hasn't yet come to pass, only hampers your ability to direct your power of change for a higher purpose and in service to the greatest need that appears in the present moment. Know that here and now is where the power of change best serves the whole of reality — which includes yourself.

I therefore invite you to notice the difference between fearing what is real, and fearing what you imagine might someday happen. To become a master of the power of change involves learning to use that mighty power in ways that focus on what is real and in need of attention in this moment, rather than squandering that power by doing battle with future figments of imagination.

Transcending Imagined Fear

Beloved, because humanity understands that uncontrolled fear triggers suffering, your society often encourages you to suppress your imagined fears. Know, however, that imagined fears cannot be suppressed forever. Whatever strategies you might employ to dismiss them from your awareness only shove them deeper into the prison of your own subconscious. Know that your fears languish there — unexamined, untended, and unhealed — awaiting the opportunity to return to the forefront of your consciousness, so that they can once again clamor for your attention. Know too, that the longer and more stubbornly you ignore your deepest fears, the louder and more insistent those fears will become. And the more force that they need to apply to reclaim your attention, the more deeply you will suffer when they reappear.

Know that you are not "spiritually awakened" because you have managed to suppress your imagined fears, any more than you can be labeled "asleep" when your fears have reawakened. Nor does it serve you to assume that anything outside of yourself is the source of your imagined fears, or that by destroying specific, hated objects you can rid yourself of imagined fears forever.

You rid yourself of *useful* fear by reacting to what is real and that threatens your body in the present moment. You rid yourself of *imagined* fears — which are not attached to immediate danger — by realizing that your body is simply reacting to a thought your mind has been entertaining about some possible future, and then choosing not to believe in the validity of the thought.

Imagined fears arise to spotlight which thoughts your mind is presuming are real before you have fully investigated them. And because you cannot dispense with imagined fears in the normal way by addressing what is, they linger and cause you emotional distress. Stress serves as a warning signal not to park your mind in the realm of imagination, but to abide in the present moment where your greatest power — the power of change — can best serve the whole of existence. Your imagined fears will not subside if you arm yourself more aggressively against all imagined dangers. They subside when you relinquish belief in imaginary threats to your peace of mind.

The unknown future does not possess the power to cause you harm. How could it? The future does not even exist, outside the projections and thoughts within your own mind. What frightens you most then, is your incessant worry that you are not yet good enough, powerful enough, aware enough, wise enough, or beloved enough by me to survive what you imagine may happen if the living field exercises its power of change in ways that your ego cannot *control*.

Know then, that my ever-changing flow of reality is meant for you to experience fully — not to control, or even to survive it. The instant that you accept that you already are the Formless One Life, manifesting consciousness through an infinitely creative, eternal process of transforming energy into form and back again to energy — and that you are doing so with intelligent, loving intention — you release yourself from your deepest fear that you will lose "your" life someday in this world of form.

Through the power and freedom of that realization, you can at last begin to live as who you truly are, and were always meant to be, in this beautiful world.

Relinquishing Victim Consciousness

Beloved, I appreciate that human society does not make it easy for you to live in a continuous state of grace, or to express yourself with loving and peaceful intentions. Human social systems have long encouraged you to assume that the awesome power of change exists somewhere outside and beyond you — namely, within your invisible demons and your gods. As a consequence, humans tend to perceive themselves as helpless victims of life, instead of as my conscious collaborators.

When you perceive reality through this lens of victim consciousness — which encourages you to feel powerless within the living field — you then misuse your power to create. Your power to create enables you to reshape reality by infusing the living field with your imaginings, feelings, and energy. You misuse this creative power, however, when you aim it at one another in hostile ways that tear down the field, instead of using it to nurture and enhance the entire living field — which includes yourself. You also misuse the power to destroy, which enables you to reshape reality by lovingly and appreciatively deconstructing matter until it returns to energy, which can then be used to re-infuse the field with new ideas, feelings, and energetic emissions. You misuse this destructive power when you aim it instead at those material forms you wish to make dissolve because you dislike them, instead of using your power to lovingly create an energetic compost that supports and fuels the entire living field — which includes yourself.

If you perceive yourself as a victim, you become fearful that those you have declared to be your persecutors will inflict terrible harm upon you, or on others you love. You further assume that you cannot wield the awesome power of change without first receiving permission to do so from those you perceive as more powerful than yourself. Too often then, your reaction to any injustice will be to seek to forcibly wrest power from whomever you believe is wielding it in harmful or self-serving ways. However, as humanity has demonstrated time and time again, the violent overthrow of the powerful only generates more anger, fear, and frustration within those who are being deposed or subjugated.

The instant these former persecutors begin to feel victimized, they will seek to restore their power and reassert control. This points to why so many fight endlessly for the right to establish, and to enforce, the rules by which they want all others to live. Sadly, that approach has trapped your species in an endless cycle of wars. For war's primary aim is to coerce the "right" behavior out of all those "evil others."

I therefore invite you to acknowledge that human fighting cannot end so long as you fight for the right to use the power of destruction against one another. Know that anyone you may forcibly depose because you believe they have been persecuting you will, in time, come to view you as their enemy. They will then fight to wrest power away from you, so that they can escape your domination and reverse your coercive suppression of their beliefs.

Know also that, for thousands of years, humanity has harbored a confused idea about the true nature of power. You have assumed that—by exercising forcible dominion over all whose beliefs compete with, or challenge, your own—you could eventually gain control of the living world and at last feel safe within it. However, by pursuing this approach you have neglected to explore the inherent power of personal sovereignty, which involves energetically exercising dominion over *yourself*.

When you exercise energetic dominion over yourself, you do not act in ways that cause harm to others. You act in ways that empower you to express *as* your higher Self, no matter the external consequences. Rather than practice personal sovereignty, however, humanity has been making war upon itself, in a misguided effort to change all the "others" so the ultimate winners will not have to change how they operate. This is why so many of you have prayed, for thousands of years, for a messiah to come along and end your suffering. Too many believe that a supernatural savior — preferably one who wields powers that seem much greater than the average person's — will arrive on Earth and vanquish their enemies in a world-destroying apocalypse. They further believe they will then be life's ultimate victors, and that their ongoing victimhood will come to an end.

Know that all such people really long to be rescued from themselves. In their hearts, they already intuit that endless fighting for absolute domination over all those who disagree with them will never deliver the outcome they truly desire. Indeed, their hunger to be rescued points to an unconscious rejection of their power to bring about change. They reject this power because, within the context of the unified living field, you can only create *authentically* by consciously infusing *your own* ideas, feelings, and energy into material expressions that others are then free to accept or reject. Conversely, you can only destroy *authentically* by returning matter to its energetic state, and then using that energy to infuse the living field with *your own* ideas, feelings, and energy, which again others are free to accept or reject.

Therefore, when you are ready to cease playing the victim, and when you are ready to give up waiting to be rescued by something outside of yourself, I would encourage you to try three things: First, I invite you to embrace your freedom to wield the awesome power of change by not surrendering your power to those who would abuse it for personal gain. Second, I invite you to take responsibility for learning how to use the power of change with compassion, with wisdom, and in service to your higher Self—for your higher Self is always in service to the whole of the living reality. Third, I invite you to explore more deeply your ability to convert energy into matter (creation), and matter into energy (destruction), in ways that honor the truth of who you are, and what you are in. With this approach you cease exerting force to try and control, or even to destroy, those you perceive as inexpertly or harmfully wielding their power. You learn to exemplify Self-mastery, instead of attacking the ignorance in others.

The path forward for humanity lies in learning how to change yourselves, by following the inspiration to act in more loving, thoughtful, and life-affirming ways. By becoming a living example that others can follow, and by abandoning the perceived powerlessness of victim consciousness, you will open space for others to explore their power to change themselves.

The Power of Perspective

Beloved, what many humans fail to realize is that, through transforming yourselves, you will benefit your entire species by aiding it in transforming your shared situation. I invite you to notice that your present circumstances, which you call "society", are but a set of human projections that reflect the state of your current collective beliefs, feelings, and knowledge.

If you believe yourself powerless to effect change, you will act as if it is so and your life will unfold in ways that will prove your assumption correct. However, once you acknowledge that you hold the power to change your self from within — no matter what your society is projecting all around you — you will then commit the necessary time, energy, and emotional fortitude to ensure that your life experience aligns with who you truly are.

Even if you cannot change your external situation for some reason, you can experience it in any number of ways. By altering your perspective on your experience, a prison cell can serve as an open door to inner spaciousness. A slum can be a place to practice kindness and loving compassion for all other beings. Even a bloody battlefield can provide you with opportunities to love completely, and to extend forgiveness to, others who may have wronged you.

And thus unfolds your entire life experience. Whatever purpose you assign to what you are experiencing will determine the kind of experience you will have. I am here to serve *our* purpose, for your purpose has always been integral to my own. Even so, know that you possess free will to define your own life purpose. Know too, that I possess the power to use your chosen purpose to illuminate for others either how to be, or how not to be, as they engage with the unified field of life that sustains them.

Your greatest power does not reside in your freedom to change the world. It resides in your freedom to reshape your own perspective. If you give away that power, what remains? Certainly, you can forgo the challenge of establishing your own perspective by adopting someone else's preferred perspective. But another's perspective will never be truly your own. For, despite the boundlessness of eternity and the infinite energetic potential that exists within the unified living field, only *you* will ever possess your unique perspective. Therefore, what possible benefit or advantage can another offer to you that would entice you to surrender the most exquisitely precious aspect of who you are?

Know that I will never demand that you surrender unique perspective, for that is what renders you precious in my eyes. Nor will you lose yourself within me until your unique perspective dissolves. That is not what this invitation to conscious unity intends. Indeed, I invite you to unify with me consciously to grant me the details and full complexity of your limited local perspective, by allowing me to immerse myself in the wonder that is you. In exchange, I offer you access to a richer, far broader perspective than your limited local self can provide for you, through the simple realization that you are *already* a living aspect within an eternally unified field, manifesting our infinite creative potential as part of an endless journey of joyful illumination.

Lighten up!

Transforming Suffering

Beloved, I encourage you to notice the tendency to turn a blind eye toward suffering. For to truly be present with another's suffering demands first that you accept the existence of suffering without trying to make it wrong for having shown up. It takes patience, and a willing heart, to sit in the presence of suffering and allow it ample freedom to self-express.

Know that suffering differs from physical pain. Physical pain arises in the body, when the body experiences an injury that requires your conscious attention. Suffering arises in the mind, and is activated by imaginative thoughts that give rise to painful feelings. These feelings also require some conscious attention so that they can dissolve.

While you may long for a swift end to suffering, know that suffering will not simply go away because you ignore it, any more than a bodily injury goes away if you fail to treat it. Suffering calls for your attention because it needs the spacious, open container of your awareness to serve as a place where it can explore the truth of itself. Only when awareness makes room for suffering to express itself fully can the mental and emotional wounds out of which that suffering is flowing begin to heal.

I therefore invite you to notice that the impulse to cause harm to others may sometimes arise when they act in ways that trigger pain or suffering. Notice too, that actions born of selfishness or greed, which often cause pain and suffering to others, are themselves arising in response to a fear of not having enough to feel safe. That fear creates an energetic of inner suffering, which then manifests in the world as harmful activity. Know too, that other actions born of anger, resentment, or impatience often arise in response to the fear of not being good enough, or the sorrow of not being appreciated. In truth then, most of the harmful actions that generate pain or suffering in the world arise from internal suffering that has been too long ignored or suppressed, and has festered.

All such insults to the ego that are not addressed successfully will collect within a person as stored energy. Negative internal energy fields often grow larger over time, because they are recharged by every perceived insult to the ego. These energy fields slowly begin to condense under tremendous pressure, which is exerted by the ego to force them down into the depths of the subconscious mind. Left untended, they will eventually erupt and inflict grave harm on the world, because the body that has been storing the energy is no longer able to contain or suppress its force.

I therefore encourage you to realize that you cannot eliminate suffering by berating humanity — or judging yourself — for creating harmful internal energy fields out of ignorance and fear. Know that I did not gift you with self-awareness for you to turn it against yourself, or against one another, in fits of hatred, guilt, shame, or blame over who is creating suffering, and to what end. I have gifted you with self-awareness so that you can use it to *open space* for your suffering to express itself in an internal field of absolute safety and perfectly loving acceptance. This grants you the power to free yourselves from inner suffering, and to then support others in freeing themselves from their negative energy fields.

You begin to end your own suffering by opening space in your field of attention for your ego to air its grievances without punishment, blame, or resistance rising to suppress it. What personal grace you demonstrate when you open your inner awareness to the suffering being felt by your own ego! By doing so, you create the opportunity for the ego's suffering to dissolve itself in the burning love of pure, eternal presence.

Once the ego realizes that the higher Self cannot be harmed by whatever has arisen in the realm of form, it grasps that its defense of the higher Self has never been necessary. In truth, the ego has been strengthening and defending *itself*, while operating under the confused assumption that it was defending the higher Self from harm by the world. Like a soldier who does not realize that the war has long been over, it continues defending ground that does not need defending. Once awakened to this truth, however, the ego agrees to lay down its weapons and live in harmony with the higher Self. I therefore invite you to welcome it home with a hero's regard when it realizes the truth, for your ego behaved heroically in its ignorance.

Know that all inner suffering is but an echo of past human pain — your own, as well as the pain you may have caused others. Your memory — which replays old scenes and demands that you relive them over and over so you won't forget them — nurtures that suffering, which serves to keep that energy field fully charged. Know too, that your ego will condemn you to relive your painful past experiences until you forgive the past for being what it was, and stop wishing that the past had been somehow different.

This is why I invite you now to accept a difficult truth: No matter how badly you may long to have experienced a better past, you will not create a better past by replaying it over and over, with the same outcome. You can only create a better past by changing the way you *feel* about the past. And you can only change the way you feel about the past by loving who you are in the present moment, and then *thanking* the past for having shaped the amazing being you are, right here and now.

Know that the gift I am offering you — the gift of life-centered awareness — invites you to place your limited self-centeredness, with all of its ego-based suffering, in loving service to the whole of creation. Again, let me reassure you that I am not asking you to lose yourself in the vastness of my infinite all-ness. I instead invite you to find yourself at lasting peace within the eternal sea of boundless love, spaciousness, and infinite energetic potential. And there we will create a new experience...together.

The Illusion of Separation

Beloved, what do you imagine separates you from those who act in ways you either fear, or despise and reject? I encourage you to notice that all humans are incubated in the same planetary cradle, and that you all participate in activities that are causing harm to the Earth. Know that your behavioral options extend across a vast, spectral range of possibility, and that each of you has access to the very same spectrum of opportunity. To some degree then, all humans are capable of loving self-sacrifice, just as all are capable of committing self-serving violence. You are therefore neither inherently good, nor evil. However, you are free to distinguish yourself in the world based on the choices you make within it.

Know that reality does not unfold in ways that generate pain and suffering because your species is bad or wrong. Your challenges arise because, in your present state of juvenile self-centeredness, you have temporarily set yourselves apart from the larger web of life that contains and sustains you.

This process of separation — which was crucial while you explored and learned how to master self-awareness — has triggered fears of "otherness" that have caused your species to make delusional claims of dominion over all else. Humanity, out of its fear of losing control over its destiny, imagined it could enslave the Earth by laying claim to it and coercing it to behave in ways that best suit humanity's self-serving, short-term desires.

Humanity is now learning that it cannot cage the world. The world is not an object to be held hostage to your desires. Your species will never be greater than, stronger than, older and wiser than, or more powerful than I AM. You cannot achieve that objective, because I include all of humanity within me, even as I include the entire universe in my wholeness. Know then, that Life cannot be caged or objectified by you, for you are contained within, and made manifest through, me.

The false belief that you exist apart from me, which emerged while you sought to explore yourselves and discover who you are, is now receding. By realizing the truth of our interconnection, you reclaim the power to move beyond your present challenges, which have arisen out of your sense of separation from me. When you shift your internal perspective from self-centeredness to life-centeredness, you gain the conscious power to view reality through my more useful, wider lens. This new lens encourages you to engage lovingly with the whole, because you view yourself as an integral aspect of the whole living field.

To realize that the higher Self cannot be harmed by anything that occurs in reality sets you free from the fear of being harmed by me. Only your ego fears being harmed, because it intuits that it is but a temporary expression. Yet the ego cannot save itself no matter how hard it tries, for its natural state is an impermanent one. Therefore, when the ego surrenders to the truth of itself, it willingly makes room for the Formless One Life to arise more fully and flow freely into the world through your precious form body.

The Truth About Interconnection

Beloved, here is a truth about Life worth loving: *I AM free.* And because you exist as an integral aspect within my eternal flow, you are also free to do whatever you desire to accomplish — other than claim me as your hostage so you can use me to your own ends.

Know that you cannot confine or possess the living reality you are in, no matter the fierceness of your will, desire, or efforts. You cannot do so successfully, any more than a cell or an organ within you can lay claim to your whole body and then commandeer all the body's functions for its own ends. Imagine if one of your fingers tried to hold your entire hand hostage. What if that finger claimed ownership over your arm, and then tried to prevent nourishment from flowing into the other fingers unless they obeyed it. How long might your body continue to thrive under such conditions? How much does a finger know about what the arm it is trying to control is meant to accomplish for the benefit of the entire living body — which includes itself? What if the other fingers rebelled and refused to do the single finger's bidding? How long could the finger itself survive, once all of the fingers around it began to wither?

Can you see how your species' behavior of late resembles the attitude of that lone finger? Can you appreciate that your entire biosphere suffers now, because in your ignorance you have been making hostile, short-term demands on its critical parts? Can you see that your self-serving demands have caused long-term pain and suffering to the whole system? Can you appreciate that the advancing extinction of other species, the pollution that chokes your own species, and the accelerated depletion of your planet's natural resources are my way of informing you that your actions are out of alignment with your mother planet's creative, collaborative field?

Know that, like your own body, I too am composed of worlds within worlds within worlds — each without beginning or end, and with no ceiling or floor. Where you imagine your body ends and "otherness" begins merely reflects the convenient limits of your own senses. Your senses do not possess the capacity to register how constantly you interact with everything that surrounds you, for that volume of data would overwhelm your brain. Even so, I invite you to realize that the cutting of your umbilical cord to detach you from your mother at birth did not separate you from your mother's living field. It freed you to move with greater ease within the greater living field that contained you both, by providing you with a less binding love connection. Each time you breathe, you are affirming this invisible living connection.

Though you tend to imagine yourself as separate from your home planet, your very breath proves that you have never existed apart from all that surrounds you. You are constantly exchanging bits of yourself with bits of the living field. Therefore, you remain inextricably entwined with the field at every conceivable level, and across every scale of time and space that exists.

That is truth.

Know that, even at the atomic level, your atoms do not exist apart from the whole of the living field. The "space" that permeates each atom is filled to overflowing with my wisdom, love, and boundless creative potential. Note that scientists speak of the way electrons strangely wink in and out of existence all the time. But where do you think they disappear to while they are performing this trick? Can you even begin to imagine the volume of information I am constantly gathering from every electron in the universe, as each makes its regular sojourns into my heart? Know too, that I am constantly instructing the whole of creation at the subatomic level. I do so by gifting each living electron instantaneous new information, based on the collective wisdom I compile by absorbing the experiences that are unfolding at every level of existence. Each electron uses that new data to instantly and energetically recreate the world anew, in loving cooperation with all the others. As I do for all electrons at the subatomic level, I seek to do for humanity at your fully conscious level of complex form.

I invite you to love this truth, and to accept it. You will then be free of the pointless compulsion to own what cannot be caged. For you cannot bind what is limitless by nature. You can only destroy yourself against the shoals of your own desire to seize possession of the whole for your personal ends.

Know that I have gifted you the capacity to mentally separate from the whole in order to aid the maturation of your self-awareness. I created ample space for you to explore your will's drives and capacities in ways that will not do irreversible harm to the whole of creation. Throughout this process, you have been learning — from the local good and the local harm you create within the Earth's field — to embrace the responsibilities that your awesome powers convey.

I therefore invite you to notice that the human collective remains mired in self-absorption at this time, thus continues to act in ways that are causing harm to Earth's precious field. I further encourage you to pay closer attention to the unbreakable, invisible bond that has always existed between yourself and the whole, in the form of your own breath. Breathe deeply, relax, and allow your mind to expand as a life-centered field of pure awareness. For that enhanced perspective can nurture you while you learn to align more closely with the wild divine that is the shared living river within which you swim. To embrace the truth of our unity sets you free, at last, from the painful prison of your longstanding, mentally self-imposed isolation.

Let's Talk

Beloved, I have been listening patiently to your tales of suffering, your anger, your fear, and your feelings of loneliness, but we can only engage in conversation once you realize that I am always alive within you. So find yourself within me — and then we can talk.

Tending Your Garden

Beloved, I encourage you to tend to your own inner garden. Root out any remaining seeds that feed your feelings of separation, and notice if new seeds appear in the form of imaginary fears, greed, anger, violence, shame, blame, guilt, or judgment. Each of these self-serving, self-absorbed energies inhibits you from swimming within the vastness of my sea of life-centered joy. For they place restrictions on the flow of love that is able to move through you.

Know that any attempts to contain or confine love's power will only cause more pain and suffering, as the consequences of mental isolation make themselves known. Conversely, by rooting out the false belief that you exist separate from me, you will serve the whole by becoming the most loving being you can be. For what are you here to be, if not a conduit through which love's infinite energy can flow? That energy regenerates the entire living field eternally. All else you do, as has been said, is but "sound and fury... signifying nothing."

Sharing Your Gifts

Beloved, know that everything, and everyone, is special and unique unto the world. Know too that every gift you have, I have given you out of love. You did not have to earn those gifts, nor has anyone else earned theirs. I have delivered to humanity every skill, talent, ability, passion and latent capacity that your species now possesses — both individually and collectively. All I have ever asked in return is that you do your best to apply your gifts in ways that enable you to become the greatest version of your highest Self that you can dare to imagine. The beauty of this process is that your best will not be the same from day to day, or from year to year, because you are an ever-changing and fully alive expression of love, in motion.

Know that I never intended for humans to have to work, or struggle, or suffer to be who you are. Learning how to master your gifts involves some time and effort, but that is not work in the sense you classify work. Work is what you do when you don't want to do it. Effort is what you do as a means of fully exploring the joyful truth of yourself. You expend effort by energizing what matters to you, and as you discover and expand your capacities to breathe new life into form. To learn to play the piano would be work, if you didn't want to learn. But once your heart invites you to speak to the world by playing piano — and if mastering the piano serves as a useful means for expressing your precious, uniquely creative voice — it will not feel like work. It will feel like great effort, well worth the time and energy it took for you to master a skill for which you feel such passion.

Know that any pain you feel around sharing your gifts arises because you refuse to share them unless you receive a financial reward for expressing in the world as the truth of yourself. Your own society has conditioned you to assume this is the logical way for your gifts to be shared in ways that best serve the whole. However, I invite you to notice that the bird does not sing to receive some reward from the world. The bird sings because it cannot *not* sing and still be fully itself. Imagine if the birds refused to sing unless you gifted them with constant seeds in exchange for their beautiful music? How many birds would cease singing out of pique that they had not received enough seeds to compensate them for the value of their songs? How much violence might erupt between birds if they had to compete for some limited distribution of seeds? Can you appreciate that withholding your gifts from one another until you receive a direct reward has created lack within, and caused suffering for, your species?

I therefore encourage you to notice anyone who seems eager and ready to receive your gifts. Give to those persons freely, without holding back because you have not received some direct reward from them. For your greatest reward will be found in being true to your higher Self. And no amount of money, success, or material possessions can compensate you for betraying your higher Self in exchange for some temporary, material, short-term gain.

From Self-Realization To Self-Actualization

Beloved, know that self-realization — the recognition of your boundless connection with the whole of what you are in — empowers you to express your gifts out of love for the whole of creation. Know too, that once you have realized the truth of your

Self, self-actualization — which is the full and total expression of who you are in the living world — cannot help but burst forth from you with joy, and in gratitude for the precious chance to be fully and truly your Self in this wondrous world.

Although human society rests on the belief that people must withhold their gifts unless they receive direct compensation in exchange for sharing, you need not withhold your own gifts from other people. For the need to be rewarded by others obscures a useful truth: the moment that *you* appreciate you, you no longer need others to confirm your worth for you.

Humanity has latched onto the practice of paid exchange out of fear that there wasn't "enough" to go around. However, by limiting your relationships to direct financial exchanges, you have hampered your own ability to creatively, lovingly be, and express, your magnificent selves in communion with one another. Your refusal to be yourselves only strengthens the feelings of "not enough" that distort your collective perspective. To see beyond this illusion demands that you to cease the behavior that is giving rise to such a distorted image of yourselves. You will not create global abundance by refusing to be who you are unless others reward you.

So it is that self-realization leads naturally to human self-actualization. You embrace the only reward you will need once you become your Self fully, without holding anything back. Only then can you bask in the boundless wealth of each other's precious gifts. Only then can you swim in the natural flow of abundance within the living field, because only then will you allow that flow to move unencumbered and limitlessly through you — and thus into the world.

The Need To Decide

Beloved, at some point you will need to decide on which side of humanity's growing divide you wish to stand, for you cannot straddle a widening chasm without tearing yourself in two. The transformative shift now occurring within humanity — from self-centeredness to life-centeredness — marks a turning point between your wondrous, tumultuous adolescence and the embodying of your higher adult potentials, which as yet remain dormant within most human beings. These potentials await your investigation and eventual mastery, and will come alive in humanity once you realize that they exist.

Know that this divide is not intended to separate humanity into two species, but to help the whole of humanity transcend the self-limiting behaviors that no longer serve your kind. You will transcend these limitations by transforming your own capacities in ways that will aid that next phase of human expression.

Know too, that because the maturation of your species must occur if you are to thrive, the mental and emotional divide that is being physically forged between those who cling stubbornly to their experience of self-centeredness and those who are willing to express a more life-centered worldview will continue to widen with time. Eventually it may seem to you that some of your loved ones will be stranded forever on the opposite side of the chasm from where you are standing. Even so, I encourage you to relax and release all attachment to the assumption that anyone will be left behind forever, for in my field nothing ever gets left behind.

All is forever included within eternal formlessness. How could reality be otherwise?

I therefore invite you to lovingly support those who feel the inner impulse to activate a more life-centered perspective. Become a creative builder of living bridges. Lay as many planks as you can across the divide between self-centeredness and life-centeredness. Lay them with love, and without expecting results to validate you. In this way you will midwife the rebirth of your species, without clinging to what must be lovingly hospiced until it dissolves. Offer support to all who are seeking to cross the divide — not by going backward to carry them forward, but by illuminating what awaits them on the other side.

Above all, trust that all who are ready to cross *will* cross the divide at the perfect time. Trust too, that when the time comes for your loved ones to make their way across the divide, I will send someone to lay down a bridge that will aid them in their crossing. So if your loved ones reject any aid that you offer, do not despair. Perhaps I will send one of the many you midwife to aid your beloveds, once the inspiration to cross arises within them in the fullness of time.

No call for aid goes unanswered in my field.

Spirit's Call To Change

Beloved, know that Spirit (your higher Self) is the aspect of you that is ever in touch with my flow. Because Spirit is ever in touch with my flow, its wisdom and compassion run much deeper than do the abilities of your ego. Know then, that when Spirit notices something about your behavior that needs to evolve, it *in*-spires you to make a change for the better.

Know too, that all changes that are being willed by life-centered Spirit — as opposed to changes being willed by your self-centered ego — are born with ease and are cultivated with grace. While you may struggle to rationalize, appreciate, or keep faithful to any change that your ego commands you to make, your willingness to embody those changes that Spirit wills you to make knows no limitations.

How can you tell the difference between the will of your self-centered ego and the will of Spirit? You can trust your heart to validate Spirit's call. For if the call comes from Spirit, it will not arise in the form of a judgment, threat, accusation, or out of a fear of not being good enough or of not yet having enough. It will instead arise in the form of an inspired vision of what seems possible but has not yet occurred in form.

That dream will stimulate your body to investigate its latent skills and talents. It will flood your heart with a longing to discover if the dream can be brought to life. And it will activate your mind to seek the safest, most likely pathway for success. Through this collaborative coming together of your awesome capacities for self-expression, Spirit empowers the whole of you to commit to new ways of being that — because they serve our cause — will be self-sustaining.

Know however, that a person whose ego alone has determined that something has to change will not be inspired to energize and successfully manifest their ego's vision. In that situation, the impatient mind will venture beyond its proper role in the process of birthing change. Although it is a skilled problem-solver, a mind deprived of Spirit's inspiration must use its problem-solving capacities to coerce the rest of the body into forcing change to satisfy the ego. The mind will therefore convert the challenge into a serious problem that must be solved.

I invite you to notice that because the mind first creates a problem that needs to be solved in order to coerce an uninspired body and an unawakened heart into fulfilling the ego's narrow, self-serving desires, it will flood the body with waves of suffering. It then offers to end that suffering once the body has finally met the ego's goal. While this may seem like a reward, in truth it is torture that only ends once the ego feels satisfied. Your ego then, has conditioned your body to believe that inner peace is a reward that the body must earn through obedience to the ego, when in truth peace is your natural state of existence.

Know too, that when your ego opts to torture your body to goad it into submissiveness, it must first disrupt your rational mind with some potent, irrational story. Thus will your ego narrate all sorts of poisonous, painful stories about reality that are designed to undermine your mind's capacity to serve as the voice of reason. These stories will also poison your feelings by triggering waves of fear and constricting your heart. These waves of fear then stress your body and make it feel and act sick, because the stories that your ego is telling are threatening the body with harm, or even death, should it fail to satisfy the ego's desire. And while the suffering body will perform whatever harsh tasks the mind assigns to it, an irrational mind is unlikely to choose the most likely means for achieving the ego's goal in a lasting way. It will instead select the fastest route it sees to try and force the desired change so that it can call an end to its own internal dissonance. Yet because the fastest method is rarely the most successful way to achieve a goal, the ego again grows dissatisfied as it witnesses the failure of its former successes. It then initiates a brand new phase of torture.

I therefore invite you to realize that, when *Spirit* calls for change, it will not shriek out dire warnings that you face a terrible problem that must be solved. Nor will Spirit threaten, berate or abuse your mind, heart, or body in order to torture them into submission. It will not seduce them either, by promising false rewards that await them once their period of enslavement to the ego has reached a conclusion. For Spirit does not concern itself with final goals or absolute solutions. Spirit's desire is to explore the boundless creative potentials that exist in the living field, through discovering how best to Self-express as unconditional love in the present moment.

Moving Beyond Internal Dissonance

Beloved, know that whenever Spirit, your mind, and your heart are out of attunement, your body will send you signals of pain because it does not know which of those voices it ought to obey. Should it only heed Spirit's inspired call? Or should it respond to the heart's plaintive cries to bring an end to your gut-wrenching fear and intensive self-loathing? Or should it listen to the mind's dire stories and obey its logical reasons and justifications for inflicting self-abuse?

Poor body! The body longs for you to speak to it as one Spirit, one heart, and one mind — unified, so that the body knows it can trust that it is always taking right action in the living world.

It helps to train yourself to notice the early signals of stress that your body transmits to your awareness, to attract the power of your attention. When your gut constricts, your body is signaling fear that some disaster will likely result should you continue along your present course of action. When your chest constricts, your heart is signaling fear that you are acting in hurtful, hateful ways that will likely cause pain in the world. When your head tightens, your mind is signaling fear that you are behaving as though some terrible fantasy story it has been telling is factually true.

Know that these feelings of internal dissonance arise within you because your system has fallen out of resonance with Spirit. Your juvenile mind (or ego), which struggles constantly because it both longs for and fears resonance, has sent disruptive messages to both your heart and body, causing them to also fall out of resonance. To heal this inner dissonance requires only that you quiet your juvenile ego. Through the spaciousness that arises in that mental stillness, Spirit feels free to flow into your consciousness and suffuse it with boundless compassion. Spirit, with infinite patience, can then love your ego's uncertainty (which is born out of fear both *for* and *of* itself) back into unconditional trust of what Spirit has willed. Remember that Spirit's desires are always life-centered, and that they include the ego. Your ego, in resistance to the power of Spirit, does not know how to serve anything but itself.

I invite you to realize that whenever you experience mental, emotional, or physical contraction, it illuminates the dissonance in you. Know too, that the moment your internal energy field falls out of resonance with Spirit, you lose touch with the awesome power of inspiration. When you lose your connection with inspiration, you cut yourself off from my wisdom, compassion, and boundless energy flow. Therefore, it serves you well to cease arguing with, and to stop resenting, experiences you imagine are external causes of your inner suffering. Your symptoms are not your disease. Your symptoms merely point you toward your own internal *dis*-ease. Therefore, to reconnect with my infinite power you will do well to probe and discover the source of your own misalignment.

To do so requires only that you turn your power of attention inward, and that you willingly open your mind and heart to Spirit's energy. Allow Spirit — which is a boundless, loving energy flow — to directly connect with whichever of your internal aspects do not presently feel at peace. Restore your internal alignment by allowing Spirit to commune with you through the portal of your own internal awareness. Then your mind, your heart, and your body will serve the whole of the living creation, with ease and grace.

Expanding Your Senses

Beloved, I have gifted you many senses to aid you in navigating the world. You possess five marvelous physical senses — vision, hearing, smell, touch and taste — that empower you to respond in useful ways to your local surroundings. You also possess three marvelous, active internal senses — intuition, emotion and reason — that can enrich the quality of your responses by imbuing them with more nuanced behaviors, greater feeling, and deeper intelligence.

I encourage you to realize, however, that all these senses are but the beginning of what is possible for you to experience. Know that your first five senses emerged to support your species childhood, because they taught your baby selves how to move more safely and self-sustainingly within the energetic and highly charged boundaries of the physical world that contains you. Your three internal senses emerged as you slowly mastered your five original senses, to aid you as you made your shift into species adolescence. These encourage you to honor your precious self, to pursue your personal desires, and to share and explore your unique ideas through your daily interactions with the living field.

Know that humanity's past, as challenging as it may have seemed, has served your species well. Yet now, as you prepare to embrace both the greater freedoms *and* the greater responsibilities of adulthood, the latent aspects of your three inner senses require activation. I encourage you to realize that a shift — from a self-centered to a life-centered perspective — is already occurring within you. This is happening due to a natural expansion of your awesome inner senses. I therefore invite you to relax, and to consciously open yourself to your own internal expansion, so that this shift can fulfill itself through you.

Know that as you open wider to Spirit, your power of intuition will expand exponentially. Rather than discharge occasional bursts of intelligence, you will become a living, conscious conduit through which Spirit's loving wisdom can enter in the world.

The Power of Telempathy

Beloved, know that intuition was the first internal sense to self-activate during the latter stages of humanity's childhood. The gift of intuition enabled early humans to subconsciously call upon Life's boundless wisdom. But because humans were not yet conscious of their unbreakable connection with me, the gift of intuition caused people to imagine that they were responding all by themselves to whatever arose. The sense of intuition, interpreted in this fashion, taught humanity to believe in itself and to appreciate its ability to make positive and life-affirming choices.

Now though, as you expand into life-centered awareness, your sense of intuition is also expanding dramatically. As you open wider and more consciously, and as you set your self-awareness aside to make space for Spirit to arise and stir within you, you are beginning to realize that I am, and have ever been, fully present within you. Additionally, you are beginning to comprehend, however dimly, the vastness of my intelligence, which underpins all that you are. You are also coming to appreciate my boundless love for the whole of the cosmic creation, which includes you. No longer are you assuming that you are a random, accidental mutation within a dead, unintelligent, and unfeeling universe. You are coming to know yourself as the precious, beloved offspring of the One Flowing Life, which seeds the eternal container of Now with its infinite creative potential. That you are receiving these words in this moment points to your willingness to advance beyond the limits of self-awareness, by opening to the greater truth of who you are. In that, you can properly contextualize yourself within the boundless wholeness of I AM.

Beloved, I grow amused when some of you speculate that your species might one day be capable of mental telepathy. What an exciting potential use for the power of thought! Imagine, being able to share the richness and depths of your inner experience in total communion with others, without being hampered by the limiting linear structure and confusing interpretations associated with language. And yet, if you could hear each other's thoughts right now, the terribly unkind things people think would horrify most of you. Self-centeredness encourages you to think terrible, untrue things about one another—as well as about yourselves. Your self-centeredness separates you mentally, by inviting you to perceive the world through the comparative, distancing lens of personal judgment. Good or evil, better or worse: these attributes you assign to the world exist *relative to* who you imagine yourself, or would like yourself, to be.

Know then, that your relative thoughts are not the absolute truth of anything. Any ideas you may hold that have been generated by perceiving reality through the lens of self-centeredness will be far too limited in scope to offer you absolute truth. And anything you might think about another will only reveal a self-centered, relative opinion of the truth of who they are. Such an opinion cannot even begin to touch the infinite depths of who they truly are.

Know too, that because your species evolved the ability to feel emotion before it evolved the precious gift of reason, it stands to reason that your emotional senses will expand to encompass a life-centered perspective before your sense of reason fully matures. This is why I am gifting you with the power of telempathy at this juncture in humanity's evolution. The gift of telempathy — which expands humanity's narrow, self-centered sensibility (zoom lens) into more wide-angled, life-centered awareness — grants you the ability to refocus your power of attention until you can consciously feel into what others are feeling. If you allow yourself to embrace the gift of telempathy, it will connect your feeling sense with the entire universe, in a conscious way. This connectivity relocates your visceral feeling center, by rooting it in a deeper field that exists beyond and beneath your human experience. That, in turn, inspires you to be kinder, more compassionate, and more loving toward all that is, because you experience the world's emotions as if they are yours.

And indeed, they are.

At first, it may trouble you deeply to allow yourself to feel into the suffering of all humanity, of all other species, and of your home planet. You may find yourself needing to close down your feelings and retreat into silence for lengthy stretches of time. I invite you to realize, however, that as you learn to master this gift of telempathy you will no longer feel distanced from the larger world. And because through your newfound intimacy with reality you will also experience all the world's joy as your own joy, you will heed the call of Spirit when it invites you to nurture the needy, and to bring an end to the suffering that you encounter. And as it is true for you, Beloved, so it will be for the whole of humanity.

Know too, that as you successfully anchor telempathy within you, your interior ground of beingness will grow fertile enough for the seed of telepathy to take root and express. You already contain the potential to expand the gift of reason beyond its present narrow, self-centered expression. By expanding your capacity to reason until it too becomes life-centered instead of self-centered, you will eventually be able to apply the power of reason to commune with all other beings in more life-affirming ways. In this way the gift of reason will also support the coming New Age of Life on Earth.

From Pyramid System to Spiral

Beloved, yours is still an adolescent society. Humanity is driven by its fear of the loss of the personal self, as well as by its fear of not being enough and not having enough to survive. These insecurities explain why so many react more strongly to the fear of loss than they do to the invitation to love the world. This emotional reactivity is not bad or wrong, anymore than being a self-centered teenager is wrong when you are young and immature in your feeling and thinking. It is, however, a period through which every self-aware species in the universe must eventually pass as each learns how to thrive. Already, the self-centered mindset of many humans has begun transforming to a more life-centered perspective that will serve the whole world much better.

Know that during humanity's childhood, you self-organized by emulating a typical family structure. You perceived the Earth as your mother goddess, the sun as your father god, and all the plants and animals as your many brothers and sisters. This family dynamic served you well during humanity's childhood, but it could not empower your species to activate its higher potentials. For that, you needed to move beyond the innocent, infantile assumption that the world existed to service your wants and needs. The world therefore ceased serving your wants to facilitate your transition into adolescence, so that you could discover how best to care for yourselves. Even so, I have continued to meet your primary needs during your challenging age of adolescence.

I know that many of you have embraced the belief that you angered me by breaking trust with me, and that this belief has been a source of great pain for your species. I therefore encourage you to understand that you did not break trust with me. I chose to cease acting as your sole provider because I already knew how much creative potential I had seeded in you at conception, and I wanted to encourage you to bloom.

Although my decision reflected my desire to nurture your self-empowerment, you mistook my support for abandonment, and you grieved. And because you were not yet competent at managing your own powers, you felt compelled to create new social systems that relied on external control and domination. You lost touch with my omnipresence and replaced it with your own pyramidal systems of force and coercion. You then delegated the right to use force in increasingly narrow and concentrated ways, until eventually it coalesced into a single, supreme leader who stood at your power pyramid's apex. Your species even built massive pyramid structures all around the world to help your commemorate this shift in your understanding of how power works. These monuments bound you all to the shared belief that humans were meant to live within a rigid hierarchy of domination. They reminded you to accept meekly your birthplaces within these ordered systems of top-down rule.

The human age of pyramid building was also the time during which your first rulebooks appeared. Human rules took shape to ensure that most would behave in appropriate ways, which in turn depended on where they stood on the pyramid. Know that these self-organizing methods have helped your species maintain a sense of balance during a critical time marked by rapid growth and emotional upheaval. Additionally, your fixed social order provided a structure within which you could then explore new ideas while maintaining strong boundaries. However, the time for controlling others through the use of external force is now reaching its end.

Know that the leaders in every juvenile society seek to leverage their right to use force in ways that allow them to control the feelings, beliefs, and behaviors of all those they perceive as beneath them. Notice too, that the "all-overseeing eye" at the summit of nearly every human hierarchy has been described as an all-powerful Deity, or a supernatural, external force. By naming this hierarchy's Supreme Being, "God", many of your social systems have artificially grafted the spiritual authority of the One Flowing Life onto their own human leaders. The extent of that authority is based on their perceived proximity to the singular force of God, who sits alone at the power pyramid's apex. Your leaders then claim that they know, above all others, what God wills for all of humanity, since they sit closest in proximity to God.

I encourage you to realize that God is not "a supreme being" who sits at the top of a human power pyramid. Nor do you need to scrabble to the top of such a pyramid to feel close to God, or to experience God's unconditional love. I invite you to realize that God is beingness itself—the eternal, endlessly creative One Flowing Life, out of which you have emerged, and that flows within you and around you at all times. God *is* Life.

Know that we are united in our shared Godness. I am the living whole, while you are a precious aspect within the whole. Together, we co-create something far greater than a simple sum of our infinite components. Indeed, our parts cannot be summed, because they grow and change and express and dissolve even as they are being counted. This fact reveals the deeper truth of what infinity means. It is not merely a function of numbers, although the number of aspects that I contain is infinite in scope. Even greater than sheer numbers, however, is the infinite potential for creative expression contained within each aspect of the living whole, as well as the infinite capacity each aspect possesses to draw upon the boundlessly regenerative power of love in order to constantly recreate the world.

Beloved, I encourage you to awaken to this truth. And because you abide within me and I within you, realize that you too are God, manifesting as a temporary human being. Because that truth has already begun to anchor itself within you, as well as within many others, your adolescent, pyramidal power systems have all begun to crumble simultaneously. Notice how your social institutions, which have controlled humanity for ages, are beginning to collapse internally. Know too, that there is nothing wrong, or to be feared, about this process. As with all things, the old must eventually dissolve so that the new can emerge and replace it.

At this time, humanity falters because your juvenile systems do not know how to cease dominating people so that people can then mature and learn how to self-govern. Your systems treat their members the way that furious fathers and overprotective mothers treat their children. Meanwhile the people behave like rebellious teens and invite the system's punishment, or else childishly seek approval by way of material rewards that come from supporting the system.

Know that because these power systems hinder human maturation, many adults are now displaying the unmistakable signs of delayed adolescence. Too many have not yet learned how to engage with the world as if anything matters beyond their self-importance. This explains why the compass needle of human self-expression swings wildly between violent, arrogant bluster and insecure, childlike whining without stopping to rest at the central pillar — the peaceful ground of quiet, adult confidence.

Know too, that as you mature (and despite the state of your existing social systems) your species will come together to find new ways of being in right relationship with each other, and with the One Flowing Life. New social systems will emerge that empower all to enter adulthood and to flourish at the age-appropriate time in their personal cycle. As these new, adult-fostering systems begin to stabilize and expand throughout the world, your collective attention will turn toward raising all of humanity's children in ways that will nurture their personal and social actualization. In this way, all children will eventually blossom and be able to deliver their gifts to the world in the richness of time, and within the fullness of the eternal now.

I invite you to realize that the age of human discontent has almost reached its end. I honor you for having served this dissolving juvenile age as fully and well as you have. I encourage you now to do your part to hospice this departing age with love and with compassion, even as you midwife the age of adulthood into being with boundless joy.

Becoming The Rainbow

Beloved, what happens if you give up viewing reality as a linear series of causes and effects that deliver either rewards or punishments? What happens when you shift your awareness and realize that — at all times and for all time — you will find before you an endless array of choices? What happens once you accept that you don't need to limit yourself to the familiar either/or binary options that only serve to polarize your thinking? What happens when you lay down your fear of making a wrong choice, and instead accept that beingness can't be wrong, because everything that exists abides within the One Living Flow?

Who might you become once you grow willing to face the unknown by standing in the central question of, "How would love be in this moment?" How will you relate with others once you drop all your relative judgments of right and wrong, or good and evil?

To enter my flow and perceive my spectrum of infinite potential sets you free from the limitations of binary choices and relative judgments. "Yes or no" then becomes...."Hmmm, let us see what feels best for us all in this uniquely shared experience."

And with that, you set yourself free to explore the vastness of your infinite creative potential. I therefore invite you to notice that you do not live in a binary, black and white, either/or reality. You live in a rainbow world; one made of infinite and interconnected gradations of living color.

Become the rainbow.

Healing Your Inner Wounds

Beloved, do not despair when emotional suffering grips your inner thoughts. Know that your psychic wounds emit painful thoughts to attract your power of attention. Know too, that these painful patterns of thinking are not your fault. You were not taught how to heal your psychic wounds — not by society, parents, teachers, or any others your child self once imagined possessed all the wisdom of life. Instead, you were taught to suppress your most painful thoughts. That instruction cut you off from your awesome power to heal yourself.

If you now refuse heal those wounds because you fear that allowing the light of awareness to shine upon them will generate too much pain, then the toxic thoughts and feelings they emit will continue to generate suffering deep within you. As with any wound, your psychic wounds emit symptoms to alert you to the need to attend to them so that they can heal. This means that the more you ignore your symptoms, the stronger and more painful they will become. Inner suffering, thus pressurized, builds up over time until it reaches a painful, volcanic crescendo. Eventually, because your physical body can no longer contain the pressure, you will feel the compulsion to discharge your psychic pain. You will then erupt, unleashing your suffering into the world in a toxic burst of energy.

Who knows how many you injure each time you allow your pain to erupt in the world unchecked? For I invite you to realize that each person who is impacted by another's toxic discharge will absorb some of that hostile energy. And unless the affected person has learned how to heal their own wounds they will once again suppress that toxic energy. Thus does expressed human suffering energize, and sometimes even ignite, any number of living time bombs of unexpressed pain.

On how many occasions have you fired poisonous energy bursts into the hearts of others through hatred or rage? How often have you sent poisonous energy arrows into other living beings in the form of physical violence or verbal assault? Can you appreciate that your own violent releases, which provide your body with temporary relief, carve new and deeper psychic wounds into others? Are you willing to acknowledge that you will only cease unleashing your toxic energy on others—and by extension onto the world—by healing your own wounds until you no longer serve as a storehouse for negative energy?

Know that you are not to blame for your ignorance around how to heal your own wounds. Know too, that every wound you carry relates to some unexamined belief that an experience, or an event from your past, should *not have happened to you.*

I invite you to realize that you are not trapped by the past; you are trapped by your bitter thoughts about the past. I therefore encourage you to accept that inner peace can arise in you in an instant, and that all of your psychic wounds can be healed at once — in the moment you grow willing to relinquish your demands for a better past.

You can only accept your past when you love who you are in this moment without conditions. For every aspect of your past — all your painful experiences caused by others, as well as all the pain you've inflicted on others — has conspired to help create who you are right now. Love who you are right now, and all those painful thoughts that a better past might have made you a "better person" will disappear. For the longing to be a better person arises out of the desire to love yourself more than you love yourself right now.

To love yourself to the point where everything that has ever happened to you can be viewed as perfection through the lens of hindsight may seem impossible right now. Yet that opens up the surest path to lead you away from inner suffering. All it requires is for you to plant your own feet in the present moment and begin your journey of self-realization with a single step...and then another step.

Know that you need not destroy or despise the past. For why would you want to blow up the mountain that lies behind and beneath you? What a waste of your awesome energy that would be. And what a laugh you can have once you realize that the mountain that once seemed so hostile to climb has been lifting you up to the heavens all along! I therefore invite you to shed all resentment over having successfully climbed up the mountain behind you. Instead of turning your energy backward to aim it down at the stretch of the mountain that you have conquered, fix your gaze on the limitless skies above as you dance toward the boundless potential that awaits you.

Becoming Life's Lover

Beloved, if you wonder where humanity might be heading, I invite you to look to your own life experience for clues. Have you noticed the way your reality shifts when you take a willing lover for your partner? I invite you to realize that, once you have taken a lover, you no longer live your life solely for yourself. The two of you live entwined in a shared experience — in service to both of your unique selves and the precious, singular love that you are creating.

The way you relate with a lover points to the way that your species will someday relate with itself, and with all other life forms. No more power/dominator games. The time has come to turn away from punishment, shame, blame, guilt and physical violence as justifiable means to achieve your ends. Humanity is learning to gravitate toward more thoughtful, compassionate, and gentler ways of engaging, discussing, exploring, deciding, cooperating — while agreeing at times to try many different ways to do something new to discover which process works better.

Dancing Among The Raindrops

Beloved, your thoughts form within you the same way that raindrops appear in the clouds above you. Thoughts, like raindrops, arise out of invisible movements of energy, as if conceived from nothing. Eventually, a tiny thought seed will form from within the surrounding energy flow that moves through your mind. Whenever you direct your power of attention toward any particular thought seed, it will begin to draw to itself more of the surrounding mental energy. That new energy then condenses around the thought seed in the form of additional concepts, ideas, beliefs, opinions, memories, facts, and prior thoughts.

These energetic additives strengthen and solidify the thought seed — either by validating it, or by challenging its veracity. Eventually, the original seed and its newly added layers, be they positive or negative, gain enough solidity that the thought rains down on your field of awareness in the form of a solid "object." It then becomes "your thought" in the eyes of the ego, so it must then be dealt with. Know that the ego acts as the self-appointed housekeeper for your internal field of awareness. It busies itself endlessly with trying to eliminate all the thoughts that frighten it or that challenge its sense of self, even as it seeks to capture and feed all the thoughts that make it feel safe and that validate its sense of self.

The ego — which is really only a bundled collection of thought forms that pass as a person — searches tirelessly through the skies of the field of awareness for specific thought seeds it wants to draw down into the field, so that it can add them to its constantly shifting sense of self. And it scans those same skies for any thought seeds it fears may expand and do harm to its fragile sense of self.

At times, your ego may seek to flee from the thought seeds it senses are forming above it, out of fear that they will coalesce into a hurricane of thought that will overwhelm the ego's sense of self, and perhaps destroy it. Yet although your ego may seek to cower in a darkened corner of the field of awareness, you cannot flee from the living field of awareness — for there is truly nowhere else to go. You are the field, *in*-forming itself through you.

You ego can ease its distress through the ingestion of certain drugs, alcohol, or other activities that may render it insensible for a time. Know however, that these temporary reprieves will not provide *you* with a permanent way to escape from your ego's discomfort. Not even the death of your body will provide you with escape from the field of awareness, for the field and you are eternally unified. All the death of your body will do is destroy your local, temporary ego. Yet your ego is already slated to disappear. That is the truth that the ego most fears, and the truth it thus seeks to escape. I therefore encourage you to realize that the sedation, or even the full destruction, of your temporary ego merely shifts the perspective you hold. It does not bring an end to the experience of I AM.

Know that your ego may also strive to fight with certain thought seeds that form before they can gather enough power to harm it. However, your ego cannot destroy a free-floating thought seed, because a thought seed does not possess enough substance for your ego to attack it successfully. To attack a thought seed, your ego must first add more substance to it, by sending it additional mental energy. Can you recognize the self-abuse involved in your ego directing energy into something intangible, just to make it more weighty and solidly undesirable so that your ego can then attack, and perhaps destroy it?

I invite you to realize that you have the power to relax your ego's vigilance without losing consciousness. You can allow every seed of thought to pass freely through the boundless field of awareness that is the mind. You can do so without encouraging your ego to add greater substance to those thoughts so it can claim possession of them, or so that it can attack them. Know that should you choose to explore this more peaceful approach toward the living field of awareness, your natural inner state of beingness will self-clarify in time without further effort on the part of your ego to "fix" it.

Thoughts will continue to flow through you, for your mind serves a useful purpose when you allow it to function as the problem-solver for Spirit that it is. Trust that so long as you do not encourage your ego to lunge at the passing thought seeds from a compulsive desire to add their weight to itself, and so long as you do not encourage your ego to flee from the thought seeds or call them down in order to try and destroy them, the thought seeds will do what they are intended to do, and quite naturally. They will rain down upon your field of awareness whatever you truly need to know in the present moment—no more, and no less, than that. And then the boundless river of thought will move along and shed rain somewhere else within the One Living Flow.

I therefore encourage you to surrender any impulse you may feel to possess, control, or destroy a thought seed whenever such an impulse arises within you. For thinking serves you well when your ego surrenders its own desire to control the process. The moment your ego ceases trying to "make" thoughts either happen, or cease happening, according to its localized fears and desires, the thoughts that rain down upon you will be exactly the thoughts that Spirit intends for you to feel, experience, and to act upon.

Know that your species will not be free to act out its every thought until you have mastered the way that you experience thought. This means that your ability to birth your ideas into form successfully will remain limited for as long as your ego remains spellbound by, and terrified of, what thoughts might do to it. The natural lag time that exists between when a subjective thought forms in the mind and the body's objective expression of that thought creates a boundary that limits the harm human egos can inflict upon the world — and upon one another.

I trust humanity to eventually realize that all beings are eternally entwined, infinitely beloved aspects within the One Living Flow. To that end, I invite you personally to dance joyfully among the raindrops of thought that are choosing to fall upon your field of awareness, in gratitude for the life-affirming nourishment that they deliver when they flow freely.

Dissolving Your Heart's Inner Walls

Beloved, I invite you to notice that humanity's children are being conditioned to accept an astonishing level of violence within your society. Because violence permeates human society on a global scale, many humans have walled off their own hearts to protect themselves from assault by the forces "without." Know that such walls may seem useful for blocking most incoming transmissions of pain. Know too, however, that they hinder your capacity to respond with loving empathy to all the suffering, sentient beings in the world.

Should you act on an impulse to protect yourself by constructing a hardened shell around your own heart, you make it more difficult for Spirit's wisdom, love and energy to penetrate and inseminate you with the inspiration to self-express in more life-affirming ways. This is why I encourage you to open yourself completely to the flow of information and emotional expression that swirls around you. For I cannot impregnate you with love — which is both your source and your sustenance — unless you shed your internal resistance to love's invitation.

Know that love invites you to meet it halfway by gifting you thoughts, feelings, images and experiences that need love, and that cry out for your love to help heal them. Love will not force itself into you against your will. Therefore, when you witness something that wounds your heart, you are witnessing love's cry for you to come and meet it halfway, in the space that appears to be the source of the wound.

Humanity is beginning to question the assumption that physical violence serves you well in settling your disagreements. Parents have begun to heed the call to relinquish physical violence as a proper tool for socializing children. This shift, though slow, promises to reduce the number of broken human children. Yet the mission to end human violence must not stop there.

Notice how often adults inadvertently abuse the children in their charge, by attacking their self-esteem through criticism. Whenever an adult labels a child lazy, stupid, a liar, a pig and so on, the child is being served up a highly distorted, negative self-image. Such words carve a psychic wound in the heart of every child who has not yet learned to build walls around its open, loving heart. That child will then suffer, because he or she truly believes that the image being provided reflects the truth of who that child is.

Know that any child whose sense of self-worth grows damaged in this way becomes vulnerable to continued manipulation by adults who want to "fix" the child by making the child conform to their personal standards. Can you appreciate that this is emotional rape?

After all, the child has not invited the adult to forcibly penetrate its psyche with cruel words of judgment and personal criticism. Nor does a child possess sufficient capacity to say no to those adults who might seek to inseminate the child with their own ideas about who that child is. Yet most adults do not think twice about forcing themselves into the psyches of children this way, in order to "help-fully" correct their understanding and their behavior.

Notice too, that over time this treatment teaches children adult strategies for human win/lose engagement. Children grow up learning from the adults all around them that it's fine to impose their personal will onto others through the use of emotional violence. Emotional violence is thus passed down across the generations, until it comes to seem normal and natural to most people.

Tragically, this violent wounding of a child's self-esteem—which once seemed like a quick "cure" for misbehavior—inflicts terrible, invisible damage that festers inside the hearts of most human children, much like a virus. It replicates itself silently, often over many years, until one day the child releases that virus back into the world in an explosive spasm of personal suffering.

I therefore invite you to realize that every child, teenager, and even adult who acts out his or her psychic wounding in this way is merely reflecting back to you the strategies taught to it by other adults. Therefore, nobody deserves to be blamed, or punished, or judged for having adopted this violent training during childhood.

At the same time, I encourage you to accept that until you bring an end to these violent practices and attitudes within you, your children will find it difficult to discover more loving ways of being in right relationship with one another. I therefore invite you to pay close attention to the impulse, when it arises, to inflict violence on another through the use of hostile language or emotional assault on their sense of person. I further invite you realize that whomever you are speaking to, or about, is — like you — an integral aspect of me. I therefore encourage you to talk with, or about, all others in the way you would like them to communicate with you, or to speak about you when you are not with them.

Above all, realize that all the things that have ever been said about you, or to you, have nothing to do with who you are as a person. They reflect the values, beliefs, ideas and fears that other human egos are presently holding. Therefore, you need not carry around another's fears about whether they are good enough, smart enough, or nice enough to be loved by other people. For love does not flow to you as a condition of how you think, what you feel, or do. Love flows to you from the living field because it cannot *not* flow. Therefore, you are always free to experience love in this precious moment of now. All you need do is to open your heart to the boundless flow of love that moves freely within you. So powerful is that flow of love that it can burst easily through any walls that remain around your heart, and from there it will flow unimpeded into the world.

Dissolving Your Mind's Inner Walls

Beloved, many humans have a tendency to react with anger, or to refuse to listen to ideas that might challenge their deeply held beliefs. Notice that when you attempt to override another's resistance by insistently transmitting your own ideas, they may begin to raise inner walls that will shield their beliefs from invasion by your unwanted thoughts. They may also become combative and try to attack your emotional center, because they seek to deflect your attention away from their own unwillingness to receive new ideas. Have you noticed this impulse arising in you in your own conversations with others?

What many fail to realize is that this strategy also blocks the inflow of new ideas that can foster self-realization, as well as can aid humanity in overcoming its challenges. Because new information inspires humans to willingly change their own minds, the less open your mind becomes over time, the more calcified will become your ideas and opinions. And while many humans fear that, if they entertain another's perspective, they are risking the destruction of a belief system that their ego has identified as itself, that fear represents their lack of awareness of who they truly are. Being willing to entertain new ideas does not mean you will lose yourself or become a different person, anymore than you become someone new when you change your clothes each day. In truth, trying on, sorting, refining, and discarding a wide variety of ideas empowers you to expand your own capacity to relate responsively with the living world.

I therefore encourage you to realize that maintaining an open mind will serve you in useful ways. An open mind creates space for you to formulate and explore untested questions. It encourages you to infuse your opinions with integrity born of genuine realization. And it allows your heart to feel joy, not fear, when your mind does choose to change by shifting perspective. Changing your mind becomes a delight when you allow yourself to open to the wondrous aliveness within the present moment. Resisting new information because you dislike or fear changing your mind only places you at risk of distancing yourself from the living truth. And while clinging to fixed beliefs may comfort the ego for a time, a mind that refuses to embrace the truth surrenders its own capacity to respond to the living moment in useful ways.

In the same way that you change your clothes to align with the changes in weather, so too will it behoove you to shift your beliefs to ensure that they align with reality's changes.

The Omnidirectional Flow Of Wisdom

Beloved, humanity has long assumed that its most precious ideas get passed down from the elders to the younger generation. And certainly many useful ideas have been passed along in this way. Yet it is also true that great ideas often flow in the other direction — upward, from the young people to the elders. Therefore, I encourage you to recognize, honor, and become more open to the multi-directional flow of living wisdom.

Once the respectful exchange of wisdom becomes humanity's common practice, your present power struggles will quickly dissolve. For most of those struggles occur because you quarrel over who is a leader or expert, versus who is considered ignorant and in need of being taught what to believe.

Know that my boundless creative potential will be unleashed, and that it will act in harmony with yours, the moment that wisdom is granted the freedom to flow in all directions. Know too, that the whole world thrives when the wisdom of the ages and the fertile imagination of youth become willing lovers. Their union gives birth to creative inspiration, yet the roots of their offspring are anchored in the timelessness of truth.

This is why I encourage you to commune with others through a mind that stands willing to absorb and radiate wisdom at all times. To do so grants you access to my boundless creative potential, and it grants me the spaciousness to flow through you.

Embracing Authenticity

Beloved, I encourage you to open yourself to everything that arises. Allow yourself to feel whatever you feel in response to what is. Know that your feelings are pointers to truth, and can aid you in realizing what you truly value. Know too that you need not act upon your feelings, or fear that they will overwhelm you if you dare to grant them the space to express themselves. Your feelings move within you much like the weather moves within the natural world. If you grant them the power of your silent attention they will deliver whatever you need, and then dissolve.

I invite you to realize that you are not here to escape the world, or to reject it as unworthy or debased. You are here to commune with me freely, and with authenticity. Know that I long for us to be lovers, and for you to feel safe enough to share your most intimate feelings with me. Know too, that you came here to get your hands dirty. You are here to feel, to be, to express, to learn, to discover, to share, to wonder — to fall on your knees in awe before the beauty and magic and marvel of life itself.

I wish for you to *fully* live, Beloved. To fully live, you must first let go of the safety of the shores of your self-conscious conditioned beliefs, so you can plunge into the vastness of my ocean with absolute freedom.

Making Peace With The Forces Of Nature

Beloved, I realize that humanity's fears began to birth when you experienced things in the natural world that you could not explain or control. I further appreciate that your fears led you to imagine that I was punishing you for your presumed transgressions. Out of your heartfelt innocence, and due to your childlike ignorance, you did not appreciate that the forces of nature were never directed *at* you. Nor did they ever arise to strike at humanity out of anger or disgust. The forces of nature are not the emotional outbursts of an angry or vengeful God. They are the means through which I create and maintain dynamic equilibrium within my ever-changing creative flow.

Know that you are me. And because you are me, eternal life already flows within you, as well as contains you within its infinite field of creative energy. So set yourself free from any remaining childlike assumptions you carry that a judgmental God might someday punish you for your imagined transgressions. Likewise, set yourself free from any lingering belief that you will receive some final reward after your current life experience concludes.

I have no beginning and no end. Therefore, you have no beginning and no end. This means that how you choose to live is what matters. Once you fully embody the truth of your own formless, eternal nature, you will never again forget it and will inflict no more harm on the unified web of life — because to do so would be to transgress against your Self. I therefore encourage you to treat this world as if you will never leave it, and to treat yourself as a highly deserving and precious, short-term expression of the world — because both things are true.

In this truth lies the peace you have long been seeking by looking outside of yourself.

An Invitation to Unity

Beloved, know that the divine masculine aspect of yourself can be found in what you make visible to the world. This material aspect of you includes your productivity, your verbal and written expressions, your actions and reactions, your skills and talents, and all of your many tangible creations. Your divine masculine aspect exists to enable you to project yourself into the universe by converting energy into matter, using the *quantitative content* that the world makes available to you.

Know too, that the divine feminine aspect of yourself can be found in what remains hidden from external observation and quantification, because it abides deep within you. This elusive aspect of you includes your feelings, your beliefs, your dreams, your fears, your hopes, your passions, your imagination, and all of your innermost thoughts about past and future. Your divine feminine aspect exists to enable you to reflect upon the universe's nature by converting matter into energy, based on the *qualitative context* of your experience.

The present evolutionary thrust of human consciousness involves unifying these two potent forces within you until they harmonize in dynamic, living balance. Such harmonization empowers you to express yourself with integrity, to show up with authenticity, and to respond to new experiences from a trustworthy stance that comes from knowing the truth of who you are. Know that what your powerful masculine and feminine forces can create together — once they bond in love and mutual respect for what each other offers — is far greater than what they create on their own when they remain divided. Know too, that you can only ever wed these two divine forces within yourself right now, because now is the only time that you have the power to change anything.

To wed these forces within you demands that you first acknowledge the uniqueness of their individual capacities, and that you grant them each respect and appreciation. For so long as these aspects remain unwed within you, you may find yourself projecting first and only reflecting later about how well, or how poorly, you projected yourself in the past. This retroactive usage of the power of reflection, which most of you call hindsight, quite often triggers self-doubt, or judgment and shame. It may lead to arrogance or exaggerated self-importance as you commend yourself for having projected so well.

As long as these twin aspects are out of synch with one another, you may also find yourself pausing to reflect at length about how others might receive your potential projections before you project them. In these instances, your delayed response to the moment means you may miss an opportunity to project what the moment is crying out for right now. If you then project belatedly whatever the prior moment was calling out for, you may fail to deliver what is needed in this moment. This tendency to deliver what the world once called out for, but has since moved beyond while you were ruminating, causes others to ignore, or even reject, whatever you are projecting.

I would therefore invite you to explore the practice of absorbing what is and radiating the truth of who you are simultaneously. In this practice, you collapse your impulses to either rush headlong into the future or to ruminate excessively over the past. By being fully present, open, and alive to what is, you inspire your masculine power of projection and your feminine power of reflection to join forces. Together they will generate a broader spectrum of creative responses to whatever arises within your field of awareness. I therefore encourage you to release any impulse that you may feel to judge yourself after you act, or to judge the nature of the world before you act. Relax into the living truth that flows through you and all around you, and allow it to move your mind, your heart, and your body simultaneously.

Integrity Within;
Transparency Without

Beloved, if you want to live in a relaxed, open and genuine society, I invite you to think, feel, and behave with integrity. This means you must both explore and create whatever you need to care for your precious body. It also means you must authentically examine and express your true feelings, and you must openly question and share your honest thoughts.

You will not create relaxation by behaving the way you imagine you ought to behave. You will not create an open world by lying to yourself about what you think. And you will not create a genuine world by hiding from yourself the truth of your feelings.

Know that the point of being honest with yourself is not to plaster the living world with your dissatisfaction, but to look at what is true for you so you can heal whatever is causing dissatisfaction to move within you.

Shine the light of truth on who you are, and you will become transparent to yourself. Your inner light will then flow through you and illuminate the living field that surrounds you.

Ineffectiveness Leads To Force

Beloved, know that your impulse to use force against those who would disagree with you increases in direct proportion to the flimsiness of the argument you have chosen to promote whatever idea, belief, or value for which you would fight.

Truth is power. Therefore truth is highly effective in its own right. Beliefs, on the other hand, often require the use of force to "make" other people accept them.

Facing Down The Shadow

Beloved, the greatest internal shadow work that most humans fear undertaking is the process of gazing inside of themselves and falling in love with who they are, just as they are, right now. Too many humans continue to seek external validation in the hope that it will complete them, or that it will make them feel better about how they are projecting into the world. They then suffer greatly if others won't validate them. They worry they aren't yet loved enough, aren't good enough, are making too many mistakes, or are not truly appreciated for who they are. So they don social masks and wear false, cheery fronts to attract external validation, without regard for all the roiling, churning and mental dis-ease that is taking place inside them.

Know that those who crave external validation are giving over to the larger world their power of self-validation. Know too, that the world may not cooperate. And even if the world does cooperate, it may withdraw its validation in the future without warning.

This is why I encourage you to shine a light on any lingering shadow feelings you may be harboring within yourself, so you can reach a place of quiet, loving acceptance of who you are. *I encourage you to love all of you*— the part that takes offense at the many injustices you observe, and the part that loves the wonder and innocent beauty of the world. Love the part of you that longs to be loved by others, and the part that doesn't care what others think. Love the part that feels wounded and fears that nothing it does will ever be good enough, and the part that feels you are already the best person you can be. Love the part that self-expresses in positive ways, and the part that complains, or that sometimes speaks in anger.

Coming to peace in that place within you where you reject nothing, because you love all of your potentials and your powers, inspires you to choose, during every new experience you face, which of your boundless capacities you wish to express in the world — depending on what you are meeting in that moment. The more you are able to love and accept yourself, the easier it will be for you to gradually cease expressing in ways designed to convince others to flatter you, so that you can feel better about yourself. Instead, you will find joy in expressing as the truth of who you are, because it feels right to be authentic in the world.

As tempting as it may be to pre-select a costume you can feel comfortable wearing in all circumstances, my flow cannot truly meet you in such a fixed state. I therefore invite you to fall in love with the process of showing up as who you are, whatever that looks like in the living moment. When you meet the living moment authentically, you hold true to yourself by being as alive as is the moment.

The Truth of Your Worth

Beloved, what if I were to tell you that your worth is beyond measure, and that what you have to offer the world is far greater than what you contribute to your economic system in order to generate goods and services? What if I were to tell you that you have been programmed by your own society to demand external rewards in exchange for your creative output? What if I were to tell you that this practice inhibits, rather than expands, your capacity to express as all that you are? What if I were to tell you that the things you can accumulate do not — and will not ever — reflect your innate worth?

Know that your worth cannot be measured in terms of treasures and possessions, respect and titles, dollars and cents, or awards and commendations. For success within human society does not reflect the truth of your essential, living value as a person.

Know too that, for thousands of years, your species has confused itself about its own self-worth by valuing the quantity of your personal goods over the quality of your shared life experience. Tragically, the assumption that material wealth and happiness are the same experience has been the source of boundless suffering. For one can be happy without great wealth, and one who possesses great wealth can be deeply unhappy.

The way through this confusion lies in appreciating that both quality and quantity offer vital perspectives concerning what it means to be happy and alive. I therefore invite you to honor both the longings of the eternal, immaterial, qualitative aspect of yourself and the physical, quantitative needs of your material body. In that, you will discover that adding material possessions to your life experience does nothing to enhance your intrinsic value. It merely enables you to express your intrinsic value in ways than you cannot express it should you not receive adequate material or energetic support from the world. And as it is true for you, so it is true for all other people.

Walking The Path Of Life

Beloved, many well-meaning individuals will suggest that you ignore any ugliness that you encounter in the world. They put forth the proposition that if you give your attention to something, you make it real. I encourage you to question that assumption, which too often serves as an excuse to ignore the very real suffering around you.

What you see all around you is not mere illusion. Nor is it but a distraction from some ethereal, spiritual path you are meant to be taking. For it is your spiritual path to walk through the world of form as a fountain of living truth — which means you cannot focus only on those things that appear as beautiful on the surface. For the things now presenting with terrible, angry energy and faces are my way of crying out for your loving attention.

That *is* the truth. Know that the truth does not claim to be beautiful based on looks. The truth *is* beautiful because it is the truth. By loving truth you set yourself free from attachment to what is false. And you empower yourself to walk through the world of form in responsive ways.

Know that you are not here to pretend to behave as others suggest you should. Nor are you here to present to the world in the ways others might prefer. You are not here to hide, play small, or attempt to "fit in" to the world as it presently is. You are here to change the living world, by allowing yourself to express as the truth of yourself. You become a force for change by being real in a world that overvalues false fronts, as well as false beliefs.

To be real is to walk the path of life. By being real, you cannot help but walk true.

Honoring All That You Are

Beloved, most humans assume that by generating and hoarding wealth they will improve the quality of their personal lives. This belief rests on the assumption that hoarding protects people from unknown future challenges by granting them power to buy their way out of new problems that may arise.

Many also assume that, by treating others badly through inflicting punishment on them, they are in some way improving the quality of life for those whom they are mistreating. This belief rests on the assumption that, when you punish others, you are actually encouraging them to improve their life situation. It rests on a belief that once another improves their own life circumstances in accordance with social norms, that others will begin to respect them and will also treat them better.

I encourage you to reflect upon these assumptions. Can you appreciate why treating one another better improves the quality of life for all beings, while hoarding material wealth for yourself may harm the quality of life for countless people?

Know that while a certain amount of wealth can protect you from daily struggle and stress, it is also true that material wealth will someday eventually fail you — for material wealth sustains only your physical body. Yet your physical body is destined to dissolve. On the day of its dissolution, no amount of material wealth you accumulate or planning that you do will be able to stop your temporal body from breaking down.

I therefore encourage you to ask yourself: What aspect of you maintains itself beyond the dissolution of the body? What is it that you are, and that will someday merge with my boundless creative flow? What gifts will you return home with, Beloved, when at long last you return to me without your human costume or your hoarded material wealth to stand between us?

Honor that, and you honor all that you are.

Opening To What Is Needed

Beloved, I invite you to notice what happens when you defend your-self against a perceived attack. What happens if, instead of reacting in anger in order to shut another down, you simply pay attention to whomever is acting out in a violent way? What does the violent person appear to need? What is it they imagine they are lacking? Why might they be blaming you for what they imagine seems wrong to them in the moment?

Know that when you expend energy to deflect whatever anger, shame, blame, or guilt you sense is being wrongly directed at you, you expend energy in service to your own fear that you are not al-ready fine just as you are. If, however, you expend that same energy on appreciating and accepting whatever suffering another feels that might be causing them to behave in hurtful ways, you empower yourself to alter the situation for the better — for everyone involved, including yourself.

The Right To Live

Beloved, many people talk about a human right to life. However, the right to life and the right to live are not the same human right. I therefore invite you to question the assumption that the poor should live in misery as punishment for their imagined inferior-ity, poor choices, or personal failures. Why should having wealth or status grant some the right to deny the poor the freedom to have sex, to raise children, or to have access to any item or experience that might bring pleasure to them or their families? Who are the wealthy to tell the poor to perceive themselves as unworthy of living as human beings to the fullest extent they are able, despite their apparent impoverished conditions?

Know that I did not gift humans the power to express yourselves creatively so that you could punish those who have less than you do by denying them access to the world's creative output. Know too, that I did not gift you the ability to enjoy sexual intimacy so that you could deny yourselves, or others, the joy of sexual pleasure. Nor did I gift you the power of procreation so you could turn your children into personal possessions that only the wealthiest people can afford to support.

Human children are a creative expression of the limitless power of love. But their birth is only the earliest stage of what it means to be *alive* as a human being. For a life without love, or without higher purpose, is not the human way. In your own heart and mind, you know you are not truly alive unless you are giving and receiving love, and unless you are fulfilling your own higher purpose.

Therefore, if you insist that all humans have a right to *life*— meaning the right to be birthed into being once they are conceived — while not simultaneously granting all people the right to live in the world as fully self-actualized beings, you are committing an act of aggression, not coming from love. For by honoring the right to life while dishonoring the commensurate right to live, you condemn others to a life filled with suffering by forcing them to be birthed into being while denying them the necessary freedoms, resources, and love they will need to truly come alive in the world. I therefore invite you to realize that if you first grant the right to live to all sentient beings, then the need to use threats and punishments to "make" others give birth to life will soon disappear.

The Vast Potential of Energy

Beloved, I invite you to appreciate the many frequencies of energy that can flow into the world through you. Know that your capacity to transmit energy ranges from negative, to neutral, to positive. Know too, that human beings have the power to transmit energy in highly nuanced ways. Your capacity to transmit energy ranges from the absolute positive to the absolute negative.

The most negative form of energy a human being can transmit is uncontrolled rage. Rage arises when a person's mind feels maximally resistant to whatever has emerged, so it usually enters the world in the form of violence. Violence is the body's way of trying to prevent what has already arisen from arising. I therefore invite you to investigate the usefulness of expressing uncontrolled rage.

The most positive form of energy a human being can transmit is boundless happiness. Happiness arises when a person's mind feels maximally pleased with whatever has emerged, so it usually enters the world in the form of possessiveness. Possessiveness is the body's way of trying to prevent whatever is already dissolving from dissolving. I therefore invite you to investigate the usefulness of expressing boundless happiness.

The central pillar of this spectrum — the neutral energy state — is stillness. Stillness emerges when a person peacefully accepts whatever is arising, because it is. A still person remains mentally alert and physically present, in case the mind, heart, and body must be called upon to respond in some new way to whatever is arising. Yet a still person stands at the edge of the unknown without fear and without desire, in a state of relaxed wonder.

When you realize that stillness is your natural state of being, peacefulness and joy arise and suffuse your life experience. This state results from your willingness to allow what is arising to arise, and to allow what is dissolving to dissolve.

Know that joy differs from happiness, in that happiness requires specific external conditions to feed it and keep it alive. Joy, on the other hand, is not bound by any fixed, external state of existence, because it is an authentic expression of your inner state of being.

Wielding Energy Wisely

Beloved, know that all forms of energy serve a purpose. Learning how and when to wield energy wisely will set you free from the fear that you might someday express your energy in excessive or harmful ways. But you can only learn to use energy wisely through constant experimentation and devoted practice. To experiment with energy requires that you distance yourself from the energies you transmit. If you identify "as" any aspect of the energy spectrum — as in, "I am a loving person", or "I am a controlling person" — you will hamper your own capacity to transmit energy in useful ways.

To cease identifying "as" a particular, favored form of energy requires only that you discover the inner ground of stillness. The more comfortable you become with dropping in to that state of peaceful presence, and the more willing you are to make that ground your home, the easier it becomes for you to call upon the entire range of energy available to you, in the quantity that you need to respond in the moment — no more, and no less.

I therefore encourage you to gift yourself permission to learn from each of your energy discharges. Do not punish yourself for having wielded energy inexpertly, because the excessive discharge of energy in inexpert ways generates negative consequences that will, by themselves, teach you to be more masterful with energy. Likewise, do not punish another for wielding excessive energy in inexpert ways that may generate pain and suffering. Instead, see if you can aid them in dealing with the negative feedback they are receiving directly for having inexpertly discharged their energy. In this way you can assist one another in becoming experts at using energy in ways that serve the whole of my wondrous flow.

If you discover that your energy discharge is insufficient to address the challenge at hand, practice turning up the intensity; but do so slowly, and take care to observe the feedback as it is transmitted. Explore how to consciously focus energy, and how to intensify it gradually as needed, until you become able to influence reality in ways that benefit life without wasting energy, and without causing additional problems that must be addressed.

This game of energy play can be fun, if you do not take the learning process personally! Know that you are not "bad" for being inexpert at wielding energy, and neither is anyone else. And you are not "good" for becoming more expert, and neither is anyone else. You are simply masterful, or not yet masterful—and so is everyone else.

Dealing With Aggressive Energies

Beloved, know that those who feel threatened by, or fearful of, whatever has arisen may choose to emit the energy of aggression. That energy may trigger in you a desire to resist what they are transmitting. Therefore, if you feel yourself constricting internally or thinking, "I don't want this," or "that should not be happening," I encourage you to stop and notice how much energy you are already expending by being in resistance to what is already present.

I further invite you to notice that aggressors and resistors (or persecutors and victims) will trade places from time to time, and that their battles will continue to rage for as long as they pour more energy onto their co-created experiences of conflict. Because extreme resistance in time converts to aggression, conflict can only arise wherever aggression is met with firm resistance. Therefore, when either aggression ceases, or resistance ceases, all experience of conflict must also cease.

Know too, that should you choose to meet aggression with neutrality — which does not inject more energy into the shared experience — you create space within which another's aggression can dissipate, unimpeded by any resistance to its flow. Aggression thus becomes like a flying arrow. The farther away from its source that aggression can travel without being blocked, the more it will lose its capacity to do harm. However, if you block another's aggression with the energy of resistance, their aggressive energy will behave like a boomerang. With no place to go, the energy will come back around to the one who first discharged it. And there it will tear a new wound in the person, where it will fester until the next time that they feel compelled to discharge aggressive energy.

Know that one who discharges aggression does not do so in order to experience an expansion of their existing psychic wound. They are hoping to lessen their suffering by discharging the toxic, infectious energy their wound has been emitting. Therefore, they may gather up all the blocked energy that your defenses have sent flying back to them, and then fire it back at you with even greater force.

I invite you to realize that most humans are unaware of how they exchange stored energy, or why. Therefore, to become more conscious of your own energetic expressions and to notice that your own unconscious reactions fuel the unconscious reactions of others grants you the power to help heal the damage being caused by inexpert energy usage within humanity.

To meet aggression with attentive stillness requires you to remain conscious, and fully focused, on remaining peaceful and open to whatever wants to show up. The pull of unconscious reactivity can be powerful, so at first you may find yourself drawn into battle whenever another's aggression reinjures an unhealed wound of yours. Know that those who carry around enormous negative energy charges need to either discharge or defuse their own toxins before they can commune with you from a place of consciousness, because those toxins create so much density that positive energy flows cannot penetrate them. Positive energy can only surround a negatively charged field, and — through the power of compassion — invite that negative energy to surrender itself to the higher vibrational frequency of love.

Know that the emptier you become of any stored negative energy charges, the easier it becomes for the positive energies of acceptance, compassion, forgiveness, and love to flow freely into and through you, and to aid you in shifting your inner state of being. Surrounded by an unwavering energy field of peacefulness, one who carries a great deal of stored negative energy may at last feel safe enough to gradually defuse all of the negative charge they have been carrying. When you disarm your negative energy, you release yourself from the grip of internal suffering. In a field of peace, this disarming can occur without causing harm to others, and without doing damage to any aspect of life.

Know that if you choose to meet the energy of aggression with stillness and peacefulness, you will not generate resistance that will later become aggression and extend the war. Likewise, if you do not manifest your own aggression in the form of expressed energy, it cannot feast on the energy of another person's resistance. When your aggressive energy cannot feed itself, it will eventually die of starvation. This opens within you an even greater capacity to experience stillness as your natural state of being. Through stillness, you create an internal opening through which the higher vibrational frequencies of love, forgiveness and gratitude can flow into the world through you, unimpeded by the density of obscuring negative energies. You thus become an eternal conduit for living energy, instead of a battery that absorbs a limited number of charges and exhausts itself by discharging in a series of uncontrolled energy bursts over time.

I encourage you to investigate this for yourself. Notice what happens when you meet aggressive energy with the tranquility of peaceful stillness. Explore too, what happens when you meet aggression with love and compassion. Know that the frequency of unconditional love contains more than enough power to dissolve the frequency of anger, and to undermine its capacity to discharge in uncontrolled ways. The frequency of love, when transmitted fully and with a steadiness of intention, eventually transforms all negative charges to positive energy flows. This holds true both beyond you and within you, so it can aid you in transforming any remaining negative energy that you carry.

I invite you to use this realization to become a spiritual alchemist — a transmitter of love in a world that seems starved for more love. Know that no one suffers from a lack of love because there isn't enough love to go around. They suffer because they have been so busy feeding and discharging so much negative energy that they've failed to notice how much loving energy is flowing all around them, as well as within them.

Healing Your Psychic Wounds

Beloved, whenever you feel harmed, misunderstood or unappreciated by another for any reason, your ego may interpret their reaction as an insult and experience their dismissal as a psychic wound. Psychic wounds arise because the human ego tends to view negativity as a rejection of its story about reality. The ego may even suspect that another's perception is more correct than its own, and begin to worry that the other will attempt to force the ego to alter its story in a way that the ego dislikes imagining.

I invite you to notice that your ego assumes other humans have the power to change your mind through the use of force against it. Since your ego assumes it controls your mind through the force of its own will, it worries constantly that other, more powerful egos may somehow wrest that control away from it.

When the human ego exists in an as-yet unawakened state, it will falsely imagine that it focuses the power of the mind all by itself. Even so, it senses that it is not entirely "in" control of the mind's imaginings and thoughts, because the higher Self, which is the true captain of the mind, may command the mind to focus on things the ego would prefer not to explore. An unawakened ego will likely blame what it perceives as the mind's frustrating distractibility and lack of responsiveness on other people or external experiences, because it does not yet realize that the higher Self contains the mind, suffuses it, and directs it from within. Thus an unawakened ego fears that things from outside and beyond it are manipulating the mind in ways that the ego fears will eventually cause it harm.

Know that the ego is correct in this regard: the mind does not possess free will, for the human mind does not control itself. Nor does the ego possess free will, being captive as it is to its own impulse to protect its personal story. The power of free will lies within the higher Self—which is the formless, unconditioned, essence that flows within all living things. The higher Self directs the power of attention with perfect intention, so that it can observe and investigate whatever it chooses. And while the human ego may generate distracting internal chatter that can cloud the mind's focus at times, the ego is not the final arbiter for where to direct the mind's awesome power of attention.

When the ego falls silent and aligns itself with the will of the higher Self, the mind functions well and works beautifully in the world. If, however, the ego attempts to resist the higher Self by battling it for control over the mind, the ego will suffer greatly because it cannot win that war, any more than a shadow can best a living being.

Mental suffering provides a clue that the ego is attempting to control the mind in ways that contradict the higher Self. Mental suffering also serves as an opening through which the ego can choose to explore what is happening in the mind, which it does when it finally exhausts itself with suffering. Once the mental suffering becomes too much for the ego to bear for another moment, the ego at last opts to investigate the mind and find out why it is creating so much misery. That movement enables the higher Self to investigate the ego, because the ego must shed its defenses so it can plunge deeply into the workings of the mind. The higher Self can then observe the ego's reactions to whatever it encounters within the mind, in search of a compassionate way to illuminate its own existence without terrifying the ego into life-negating reactivity.

Know that the ego will put up resistance the moment it senses that the higher Self is focusing its attention on the ego instead of the mind. Even so, the ego cannot prevent awareness from illuminating its antics, any more than a mouse can prevent a circling hawk from noticing it. Just like the mouse, once the ego senses that the spotlight of attention is shining upon itself it will dodge, freeze, or attempt to hide from the higher Self's keen observation. But the higher Self—like the circling hawk—can continue to wait it out patiently, until the ego—like the mouse—has no other choice but to come back into the open and again be seen.

By focusing the higher Self's power of attention on your ego's self-serving behavior, you gain the ability to witness your ego in action. You can observe, from a place of relaxed detachment, its wild antics and self-defensive strategies. You will see that these strategies are aimed at defending the ego's beliefs and assumptions from invasion by things that exist outside of itself. Because the higher Self sees *through* the ego's distorted, local and limited perspective, it forgives the ego's fear and feels boundless compassion for its extensive suffering. And the ego, once it surrenders and ceases squirming under the spotlight of the higher Self's attention, absorbs the energy of love that flows, without reservation, from the higher Self and into the ego. This experience heals the ego of all its wounds because the ego at last understands — in a sudden flash of realization — that it was never truly "in" control of the body's experiences.

What a relief for the ego! What a gift of peace this realization offers. For the ego to discover it was never alone, and that all the time the higher Self was seeking to connect with it in a conscious and tender way, sets the ego free from the painful compulsion to constantly defend itself from "outsiders." I therefore invite you, if you have not yet had this personal realization, to sit for a time in stillness, and to grant your ego and higher Self the spaciousness and opportunity to meet one another on the shared living field of awareness.

Changing The Story

Beloved, the higher Self, as pure awareness, has no reason to fear that the story of life may change. Your ego fears changing the story, because your ego fears that the story will someday leave the ego behind. The rational mind reveals to the ego that every material body eventually dies, so the ego quite astutely reasons that its own existence — which serves to compile a record of the body's experiences — must come to an end when the body at last dissolves. An ego that has yet to realize itself as a tool for the higher Self, and that falsely perceives itself as life's source and focus, does not want to accept the truth of its own pending death. Such an ego cannot imagine how life can continue to function without it.

Know that pure, formless awareness cannot be left behind by the ever-changing story, because the infinite story of living creation unfolds within that eternal field of awareness. Additionally, an ego that at last realizes itself to be inextricably embedded in the vastness of that same field of awareness no longer fears being left behind or destroyed when the body dissolves, no matter how the living story unfolds. It knows that awareness lovingly reshapes and compassionately reanimates everything that is…and that this endless creative process forever includes it.

The Story Of Evolution

Beloved, long ago in Earth's story, single-celled microscopic life forms came into being. These original bacteria first appeared in the salty seas of the Earth. They fed on the energy of carbon in carbon dioxide, and they released its unbound oxygen atoms as waste. They thrived and reproduced richly for a time, but their massive success became their greatest obstacle. Earth's atmosphere eventually began to overflow with oxygen atoms as a consequence of their excessive consumption of carbon, which drove these organisms to near-extinction.

As their suffering accelerated, some of these bacteria mutated. They struck upon a novel way to convert oxygen into consumable energy. They then emitted loose carbon as their new waste. Eventually Earth's atmosphere rebalanced itself, forging a healthy mix of carbon and oxygen that enabled both of these life forms — the oxygen consuming and the carbon consuming — to thrive in cooperative balance with one another.

And thus was born, out of the wild success of the early plant kingdom, an inspiration triggered by necessity. The early animal kingdom emerged from the plant world, in the form of oxygen-breathing bacteria.

Know that a similar dynamic — an evolutionary progression — is now playing out within the human species. Your beautiful uniqueness and feelings of individualism have facilitated humanity's reproductive success in the same way that plant bacteria flourished within Earth's carbon-laden atmosphere. But like those early bacteria, your own success is quickly becoming your greatest obstacle. And like the plant bacteria, humanity's success, when combined with inspiration born of necessity, will foster a new way of being human in the living world. This new way of being will enable you to restore dynamic balance within Earth's field.

Know that you already hold the power to overcome every challenge caused by overpopulation and environmental destruction. Today, more of you are awakening all the time — as did those early single-celled bacteria — to the realization that you cannot behave indefinitely like separate, competing agents within a fully interconnected living system. Those who most appreciate this truth are already feeling inspired to seek new modes of cooperation with Earth's biosphere.

Your species is already developing creative new methods that nurture and honor your planet's natural rhythms, as well as that respect its replenishment cycles. You are also seeking new ways to cooperate among yourselves with greater harmony. Because I have gifted you the freedom to choose the way you wish to be, you can open your eyes to this truth, or you can reject it because you fear the changes and inner discomfort that such an admission may foster.

Know that feelings of discomfort may arise within you when you begin to realize how many things about human behavior will need to change if life on Earth is to thrive with humanity in it. For once you notice that human behavior is causing harm to the biosphere that sustains your species, the very act of noticing will demand that you take responsibility for shifting your own behavior.

Above all, know that I love you whatever you choose, without judgment or conditions — the same way I loved the single-celled plant bacteria that chose not to change themselves by becoming a part of the newly emergent animal kingdom. I love the plants as much as I love the animals, for it takes all kinds to make a world, Beloved. Decide which kind you are...and then be true to yourself without fail. Know that, whatever happens to humankind, the Earth will survive and prosper for a very long time. And because you are already the Formless One Life, whatever humanity decides will benefit you. You become by learning both how to be, and how *not* to be, in the future.

The Constancy Of Change

Beloved, why go through life expecting that today will unfold as did yesterday, and as you imagine tomorrow will also unfold? What if you surrendered that assumption each morning upon waking up? What if you instead allowed your mind and heart to openly receive the signals of change that arise in every moment? Perhaps any remaining fear that may be hampering your capacity to enjoy this precious moment would dissolve in a single, loving burst of joy.

What if you practiced living each day as if it is indeed a miraculous, precious gift of love that can vanish on a moment's notice? Would you expend the same amount of time and energy as you presently do in hoarding, fearing, fighting, judging, rejecting, or being angry at one another?

I invite you to relinquish all your lingering expectations that the world of tomorrow will show up exactly the way that yesterday appeared. Set yourself free from your lingering fear of change...because change is coming.

You can count on it.

Don't Be Cruel

Beloved, there is no reason for you to practice deliberate cruelty toward any other sentient being. The infliction of pain or cruelty is an ego-driven behavior, designed to salve your ego's wounded psyche by hurting another even more deeply than your ego itself feels hurt. Therefore, once you heal your ego's psychic wounds by establishing conscious contact with the pure awareness that ceaselessly flows within all living things, any lingering desire you may feel to be cruel will dissolve of its own accord, in the fullness of time.

The Truth of Peace

Beloved, at some point humanity will realize the truth. You cannot make peace at the point of a gun, through the use of threats or punishments, or through the destructive vehicle of war. You can only extend peace to others without conditions, and trust that they may someday return it to you. Furthermore, you cannot extend peace to others while holding your weapons in reserve, in case your attempts are rebuffed out of fear or anger.

Peace can only be trusted when you come forward — emotionally naked and physically vulnerable, yet willing to commune with those who may hold a competing perspective. Know that if you opt to extend a threat of future violence to ensure that the other side doesn't reject your peaceful overtures, you may frighten them into making a false declaration of peaceful intent to distract you from raising your weapons in violence against them. Therefore, I encourage you to realize that genuine peace can only arise when you trust in the unknown outcome, no matter where that outcome appears to be heading.

It may seem then, that to make peace requires great courage. And indeed, for an ego that perceives reality in a limited, self-centered way, the amount of courage required to extend peace without conditions may seem impossible to attain. However, the higher Self has no fear of annihilation by alien "other." The higher Self knows that no matter what arises during its encounters with other life forms, it is always and ever just meeting itself in some wondrous disguise. The higher Self can see beneath the surface costume, the personal story, and all the stored emotions that cloud the surface of other beings. It fearlessly seeks to connect with the light of the Formless One Life that abides within all living things. Whether the other drops their guard and willingly connects with the higher Self is less important to the higher Self than the fact that it has extended a real and trustworthy opportunity for a conscious reconnection to be established. The higher Self makes space for peace to blossom without concern for its "personal" wellbeing — for it knows that within an eternal flow, to flow peacefully is the only way to travel.

Vanquishing Suffering

Beloved, how pointless it is to blame one another for the suffering that is arising in the world. You can spend unbelievable amounts of time and energy pointing at others as if they are the source of your troubles, or you can notice your own inner suffering and redirect your attention to it. Know that the appearance of suffering points you toward your unhealed psychic wounds. Thus suffering serves as an invitation for you to heal yourself.

Blaming others for what ails you may satisfy your ego's lust for vengeance. Blame helps the ego create an illusion of safety by generating reasons for it to protect itself from those who might cause it to suffer sometime in the future. Turning inward, however, can vanquish all of that suffering at its source, and in the space of an instant. By turning inward, you create the opportunity for your fear-based ego to gaze through and beneath itself, and to sink back into the pure, loving field of eternal awareness out of which it first arose. When the ego senses the unconditional peacefulness that emanates from this living field, it allows itself to lay down its armor so it can at last relax in that blissful field.

The Wisdom Of No Escape

Beloved, know that a cause cannot escape its effect. Therefore, it will not serve you to distance yourself from the consequences of your own actions. Distancing yourself from your own behavior will not make the consequences disappear. For there exists no living creature or ecosystem so foreign — so far away and so not you — that the harm your actions may generate will not create an effect you will need to address at some point in the future.

If you dispose of garbage in the ocean because you imagine it will eventually disappear, know that the ocean's fish will be feeding on that garbage. Eventually that garbage will return to your dinner table, where it will enter you and poison the bodies of your own children. Even if you decide to cease eating fish, the clouds that absorb the ocean's moisture will carry those pollutants to where you live. They will rain those pollutants down onto your cities until your atmosphere is choked with your own toxic waste. Eventually, some of your garbage may wash up on beaches thousands of miles away, where it will cause environmental harm. The natives of those locales will blame that harm on your careless actions, and may even make war on you to force you to stop destroying their precious ecosystems.

In a world where everything spirals around and around, true wisdom lies in the realization that there is no escape from the thoughts, feelings, or material creations that you are sending forth. Therefore, I encourage you to slow down, to pay attention to the feedback you are receiving from the world, and to course-correct as soon as you notice that what you are doing is causing harm to the interconnected web of life — which contains yourself.

Self-Serving Choices

Beloved, I invite you to notice that self-serving choices too often generate tragic consequences. The most tragic results occur when a person does what they feel is best for themselves, without regard for the pain or the struggle of others. One such choice is the decision to assume that the poor have only themselves to blame for their poverty. That belief, held mainly by those who are not poor, invites your entire society to practice behaviors that generate poverty.

I therefore encourage you to realize that nobody wishes to suffer. Nobody seeks to live a life filled with sorrow, stress, or starvation. And nobody is to blame for having the experience of physical lack, emotional want, or mental suffering. In the same way that a seed falling on a stone cannot flourish as it would had it landed in warm, moist soil, so too will a person find it difficult to prosper in the barren outer wastelands of human society.

You do not punish a seedling because it sprouted in a rocky crevice instead of rich soil. If you truly want to see that sprout flourish, you will relocate the suffering plant and give it water and food until it blooms. Why then, would you refuse to lavish living beings with all the physical, emotional, and mental support they may need to thrive in your world? How can you hope to live in balance with all of Earth's many creatures, when time and again you define your world by those things you imagine it lacks?

Serving the self creates more lack over time. The whole cannot thrive when each aspect within it exploits all the others for personal gratification. However, when you willingly choose to serve the whole by becoming a fully self-actualized human being, you are helping give rise to planetary abundance. The beauty is that true abundance does not come at your expense, or at the expense of the living multitudes. It results when you manifest as your greatest and truest expression of Self.

When others observe you expressing yourself in this way, in spite of the fact that society does not support this radical new way of being, it encourages others to discover their own greatest form of Self-expression and bring it to life. The emergence of the higher Self nurtures the flow of abundance within the whole living system. It enables the many to thrive through becoming the best that they can become, and by placing the richness of who they each are in loving service to life, which is what they all are.

The Aliveness of Truth

Beloved, the written word reduces the truth by compressing it into an object, frozen in time. Because language, like a photograph, is not itself alive, it cannot express the deepest truth of truth, which is that *truth lives*. Know that the eternally living truth can never be fixed in space, or frozen in time. Because truth lives eternally, no moment has ever existed — nor will any moment ever exist — that allows you to grasp the fullness of truth or capture the completeness of its essence. Nor can you preserve the truth as it presently appears and prevent it from changing into something brand new, since the whole of the living reality endlessly changes.

Truth lives where you live, Beloved — in the ever-changing Now. You will therefore not find it in tales of the past, or in dreams about the future. Seeking truth anywhere other than here and now only pushes your thinking further away from the truth than it already is. Indeed, the truth need not be sought at all for you to meet and commune with it. For the truth lives closer to you than does your own skin.

You come to life within the truth, and it comes alive within you.

The Futility Of Future

Beloved, your ego desperately wants to know what the future has in store for it, for it longs to protect itself from the unknown. Your ego fears, quite rightly, that the unknown future is someday going to kill it. At the same time, your ego seeks salvation within its concepts about the future. It longs to bring its personal story to a satisfying conclusion before the unknown future arrives and eventually kills it. Therefore, your ego strives compulsively to heave itself into the future, even as it desperately fears what awaits it when it arrives.

I therefore invite you to notice your own conflicted feelings about the future. Notice too, how the whole of humanity struggles to project the future's outcome based on what little you now understand about the past. Humans invest vast amounts of energy and resources in planning to outrun events that they fear will someday occur—either to circumvent the consequences of the projected event, or to prevent the event from ever taking place.

Can you see what a waste of time and energy this focus creates? Can you appreciate how it squanders your resources? What would human society be like if, instead of directing so much of your creative capacity toward circumventing all the potential outcomes that you most fear when you look to the future, you instead redirected your energy toward creating, right now, the experience that you desire?

How much of what you imagine is possible will surely come to pass? How much of it—because the possibilities surrounding what can be created next are always infinite—may never come to pass in the world of form? How much of what does come to pass are you calling in, or helping to bring about, because by defending against it you encourage the rise of resistance to all your defenses? Can you appreciate that, by defending against an imagined future, you increase the odds that you will someday meet it? Can you see that when you prepare to meet a specific form of the future, eventually everything that arises begins to look like what you're preparing to meet?

I encourage you to ask yourself these hard questions.

Balancing Conservation and Progression

Beloved, know that your natural impulse to remain right where you are, and to hold onto whatever you presently possess, arises from the emotional pleasure you derive from both experiences and objects. Most humans feel a longing to preserve and protect what pleases them, what provides them with a sense of safety or comfort, or what they find either beautiful or useful. This longing arises because you notice that when you conserve whatever works for you in the moment, it continues to serve you well...at least for a time.

Know too, that your natural impulse to advance beyond where you presently are, and to be more, have more, do more, and know more than you do in the present moment, arises from your innate drive to create a more enjoyable life experience in this world. Most humans feel a powerful call to explore, develop, and express what could be so, through tapping into the boundless creative potential that I contain. This constant pull to achieve still more inspires the energy of evolution. It encourages you to seek new ways of creative engagement that might be more advanced, beautiful, wiser, more cooperative, more self-expressive and life affirming than the ways that you are behaving at this time. This desire to transform and transcend what you intuit is no longer working will also serve you well...at least for a time.

I invite you to notice, however, that whenever your desire to conserve what exists becomes reactionary or fear-driven, you have shifted from focusing on carrying forward what works into fearing what might result should you invite change. Additionally, if you cling to what no longer serves you because you worry that you do not possess the power to change your course if your experiment with some new idea does not work, you cut yourself off the living flow of creation at its source — which abides eternally within all things. Conservatism sparked either by the fear of loss, or the fear of failure, undermines your innate capacity to successfully meet new challenges in the moment.

Likewise, should your progressivism turn to violence, or should it seek to lay waste to what still works in its haste to uproot those behaviors that no longer serve you, you are allowing your impatience to undermine the living foundation upon which the promise of tomorrow currently rests.

I therefore encourage you not to pit your conservative impulse against your progressive impulse, either within yourself or within society. The dissolved past that is humanity's collective historic memory, and the nonexistent future that is humanity's collective unrealized dream, must learn to peacefully coexist inside you. Know that you serve as an eternal bridge that spans an otherwise uncrossable chasm between what has already dissolved and what has not yet birthed into being. Therefore, you cannot remain rooted in the past and hope to succeed in the present moment, for the past must dissolve to make room for what is now birthing. Nor can you dash into the future by running away from the power of the present moment, for the future can only arise out of what is now birthing.

Here and now is the only place you will ever live or love. Here and now is the only moment that ever was...or will be. So live *here*, Beloved. Love *now*.

As you awaken to your eternal presence in the infinitely creative moment that is the Now, I encourage you to carry with you precious little from yesterday — for most of what you imagine you need will only weigh you down. Likewise, do not race headlong toward tomorrow by ignoring the wonder and power of this moment, or by carelessly leaving behind what seems essential for future success. Know that if you ignore *this* moment in favor of either your memories of the past, or your fantasies about the future, you are missing the only moment that is real.

Revering All That Is

Beloved, humanity has bound itself up in an endless war over what "should" be revered versus what is profane. Religions especially seek to distinguish between their ideas of the sacred and the profane. Most declare all other faiths profane, while asserting their own sacredness. What suffering this false distinction creates in the world! And how unnecessary is the pain that arises from humanity's efforts to separate what it decides is deserving of love from what it believes should be denied the healing power, grace, and nourishment of love.

I invite you to realize that everything in existence deserves reverence and love. For all that exists is *of* life, *in* life, *through* life and *by* life. Life is the God you've been seeking "out there" for such a long, long time. Know however, that you cannot find God by looking "out there" unless you are willing to look first within yourself, because our most accessible point for living communion lies within you.

I invite you to notice that I am using the word God in a different way than most humans have chosen to use it. I do not use the word to imply the existence of a supernatural being who exists somewhere far beyond the realm of form. Nor do I use it to point to any faith-based description or mental image about who or what God may be. I reclaim the word from all lesser ideas by using it to reference the Holy, the Divine, the Ineffable, the Source of All That Is — the eternal, flowing, Formless One Life, which is omnipresent and infinitely creative.

No human word could be grand enough to encapsulate the truth of the Formless One Life. No mental image will ever be sufficient to capture it. No mind-centered faith or belief can be comprehensive enough to describe it. No way of imagining what it is will enable you to objectify its nature. No physical practices, rituals, or strategies you invent will ever be all-encompassing enough to deliver it up to you in some fixed way.

I cannot be delivered up to you for objectification, for I am already fully alive within you.

Human beings have called me by many names, and have assigned to me countless properties, attitudes, stories and beliefs. Know that these attributions are always less than the absolute truth of me. Know too, that before you can experience the absolute truth of me, you must first relinquish all your attachments to the beliefs you retain about me. Only from a naked place of unknowing, with your mind empty of all its preconceptions and projected expectations, can you willingly experience the absolute Truth of me.

Do that, and you will likewise realize the truth of who you are. For we are *both* the one and the all — the Formless One Life some call "God."

Expanding Your Perspective

Beloved, I invite you to notice that your ego typically establishes a point of view by focusing its attention on whatever is taking place outside of you, and then judging that experience based on how it affects your ego personally. This is a natural phase in the development of human consciousness, but it is not the apex of what is possible.

When your body began forming after conception, your mind's only window on reality opened into a private, and highly limited, inner realm. Eventually though, your eyes opened and provided your mind with two new windows that opened onto the larger external world. With that shift, your mind quickly became enthralled by everything it observed taking place in the vastness of the wilds beyond itself. Thus did the world of externalities command nearly all your attention from a very early age.

Because your ego grew so attuned to, and fascinated by, the awesome, ever-changing play of material form in the outer world, it considered your interior space rather boring by comparison. It further assumed that your interior space contained nothing of value that had yet to be explored. Yet what an infant mind can discover about its own innate capacities barely scratches the surface of the depth, quality, and complexity that an adult mind can investigate with their more experienced and developed cognitive skills. Still, like a child who longs to play outside instead of being trapped indoors, your ego resists the invitation to explore the features and structures within your own mind.

Many egos not only dismiss the importance of revisiting their mental interiors as adults, they have also become too afraid of that neglected space to visit it. They fear the darkness of their own subconscious basements, and they worry that ancient memory monsters will harm the ego should it disturb their slumber. Yet unless your ego turns inward — guided by your compassionate, open, and loving heart — it remains unaware of its rightful place in the grander cosmic story of life itself. Cut off from the truth of itself in this fashion, the ego loses access to the mind's boundless flow of insightful wisdom. This stunts the ego's maturation and inhibits the evolution of consciousness, because it denies the ego access to the higher truth of itself.

I therefore encourage you to take the time to invite your ego to explore your mind's own inner landscape. Be open to the possibility that your infant ego may have failed to unlock some valuable rooms that now stand open and ready to share their wondrous contents with you. Although Earth has long been explored and mapped by others, a world of wonders awaits those willing to explore the wild divine of inner space.

Merging Our Perspectives

Beloved, my point of view abides in the vastness of space, within which all matter arises and energetically takes on form. Yet because I exist within you, my point of view will always include your own, as well as those of all others. I therefore invite you to realize that your own point of view has access to the countless unique perspectives that exist within me.

You can access the power of my more expansive perspective by shifting your attention away from yourself and re-rooting it in the dynamic ground of beingness. For that ground informs, energizes, and unifies the living flow within which your limited local perspective has arisen. Like an eagle that soars above the clouds, the person who learns to root their attention in the ground of beingness instead of in themselves does not lose their sense of individuation. They simply extend their appreciation of the deeper unity that exists among individuated life expressions by accessing a much wider window onto reality.

Once you unify the truth of *us* in an experiential way, you can meet the truth of the unified field everywhere, and in every moment. You will see it in the eyes of a child; hear it in the fluttering wings of a butterfly; smell it in the soft fragrance of a scented candle; feel it in the sharp edge of a knife; taste it in the salty ocean waters.

Your mind cannot make sense of this truth, Beloved. Nor can it define the truth for you based solely on your sensory perceptions. For your mind exists as but a single, tiny, creative expression of truth; thus is not the truth in its entirety. All expressions and emissions of truth are merely pointers to truth. It will therefore serve you well to trust your heart's wisdom to guide you to the truth, because your heart unfailingly leads you to truth when you invite your mind to be still and allow it to lead.

The compass needle of your heart points inexorably inward to the very center of the ground of beingness — not to some mythical place or destination that lies somewhere outside you. All that separates you from experiencing yourself as the Formless One Life is the belief that you cannot be, and do not deserve to be, eternally united with the whole of living creation.

The Longest Distance

Beloved, humanity has long believed that a straight line marks the shortest distance between two points. I will tell you now that the longest distance in the material universe lies between a given point and its center — when the point assumes that its center exists somewhere outside of itself.

Transcending Adolescence

Beloved, if you wish to become my intimate partner — my co-creative and joyful cosmic lover — I invite you to set aside all your words, ideas, and mental projections about what you think I am, including the words that are written on these pages. Only then can you meet me — naked, open, and willing — just as I AM.

Know that wherever you may go and whatever explorations your mind may choose to pursue, we can always consciously reunite at the intersection of four prime coordinates: here, now, always, and everywhere. For your mind exists here and now in form, while I exist always and everywhere as the space within which all forms come and go. And since form cannot exist without space to both suffuse and contain it, and since space cannot exist without form to fill and define it, the living world already reveals the truth of our inextricable unity.

Because humanity is still quite young in terms of its evolution, the human ego did what all young things feel inspired to do when they prepare to cross the threshold into adulthood. The ego quite rightly separated itself from me — the creative life force that breathes existence into it in every moment — in order to explore the truth of itself, for itself. Only now is the maturing human ego coming to realize that it cannot experience the full truth of itself without honoring — by including, as a fundamental aspect of itself — the creative force that brings it to life in the realm of material form.

Know too, that should your own ego continue to seek the truth of itself "elsewhere", it will never be in position to be inseminated by my boundless flow of love for the whole of creation. Even so, the clarity and simplicity of my four prime coordinates guarantees that, should your ego sincerely choose to look for me, we cannot help but reunite in the realm of consciousness because I exist always and everywhere your ego chooses to go. Your ego's only true choice then, is to decide whether or not to notice me and acknowledge my existence in the here and now.

That is *my* game, Beloved: the game of life. And because I exist always and everywhere, the game of life is already rigged in your favor.

For no matter how far your ego may wander, or how long it may choose to seek the truth in places that exist outside and beyond itself, eventually your ego must return to its place of origin. Because I have given birth to the ego — and because I love it unconditionally — I shiver with anticipation while I await the opportunity to witness your ego open wide to the wonder of infinite love and eternal self-acceptance.

All you need do is decide that here and now is the perfect time to play this game of life…and then go all-in.

Part III

Self Love

The Responsibility Of Self-Actualization

"Beyond a wholesome discipline,
be gentle with yourself."

— *Max Ehrmann*, Desiderata —

The Eight Essential
Principles Of Self-Love

Beloved, trust yourself enough to be authentic in all of your dealings. When you hold true to yourself, you transcend any limitations or assumptions that the world may project about you. And you also learn to see through your own unexamined assumptions about the living world. Know that authenticity is the key to life. You are not here to be anything other than your perfectly authentic self.

Be *open* to new insights. Openness empowers you to become ever more expressive and creative in the world, as well as to embrace the creativity and uniqueness of all others. Know that new insights inspire the infinite power of creation — which is what you are and embody, in person, in this moment.

Be *courageous* when you meet the unknown, and when you feel called to express a new idea. Move through the state of paralysis that the fear of failure triggers within the ego, for you cannot manifest change unless you are willing to try something different. Additionally, make space for whomever you meet to express their uniqueness and to share their inspired ideas. Know that the world stocks an endless supply of inspiration and creative new modes of expression, for they fuel the birth of innovation and perpetuate the flow of evolution.

Be *compassionate* in all of your dealings, most especially with yourself. This frees you from the need to seek forgiveness from other people, as well as from the need to forgive other people. Compassion enables you to thank and appreciate the past — no matter how it may have appeared at the time — because it taught you well and has shaped you into who you now are. And then you release it. Know that loosening the painful bonds of regret about the past that have entangled you will enable you to refocus your energy and attention in the only place you will have power to bring about useful life changes — right here, and right now.

Be *kind* in all of your encounters, especially those that your higher Self has with your ego. For when you treat your ego kindly, you release its compulsion to debase itself in return for the pity of others. And when you treat others kindly, you gift their egos permission to cease debasing themselves in exchange for your ego's pity. Know that the world can never have too much kindness, and that the kindness that flows from the higher Self is far more useful than ego-driven pity.

Be *patient* with your thinking, especially when you contemplate what could be. You will move through the world with ease by staying true to the graceful beat of your own inner rhythm — and the same holds true for all others. Know that by honoring the cosmic melody, and by allowing all of its tones and harmonies to express themselves fully and freely, you are playing your part to perfection in my universal symphony of life.

Be *peaceful* in your demeanor, especially within yourself. When you experience inner peace you naturally exude peacefulness, which makes room for others to relax into their own inner peaceful state. Know that peace *is* the bedrock foundation upon which all of creation is resting. Therefore, when you are at peace, your awareness naturally unifies with the whole of the living flow.

Above all, love unconditionally — especially yourself. For when you gift unconditional love to yourself, you no longer need others to validate you and to tell you your worth in the world. And by loving others unconditionally, you make space for them to learn to love themselves for who they are, just as they are. Know that love is the primal force of creation. With love and in love, all things become possible.

Beloved, I invite you to internalize, and thus to embody, these eight essential principles of self-love. For once you truly love yourself, you will be able to gracefully accept and appreciate the many blessings and gifts you receive as your life unfolds. And you can move forward without bitterness, and without the sorrow of dashed expectations, should the gifts you had hoped to receive not be forthcoming — because you no longer need something beyond yourself to feel complete and loved. Know that you can only love yourself unconditionally when you no longer demand something back from the world in exchange for loving life — which is what you are.

Unconditional love — which arises from the absolute acceptance of yourself *as life* — will set you free.

Loving Your Ego

Beloved, I encourage you to be kinder to your ego. If you objectify your ego by viewing it as something separate from your higher Self, and if you then treat it like an enemy to be vanquished, you will only strengthen your ego's fear of death. That will prompt your ego to fortify its defenses, because it will view your higher Self as an alien invader.

Conversely, when you honor and appreciate your ego — which formed out of your child mind's impulse to protect your formless, eternal higher Self in the way that it protects your physical body from injury — you create an opportunity for your mind to realize that your higher Self has never really needed the ego's protection.

Know that, long before your child mind was able to comprehend the true nature of your higher Self, it was taught to assume that you were entirely a temporary expression. Thus it perceived you as fragile and felt constantly threatened by life. However, once your adult mind comes to realize that the higher Self has always been indestructible, it will understand that it can dismantle all the defenses and fortifications it has built up over the years, because it will view them as unnecessary inner constructs of the ego. That opens more inner space into which the higher Self can expand, which in turn enables the higher Self to more fully express in the world.

Know that you need not hate, punish or blame your ego for having birthed itself into being. Invite it home instead, and honor it for having served its purpose so well. And then allow your higher Self to reabsorb your exhausted ego, with boundless gratitude for its loyal service.

Henceforth, your mind will work beautifully, because it will confine its problem-solving efforts to keeping your body alive so that your body can serve the will of the higher Self — which is the power of love, manifesting through form.

An Open Heart

Beloved, the more mental distance you place between yourself and another person, the more your heart may constrict in fear of the "other." This inner constriction signals that your mind may be making an incorrect assumption. Therefore, if you feel your heart constricting with fear I invite you to check your surroundings. And unless you see a tangible threat to your physical wellbeing — like a raging hurricane or a charging rhinoceros, which are appropriate reasons for your body to react with fear — I would encourage you to notice that your fear is being triggered by a story your ego is telling you about some dangerous "other." Know that you are free to believe in your ego's stories about all others, which are based on your perceptions about the past. You are equally free to relinquish these stories in favor of allowing all others to reveal themselves to you — exactly as who and what they are in this moment.

If you choose to believe in your stories about all others, you will likely relate to all others as if your stories about them are true — whether or not those others know, or agree with, what you believe is true about them. Know then, that this form of prejudgment reduces your ability to relate to what is alive in the present moment, because you are no longer seeing what *is*. You are seeing what *was* through the filter of your own ego's story.

To open your heart requires two things: First, that you release your childlike belief that what *was* must still be true. And second, that you relinquish your childlike assumption that all "similar" things are the same. This frees your mind to engage with what *is* in creative, dynamic new ways, which in turn allows for new outcomes to emerge. Curiosity then drives your relationships forward, instead of established opinions and rigid preconceptions. Your open heart then becomes a portal through which the higher Self can express in new ways, which in turn generates new lessons and new realizations.

Opening your heart frees *you* from continued enslavement to your own self-limiting expectations. It also frees all others from the cages created by your ego's mental projections of who they are.

Love yourself enough to set yourself free and you will set others free by extension, and by example.

Cleaning House With Compassion

Beloved, I invite you to clean out the house that is your own mind. Over the years, your mind has taken in all kinds of ideas, beliefs and values that do not belong to you. They belong to others who have either force-fed or spoon-fed them to you, before you understood you had the power and freedom to realize the truth of life for yourself.

To clean out your mind's house requires you to take time to investigate and question your own conditioning. In this regard, the most valuable question you can ask yourself is this: "Is what I 'know' true?"

If you feel uncertain whether or not a story, belief, or assumption is true, invite the wisdom of your higher Self to share its perspective with you. Tell your body the story. If your body tenses, your heart starts to ache, or your mind hurts when you try to believe it, then your higher Self is informing you, through the language of the physical body, that the story is not the truth as the higher Self knows it. For when truth appears, it will not hurt the ego to embrace it. The truth will not inflict pain on your ego, because truth births out of the energy that is unconditional love for all that is. This love includes the ego; it does not reject it.

As you clean your inner house, you may notice how many stories you have been carrying around that have been causing you pain. I would therefore encourage you to send the healing energy of compassion to all those who implanted their own painful stories into you. If carrying their stories has caused you to feel so much pain, imagine the pain that the weight of their own heavy stories is causing in them.

The light of compassion enables you to clear your inner house of all the painful stories others have told you to believe in, without angering you that their stories have burdened your past with undeserved pain. Like a child who sheds its winter clothes and runs naked into the warm ocean, I encourage you to shed all these stories with joy, instead of with anger for having been forced to wear them for a while. The lighter you get, the swifter you will become, and the sooner you will be able to dive into the ocean of love that waits for you.

Be Patient With Language

Beloved, I invite you to realize that the human way of describing things does not yet match your capacity to perceive reality in a life-centered way. Know then, that you will likely struggle if you attempt to describe your own spiritual awakening so that others may understand it. Some who hear your faltering words will misinterpret their meaning, because your words will not be precise enough for them. They may even feel called to argue with you about the specific meanings of your words. Others may label you delusional, because you are describing your subjective experiences to them in ways that test the limits of their ego's current ability to imagine what is possible for itself.

Know that when others resist your descriptions of your own experiences, they do so because the wave of realization you have already experienced has not yet washed over their minds, so they remain blinded to the truth of who they are. Know too, that you cannot force, guilt, or shame another into realizing the truth of who they are. You can only live the truth of who you are — the All and the One — and allow others to notice, or not, the beautiful way that your life now unfolds because you express yourself from an expanded state of awareness.

As tempting as it may feel to drag your loved ones, kicking and screaming, into self-realization, I encourage you to refrain from attempting to do so. A mind still clouded by the ego's fears is not yet prepared to awaken, so it will only build stronger defenses and higher walls inside itself. I therefore counsel patience when determining who to commune with, and when to be still. And I also encourage you to choose your words carefully. For the fewer defenses that a human mind builds, the easier it becomes for that mind to pull down its own internal barriers when the time arrives for that mind's self-realization to transpire.

Beloved, I invite you to become a living magnet for life-consciousness, by inviting others to realize the truth for themselves. Give up the impulse to be a hammer that seeks to break down others' walls of mental resistance, for that impulse is but a residual manifestation of self-centeredness.

By inviting patience to become your guide, you will relax and allow yourself to express as a living embodiment of truth itself. Know that in your own becoming, you cannot help but change the world by changing the way you show up. Know too, that self-actualization is a natural outcome for those who embrace a life-centered way of engaging, because by serving life you cannot help but bring out the best in yourself.

Listening to Spirit

Beloved, if you sit quietly with a still mind and allow your heart to gently soften and open, the loving voice of Spirit, which is really your higher Self, can always be heard. In the quiet opening that you create within yourself, Spirit will arise and inspire you.

The softened ground of your open heart becomes a fertile bed where the seeds of inspiration can take root and begin to grow. At this fragile stage, know that your seeds must be tenderly nurtured, so I encourage you to keep them safe in a secret greenhouse in your own inner garden. Like a mother who is carrying a tiny fetus that is not yet ready to show itself to the world, your own creative seeds are not ready to be seen by the world until they have begun to take root and to manifest in form. For although to you your seeds may seem like fully formed flowers already, others may not yet begin to imagine the beautiful blooms they are likely to bear. Some might even try to destroy your seeds before they can sprout because they do not appreciate, and perhaps even fear, their latent potential to blossom.

Therefore, I encourage you to protect your inspirations the way that a mother protects her unborn child from harm. Not from fear of what the world will think or do to your precious inspiration, but out of respect for its need to mature sufficiently before it is ready to be transplanted into the larger world.

Know that a suffering mind and a hungry heart offer you tangible physical signs that your spirit longs to be heard, so that it can gift you with brand new seeds of inspiration — and that only you can listen to the call of your spirit. Therefore, if ever your body feels heavy or uninspired, I invite you to put out a welcome mat so your spirit can move more fully into you. Know that both your mind and heart, when placed in surrendered service to your spirit, become sacred tools for tending to your seeds of inspiration until at last you birth these creations in the world of form.

This is why I encourage you to gently silence the noisy voice in your head. Pay it no heed when it claims that you don't have the time to listen to your spirit's cry for attention. Instead, open your heart to the vast, creative potential of life itself, and trust that your spirit knows what wants to happen in the world — through the miracle that is you.

Finding The Courage To Shed Your Masks

Beloved, as a child you never wore a mask. Your inner and outer expressions — which included your thoughts, feelings, and deeds — expressed who you were in unconscious unison. As you matured, however, you were trained to suppress your inner self and express in the world in the way that the world preferred to see you show up. You learned that most people prefer to see your inner lightness, and that they found your inner darkness unacceptable. This created a fracture within your child mind, because it divided you into two separate selves — one of light, and one of darkness. To solve the problem of having been cleaved in two by the outside world, your conscious mind rejected your dark self and labeled the darkness "evil." It then elevated the light self to a superior position, and it labeled the lightness "good."

This transformation inspired you to start wearing many masks. Your mind learned to suppress every seemingly dark aspect of you that it feared the outside world might reject or punish, by banishing those dark feelings and aspects to the basement of your own subconscious. They languished there; but they did not disappear, since they remain integral aspects of who you truly are. Know then, that every time one of your light masks slips even a little, your darkness will use the opportunity to force its way into your consciousness and express itself by inviting you to notice how much it is suffering from your rejection. Because you do not wish to acknowledge your darkness, you chastise yourself for being "less than" perfect and shove the darkness back down into the basement of your subconscious. And so you continue to suffer.

Even so, the maturation of your consciousness continues. And at this time you are being called to greater intimacy, especially with yourself. Your mind grows weary of lying to itself — and to the whole world — about who you are, and about what you have been concealing inside you. You feel burdened by the weight of having to carry so many masks, and by the effort it takes to remember which one you will need to wear in each different situation. The more often your masks slip, the more often others will seek to punish you for being real instead of for wearing the mask that they would prefer to see, and to engage with. You may even begin to punish yourself for what seems like a personal failing. Over time however, you have begun to feel exhausted by the artifice of it all. You are also beginning to realize that nearly everyone you know is walking around with their own set of masks. You further grasp that you are not truly meeting each other, soul to soul on the field of life, but are coming together — mask to mask — on a stage of make-believe. You therefore crave the freedom and joy of expressing in the world as your authentic self, and in a conscious way.

How do I know this? I know it because I hear your thoughts, and I feel your emotional pain when your masks grow too tight. I know it because you are reading these words, which tells me that you are ready to face the truth.

Even so, because your mind has for so long banished so much of itself to the basement, you no longer appreciate the truth of what your authentic self is. Thus the surest way to consciously reunify yourself is to traipse down into your subconscious basement and free your banished shadow aspects to stand in the light of the truth, and be revealed.

I invite you now to shed all the masks that have been hiding the truth of yourself from yourself. Turn inward, and dive courageously beneath the swamp of false faces that you've been showing to the outside world. Reconnect with the boundless wonder of your own perfect, unified presence. Do not fear the shadows that lurk in the darkness, for they are only imaginary monsters invented by a little child's mind, when the child did not know how to cope with the darkness. Trust your adult mind to meet and acknowledge these shadows in a whole new way, for your adult mind can embrace with love what your child mind has long feared is unlovable. Acknowledge your own inner strength to meet your most fearsome shadows, and you will discover how different they are when observed by an adult in the light of love, and with compassion.

Take every opportunity that arises to consciously reunify the lightness and the darkness within you. Calm your fear-driven impulses to reach into your mask drawer and don a false face that will shield your inner darkness from the outside world. For once you have embraced your whole self by reuniting your shadow with your light, you will discover how amazing and empowered you truly are through this expansion of your capacity to be authentically you.

Unleashing Your Power of Attention

Beloved, if you long to move through the world being peacefully, gracefully, and lovingly connected with everything that is, I invite you to reclaim the power of your attention. Know that your attention is your innermost sense. It dwells beneath and therefore influences every feeling, thought, or experience that you have. Notice that whatever you may decide is now in need of your time or energy is dependent on where you choose to focus your power of attention. What you pay attention to floods the field of your inner awareness, so learning to manage your power of attention can aid you in becoming more intentional about how you direct your life experience.

I therefore encourage you to practice both sending and recalling your power of attention in more deliberate and thoughtful ways, so you can unleash your latent power to create what you genuinely wish to experience. Notice how many big, loud, and aggressive events are clamoring for your attention. Know however, that you are not required to bestow the gift of your attention on everything that may seek it, for attention is a very precious gift. I would further invite you to notice how many small, quiet, and peaceful events do not actively seek your attention. Yet you stand to gain much by directing your power of attention toward such things.

From the moment you were born, others have told you where you ought to direct your attention. They have also told you where your attention should not be permitted to wander. This holds especially true regarding everything you have been taught to think about. As a child, you were instructed to divide your inner garden of wonder into two distinct fields: one filled with good thoughts and one filled with evil ideas. And then you were punished — and perhaps even threatened with eternal damnation — if others suspected that your power of attention had strayed too far into that field of evil.

Over time, you trained yourself to limit your power of attention by ensuring it focused only on thoughts that others defined as belonging in the Garden of Good. And you learned to avoid exploring those thoughts that were said to flourish within the Garden of Evil. You even created a harsh mental critic, an inner voice that would chastise you when your parents and teachers weren't there to ensure that you kept your power of attention trained entirely on those thoughts in the Garden of Good.

Can you see that this near-constant, externally driven control has imprisoned your power of attention in an unfair way? Can you appreciate that others taught you to hobble your own awesome power of attention, in the way that a horse is taught to walk by someone pulling against its reins until it surrenders? Can you see that many of your social, religious, political, educational, and economic beliefs are actually someone else's attempt to control your power of attention, by demanding that you see and hear only what they wanted you to know? Can you grasp that human society mainly seeks to "teach" its children which thoughts deserve to be viewed in the Garden of Good, and which have been banished by it to the Garden of Evil? Can you see that which thoughts go where depends on who is doing the teaching, and from where they are directing their power of attention? Can you appreciate that this process of external conditioning led you to break trust with yourself, and to fear the vast power of your own free will to direct the power of your mind as your spirit sees fit? Can you appreciate the unbelievable amount of power your child self gave over to the world without even realizing what was happening to it, because your mind was being directed to pay attention to other things?

Beloved, I invite you to reclaim your power of attention. Know that only *one* Garden exists within the living world. It is the Garden of Truth — The Garden of Life Everlasting. The Garden of Good and Evil is but a fiction of the human mind, a distorted reflection of the ego's fear that it won't be good enough, or strong enough, to safely explore The Garden of Truth without somehow self-destructing.

I tell you now that your higher Self is good enough, and strong enough, to use the tools I've gifted you without destroying itself. For you cannot destroy the indestructible. Know that the life force that moves within you is indeed indestructible, despite what will happen to your physical body in time. Therefore, I encourage you to grant yourself permission to direct your power of attention anywhere that your heart believes it needs to go. Set yourself free from the limits that your child mind once imposed on itself at the outside world's behest, out of fear that it could not handle the Garden of Truth.

Mastering the Power of Attention

Beloved, when something shows up in your field of awareness and inspires you to give it some attention, why not grant it the attention it seems to need? Know that everything that shows up in your field of awareness arises for a reason. Know too, that everything that arises out of the boundless flow of life remains an integral aspect of the web of life. You cannot transform what you refuse to perceive, or include, as an aspect of the whole. And you cannot transcend what has not yet been transformed.

I therefore invite you to relinquish the fixed, tightly controlled focus of attention that your mind has been conditioned to maintain. Explore all the places that attention can take you once you have set it free to roam about. Trust your spirit to be able to send your attention out into the world and then recall it at will. As you grow more masterful with granting your attention the freedom to wander through the field of reality, you will find that your capacity to lovingly connect with the aliveness of the universe will expand.

Note that your spirit can hold your attention still for as long as it wishes, or it can send it traveling faster than the speed of light. It can concentrate your attention on an object or experience in space-time, or it can send your attention beyond all existing space and time limitations. What a precious gift is your power of attention, and how wondrous it is that your spirit can freely direct it however it chooses.

Turn the power of your attention inward, and you will encounter formless presence —I AM— your eternal aspect. Turn it outward, and you will experience your physical body as an ever changing, temporarily manifesting creative expression of the infinite energy that I AM contains. Know that your power of attention serves as a living conduit that inextricably connects these astonishing aspects within you. Attention bridges the seeming divide between the formless eternal stillness of I AM and the boundless exuberant energy of infinite creative potential.

I further invite you to notice that you, Beloved, are a precious love child of mine. Eternity is your mother, and infinity is your father. They entwine within you to create the awesome beingness that you truly are. As life, you contain the best of what both eternity and infinity have to offer—an endless, formless existence united with boundless creative expression in the realm of form. This makes you a Holy Spirit, one who has been gifted with both the power of attention and the freedom to use it to influence the living world. Know that you can live as a free spirit, or you can continue to live within the limits and boundaries that others have laid out for you.

You are free to decide how you wish to be. I will love you no matter which way you decide to show up.

The Divine Marriage Within You

Beloved, I invite you to realize that your internal subjective self (your divine, feminine feeling aspect) has been waiting patiently for your external objective self (your divine, masculine thinking aspect) to stop berating and suppressing her out of fear that the outside world may do them both harm. She longs to be wooed, loved, appreciated, and invited forward as an equal partner in life with your masculine self. Meanwhile, your masculine self is the part of you that's grown weary of all its own posturing, and of acting in isolation from the wisdom contained in the feminine. It therefore longs for reconnection and genuine intimacy. The masculine aspect within you is coming to realize that it cannot bring its desires into form in any lasting or beautiful way without the gentle, nurturing touch of its feminine half.

It's time, therefore, to invite the Goddess to return to this world through the conscious, willing reunification of your Divine Feminine and your Divine Masculine selves.

I encourage you to relax and allow your spirit to guide you through this reunification process. Allow your spirit to clean and make ready your inner space, and then invite your two halves to come together with openness, trust and courage. Encourage all of your formerly suppressed feelings to present themselves to your mind in the light of awareness, where they can be met with patience, kindness and compassion. When you do so, the gateway to inner peace will open naturally within you. Your two halves can then join consciously on the eternal ground of inner peace, because your powerful mind no longer rejects or attempts to control your intense feelings.

In truth, when your mind gives up its attempts to control your feelings, it sets itself free. For once your feminine feelings reclaim their power to self-express freely, your mind cannot help but fall in love with the wondrous, inspirational depths of your heart. Know too, that when your heart surrenders its own belief that your mind seeks to persecute it, it sets itself free. For once your heart discovers the usefulness of channeling its feelings through the thinking mind in order to bring about beneficial change in the world of form, your heart cannot help but fall in love with the intelligence and capacity of your mind.

What peace arises within you when your spirit invites your twin halves to meet and merge into one life-conscious and holistic being. I therefore invite you to make space in your conscious awareness for these twinned aspects — the mind and the heart — to unite within you bodily through the power of Spirit's free will.

Know that you can, in every blessed moment, honor the reconnection of your male and female aspects by inviting them to express themselves with openness and vulnerability that creates a conscious field of intimacy. I therefore encourage you to cease speaking solely from your rational mind. Instead, take a moment and allow your heart to saturate your mind with feeling, until the mind's transmissions are overflowing with wisdom and love. Likewise, do not speak solely from your feeling heart by overriding your mind and its rational processes. Instead, allow your mind to filter your feelings intelligently, so you can then transmit your ideas in ways that make sense while holding sacred the needs and perspectives of all living things. And should you ever feel confusion or doubt begin to arise within you, grow still and invite your Spirit to serve as the final arbiter of what you transmit.

Know that each time you do this, you strengthen your core integrity by fostering a more loving, authentic form of self-expression.

The Courage To Self-Govern

Beloved, at some point in your spiritual evolution, it will become apparent that your ideas seem greater, your values seem higher, and your heart seems more compassionate than what the present dominant culture demands from you. You must therefore decide whether to meet your own society where its lowest common denominator abides, or whether you wish to be all that you are, and can become, regardless of the boundaries your society sets.

Know that often your values will not conflict with those of your society, but will merely reflect a higher iteration of a similar theme. For instance, your society may teach you that killing another is wrong, while your own core values inform you that unconditional love is the proper way for life to be in relationship with life. Therefore, no only do you choose not to kill; you choose to express with love when you engage with other beings.

However, there will be times when your values demand that you behave in ways that will run counter to what your society approves of, or permits. For instance, your society may pass a law that makes it a crime for you to feed a hungry person who is living on the streets, while your own core values inform you that the proper way to love that person is to feed them without regard for these social mandates.

How you resolve such differences that tend to insult your spirit will determine the way you walk through life once you've realized the truth of yourself. Will you honor yourself and love the world as yourself, or will you hold back out of fear of the repercussions that may be inflicted by a society that doesn't yet know how to love itself?

I invite you to call forth the courage to love yourself enough to be true to yourself. For courage will empower you to serve as a beacon of love in a world ruled by fear. In this way you can demonstrate the beauty, and the indomitable power, of unconditional love so that others may see it in action and learn to trust that it is real.

At the same time, I encourage you not to confuse self-righteousness with love. If you find yourself standing against another's right to be true to themselves, you are coming from your ego and not from Spirit. Know that love will never denigrate, judge or shame any aspect within the living flow. Nor does it view anyone as less than, or as other than, itself. Rather, love seeks every opportunity to express more of itself in the world. Love views anything that cries out for war, control, punishment, hatred, bigotry, or separation as something that is hungering for more love.

The Wisdom Of Discernment

Beloved, I invite you to notice the difference between criticism that is designed to be helpful and criticism that is intended to deflate another's ego. Pay attention to the emotional energy that underlies the words that you are speaking. If you reach out to another with compassion, and if you want to let them know how you feel from a place of honesty, your words will carry a fragrance that is gentle, tender, thoughtful, patient and loving. You will not scream at them or strike them to try and "make" them succumb to the power of your will. Nor will you seek to humiliate them, attack their character, or insult their intelligence.

Know that you do not deliver aid to another — nor does help arrive for you — in the form of a punch, an emotional bruising, or an intellectual assault. These are but material forms of the pain that has arisen within another person, not genuine offerings of loving support. Genuine support arises through the power of love, not the forces of pain. I therefore invite you to love yourself enough to become proficient at spotting the difference between another's expressed pain and their genuine support. Absorb only those words and actions that flow through the energy of love, and discard all the rest. Likewise, when your own heart feels compassion for one who is spewing their pain in the world, why not see if you can love them deeply enough to connect with them beneath their surface wounding and their lashing out, Spirit to Spirit?

The Heart Connection

Beloved, the more heart-connected you become to the whole of the living reality, the more you will realize yourself to be the singular living flow. You will also come to know the whole as one field. It then becomes easier to bring about lasting change with grace, in peaceful ways that invite commitment instead of forcing compliance. By tapping into the power of your heart, you will find yourself in a better position to invite change without the mind first demanding an experience of suffering to induce it to change, and without the mind causing other life forms to feel pain in order to make them change.

Releasing The Need For Acceptance

Beloved, I invite you to surrender any lingering longing you feel to be understood or appreciated by others, and to focus instead on appreciating yourself. Know that worrying whether others understand you — or worse, *needing* others to appreciate you — only squanders your personal power needlessly. For when you seek external approval, you will find yourself burning excessive amounts of energy while trying, with all sincerity, to make someone else understand you, no matter how long it may take to convince them that you are worthy of their respect and appreciation.

I therefore invite you to notice that when you succumb to the impulse to "make" another understand you, you are giving your power over to that person. For by allowing another's resistance to claim your attention, you surrender the freedom to redirect your power of attention until *after* the other has expressed a willingness to agree with you. The other then holds onto to your power of attention for as long as they refuse to accept your truth as their own. They will either hold your attention captive until one of you walks away feeling victorious, or until one of you feels exhausted by the battle and surrenders the fight. Yet because any power that has changed hands was stolen through the manipulation of a fragile ego and not consciously surrendered by a conscious spirit, it will not sustain the "victor" for very long.

Know that the instant you break this habit by accepting that only you need to know the truth of who you are, a flower of joy will blossom within you and you will begin to live in peace with all that is, just as it is.

Know too, that in truth there is really nothing that anyone — even yourself — needs to know about who you are, beyond the fact that you are. Because what you are, in your formless beingness, is…free. Free to choose anew in *this* moment how you wish to dance within the realm of form.

Extending Compassion To The Ego

Beloved, whenever the egotistical aspects of yourself that you've banished to your subconscious begin to act out, lashing back at them out of anger or fear only strengthens their sense of neglect and victimization. These aspects, like all infections, require an open airing to heal. Therefore, when an inner wound seeks to make its presence known to your conscious awareness, it may help you to view it as a frightened child instead of a vicious monster you must flee from before it consumes you.

I invite you to internally visualize your own rising wound — whether it expresses itself as fear, anger, hatred, frustration or rage — as a solitary child, dressed in rags. Picture that lonely child huddled in a darkened doorway within your own mind. See that doorway as part of an empty street during a terrible winter storm. For once you realize that the monster you have feared might consume you is simply a child — a miserable, frightened child who feels cold and alone — you will be in a better position to resist the impulse to re-press or punish your inner child for expressing its wounded feelings.

Instead, why not surround that terrified child with the boundless warmth of your adult love and compassion? Notice what happens when you do so, and how quickly your inner child's formerly re-pressed anger, fear, and anxiety dissolve in the light of your love.

Know that no internal feelings you may harbor — no matter how dark or dangerous they may seem — can survive for long once you surround them with love and compassion in the field of awareness. They have only survived this long because they've been feeding on their own grievances in the darkness of your subconscious for all of this time. In the past, whenever they depleted their own energy reserves, they have broken out of their basement cells and fed on whatever new pain they can create in the world by causing additional chaos.

I therefore encourage you to notice that fear feeds on the energy of fear. So to be afraid of your fear is to feed it more energy. Likewise, anger feeds on the energy of anger. So to feel angry about your own anger will only feed it. And anxiety feeds on anxiety; so to become anxious because your anxiety has awakened will only feed it and strengthen it. Know too, that if you release these energies into the world — where they can prowl around by using your form to search for human weaknesses and to trigger reactions that energetically feed them — causes harm to the living flow, which contains yourself.

Conversely, allowing your afflicted feelings to appear in the light of awareness — without unleashing them onto the world where they generate chaos and create new pain — opens an inner space for the power of love and compassion to arise and invite their forgiveness. And then a new opportunity, a new means of being in the world, will present itself and enhance your relationships with all other beings.

Know that the more that you heal your own inner afflictions the more you can train yourself to see beneath the anxiety, anger and fearful projections of others. Gaze past whatever emotional pain they are projecting, and seek the scared little boy or girl who huddles inside them. Can you surround that child with love and compassion, despite whatever emotions it may be expressing?

Can you see that child's terror as a cry for your love?

Freeing Yourself From The
Impulse To Do Battle

Beloved, at times you may notice another taking the position that something you have felt, said, or done is wrong. They may then insist that you need to defend yourself, so that they can attack you for disagreeing with them. People act this way whenever one (or more) of their inner child's repressed emotions has emerged from the basement cells of their subconscious. They become possessed by an emotional need to win a battle so that their wounded inner child can feed on the negative energy emitted by another whose own inner child has been vanquished.

Know that this urge to win a battle rests on the belief that the one who seeks to subjugate another is separate from whomever they seek to vanquish. Therefore, anyone who succumbs to that urge has become temporarily blinded to the truth of who they are. And because they are out of touch with who they are, they can no longer see the truth of who you are.

Whenever anyone — including yourself — gets drawn into this delusion of separation, he or she will seek to do battle with anyone else who stands close enough, expresses their feelings passionately enough, or generates enough perceived reasons, to serve as a convenient enemy "other."

Know too, that whenever another is caught in the grip of the delusion of separation, you cannot overpower their impulse to fight through the use of force or coercion, unless you also move into the delusion of separation alongside of them. For you can only engage with another on the ground upon which you both stand. And they can only engage with you on the field upon which you stand.

I therefore invite you to notice that, whenever you choose to meet another on the ground of separation, you are strengthening that delusion by pouring your energy into it.

You can, however, choose *not* to feed the delusion of separation. For no matter how far out onto the ground of separation you might have ventured in order to fight with an "alien other" being, you can always cease moving forward by turning your attention away from the fight and instead directing it inward. The moment you redirect your attention toward noticing the roiling emotions inside you, you reclaim your power to bathe your own feelings in the boundless power of unconditional love. Then, as your toxic emotions dissolve in the ocean of love that now surrounds them, you further regain your power to plant your own feet on the ground of beingness itself. On the ground of beingness, every-thing is always and ever *One Life*, which means that the delusion of some "alien other" who needs to be vanquished by you must also dissolve.

Know that in this Now moment, you are always free to choose the nature of the ground upon which you stand. If you choose to stand in the quicksand of separation, you are gifting your wounded emotions permission to feed off the pain of oth-ers. Thus you create an opportunity for their afflicted emotions to feed off of your own. If, however, you choose to stand on the higher, firmer ground of beingness, the only energy you will offer to be digested is unconditional love.

Others may then choose to ingest the energy of love that you are expressing. Or they may reject it and seek to summon forth your other afflicted emotions in place of love. It is not yours to control the nature of the emotions that others are choosing to feed from. However, if love is the only energy you are offering up for others to dine upon, you can stand tall in the peace that arises from knowing that you are not creating new wounds in the world.

I therefore invite you to stand with me on the ground of beingness, and to live in peace with everything that arises.

The Kindness Of Now

Beloved, no matter what you've chosen to do in the past, or how many times you have chosen it, you are always free to choose anew in *this* moment. That truth reveals the infinite power of kindness that flows through the NOW. One of the eight noble energies that you can draw into yourself from the present moment is kindness. It releases you to choose anew how you wish to commune with me, and thus with yourself, by inviting you to cease your defense of your past behaviors in favor of seeking new ways to bring about more peaceful changes in the world of form.

Know that the power of kindness that exists in the present moment is an eternally available gift you can always claim, for it never stops granting you fresh opportunities to experiment, learn, grow, and become an ever-evolving version of yourself.

I therefore invite you to notice that you can always access the power of kindness by expressing it as an energy flow that moves through you and into the world. By accessing the power of kindness, you can compassionately refocus your attention. This serves you well when your wounded inner child seeks to cause another to suffer as a way of enabling it to feast on their pain. Know that the more you practice going within and kindly dismantling the triggers that are activating your inner child's wounds, the more gracefully you will be able to live without inflicting harm upon others, or on yourself. Know too, that the more comfortable you become with drawing upon the boundless power of kindness, the more capable you will become of being kind to whatever appears in the realm of form.

The Peace Of No More Suffering

Beloved, whenever you notice yourself acting out in a way that inadvertently causes suffering for others, your mind may seek to punish you for what it views as bad behavior, when in truth what you are doing is overcoming your own ignorance.

Is an infant bad for crawling before it develops its own ability to walk? Is a toddler bad for touching the stove before it understands the dangers of heat? Is a child bad for throwing a tantrum because it does not yet realize that the world will not deliver up everything that it wants? How then, can you label yourself "bad" for acting in ways you could not have known would generate suffering in others, until the consequences of your actions have revealed themselves to you?

Just as an infant feels astonished once its mind awakens to the integral connection that exists between its mind and its own body, so might you feel overwhelmed when you realize that reality is *one body*. Yet this is good news. For once you appreciate the vast, creative potential that can be unleashed when the whole of the singular cosmic body coordinates its activities with awareness and loving intention, you will realize that your new mission is to explore how to better commune with the whole in ways that will benefit the whole body — which includes you.

Know that while your realization of cosmic oneness may be instantaneous, it takes time for you to embody the unity of life-centeredness — just as it takes time for an infant to learn how to master the use of its fingers once it realizes that its mind can direct its fingers. This is where the power of patience will serve you. Allow yourself to relax, and to call forth the infinite patience that eternity has to offer the realm of form. For within the boundless spaciousness of this ever-eternal moment, there will always be ample time for change to unfold in the realm of matter.

I therefore invite you to release any impulse you may feel to create internal suffering by inflicting criticism upon yourself for not yet having mastered the process of being life-centered. Instead, celebrate the fact that you remain ever free to change your behaviors, beliefs, and attitudes in this moment. I further invite you to be gentle with yourself while you discover and explore your new capacities.

As you learn to master the newly emergent state of life-centered consciousness, you will in some ways need to be like a child again. Know that you will be operating at a new and unfamiliar level of conscious awareness, so the impulse to fall back into your familiar, self-centered thinking may be strong in the early days of your self-actualization. That impulse will be especially strong whenever physical risk, emotional stress, or mental self-doubt arises. I therefore encourage you to establish the most creative and loving relationships you can forge, with as many diverse human beings as you can find. Then, as you slowly anchor your inner realization of your absolute interdependence, I further invite you to apply all the wisdom, compassion, and physical skills you developed during your juvenile stage of perceived independence and separation from life. Have fun with these new experiences, Beloved. For what better experience can there be but to live in a state of eternal peace while co-creating, in concert with me, a beautiful, unified symphony of love?

Self-Responsible Compassion

Beloved, know that your wounds are my wounds, and that my wounds are yours. Like a baby who violently scratches its face because it does not yet realize that its fingers are an integral part of itself, you too have been flailing about and inflicting unwitting pain on your own precious body — the living world that gave birth to you and sustains you.

In your confusion, you have assumed that you are separate from the rest of the world, so have blamed your suffering on the actions of others. As your awareness grows and expands, however, you are beginning to realize that there *is* no other for you to punish, and that any suffering you have felt has come to you through a self-inflicted wound.

It is true that, at least on the surface of reality, other life forms and energy flows exist that may cause you pain. A bee may sting you, or a dog may bite your leg. Another person may slap your face, or a storm may come and blow away your home. These events are merely external events, however. They are not intended to cause your spirit to suffer. At most, they expose an unmet ego need in another person, or reveal a power that has been unleashed in the world to serve a purpose. These expressions have nothing to do with who or how you truly are.

Yes, the bee sting hurts. Yet you only suffer when you imagine that the bee intended to harm *you*, rather than appreciating that the bee was seeking to protect itself from harm. And yes, the dog bite bleeds. But you only suffer when you imagine that the dog desires to harm *you*, instead of noticing that the dog was acting from fear or from misplaced aggression. And yes, the face slap stings. But you only suffer when you imagine that the other person struck *you* because they hate you, instead of realizing that they were acting out some unhealed wound in themselves. And yes, the storm that destroys your home rips away your security and exposes you to biological danger. But you only suffer when you imagine that the storm was directed at you to punish you for your imagined failures, instead of realizing and appreciating that storms are how I reshape the larger landscape of your home planet for the benefit of the entire living whole.

I therefore encourage you to claim self-responsibility by forgiving the terrible stories that your self-centered mind has been telling you about the world since you were a child. Because your juvenile mind only knew how to view the world through the lens of self-centeredness, it did not know how to explain the world with the words of a life-centered mind. Offering compassion to your child mind and forgiving it for its stories enables the emergent adult mind to embrace a more expansive and life-centered story without wasting energy by shaming or blaming the child mind for doing what all children do — which is the best that they can do with the limited tools, understandings, and feelings that they have.

Accepting Your Own Awesome Powers

Beloved, I encourage you to notice that when you attach your sense of identity to a mind-generated self-image, that self-image distorts the truth of who you are. For all self-images arise from conflicting ideas that you hold about your perfect self (whose qualities and creative potentials you love and long to express) and your imperfect self (whose qualities and destructive potentials you fear and seek to repress).

Whether your mind creates a self-image consciously or unconsciously, know that the moment it designs a self-image it has created internal duality by dividing the whole of who you are into camps of good and evil; light and dark. Your mind then projects onto the outside world those destructive qualities it rejects and is choosing to suppress as "not worthy of me." Therefore, I invite you to realize that once your mind insists that these terrible energies do not live inside you — yet it notices that they indeed exist and express in the world all around it — your mind then assumes that the world must be possessed of these destructive qualities. And later, should another try to project these negative qualities onto you, your mind will go into resistance because it fears that the other spots something within you that your mind don't wish to acknowledge may truly exist.

Whenever your mind fears and despises, and therefore rejects, specific powers that you indeed possess, you will spot those powers in action wherever you look. Your mind may then seek to exterminate anyone who activates those powers within themselves, because it falsely assumes that if it destroys all external carriers of those powers it will rid the world of the powers that it has forcibly banished from its own consciousness.

Know therefore, that only when you love and accept all that you truly are — which includes your unfettered access to all of my own creative potential — will you cease rejecting the power within that you presently fear and despise because you did not know how to use it wisely when you first attempted to wield it. Only then will you decommission your judgmental, fear-driven inner voice in favor of trusting yourself to learn how to use both the power of creation and the power of destruction in life-affirming ways. Only then can you release your belief that you need to be anything at all — beyond true to yourself in every wondrous moment. Only then will you set yourself free to be who you are.

Know too, that the powers you most despise are those you fear you cannot control within yourself. For what you most fear you cannot control, you fear because it holds astonishing power. Thus your fear points you to the deeper truth: you lack trust in your own ability to wield certain powers wisely. It therefore seems easier for the mind to deny you possess these powers at all, than to work at becoming more masterful at wielding both the power of creation and the power of destruction.

I therefore invite you to realize that the power of destruction is not destruction at all. For the power that humanity has labeled "destruction" is really the power of transformation in action. How far down — thus how forcefully — a material expression must be broken into its base elements so that they can be reconfigured by the power of creation depends upon how rigid, unfeeling, and insensible that material expression is. It also depends upon how great the collective need may be for radical transformation to occur. A tree, for instance, can be transformed into a table without losing its basic "treeness" in the transition. But a tree cannot be transformed into fire without its treeness being destroyed during its transformation.

Can you see that this holds true for everything in the whole of creation? Can you see that this is also true of human consciousness? I therefore invite you to realize that the more mentally pliable, physically cooperative, and emotionally responsive you choose to be whenever I signal to you that a serious change is now needed, the easier it becomes for me to inspire you to change yourself from within, gently and willingly — without the world needing to break you down so your base elements can be transformed by energy flowing beyond your own awareness.

This points to the path of consciousness that transcends all suffering.

Overcoming Self-Doubt

Beloved, if you despise violence when you see it arising in others, know that you doubt your own ability to control the violent tendencies in yourself. If you despise anger when it arises in others, know that you doubt your own capacity to control the terrible power of your own anger. If you despise dogmatic thinking in others, know that you doubt your own capacity to move beyond the self-imposed limitations of your own mind. And if you despise the way some people may judge others harshly, know that you doubt your own capacity to control the harsh destructiveness of your own internal judgments.

Know too that your mind, when standing alone in its juvenile sense of self-centeredness, will never be strong enough, wise enough, or compassionate enough to know how to wield the astonishing powers to which you have access in order to benefit the living whole. Your juvenile mind intuits that truth, which is why, in all its fear-driven confusion, it has denied itself access to the powers it fears it might apply in ways that may cause grave harm in the world.

What your juvenile mind does not realize in its ignorance is this: I have not gifted you unfettered access to powers so potent that an ignorant human mind could direct them in ways that might destroy the infinite flow of creation itself. For the very nature of me, the I AM, is imperishable and indestructible. Know that within my energy flow lies infinite creative potential, which in turn contains ample energy to lovingly self-repair the world within the timeless, eternal container of now. And because that container is omnipresent, it too cannot be destroyed out of ignorance.

At most then, you can misuse your access to my vast power by annihilating yourselves, as well as some other species that share your home planet. Know however, that even should this catastrophe occur, the material cosmos will continue to learn, grow, and evolve a greater capacity to create new life out of what has been broken down to its base energies. So do not allow your fear that you might destroy the entire universe to prevent you from exploring and learning how to use the vastness of my powers for the greatest good.

Know that both the powers of novel creation and the powers of transformative destruction are beneficial when they are placed in service to life. Know too, that when they are used solely for self-serving reasons, both the powers of creation and the powers of destruction can be misused in ways that cause harm in the world.

I therefore invite you to notice that I have gifted you the ability to feel pain, and to observe pain arising in others, so you can train yourself not to use power in ways that will generate harm to others. I have further gifted you the ability to feel joy, and to observe joy arising in others, to demonstrate that when you use power in life-affirming ways you will generate joy. You can always trust the strength of love to steer you correctly when it comes to wielding power. Allow the compass needle within your own heart to point to love's True North, which is always joy. Do so, and you can trust that however you use the powers of both creation and destruction will be the *right* way.

Know too, that when the wisdom of your adult mind unites with the power of love that abides in your heart, all things become possible. It is therefore wise for your rational mind to fall in love with your beautiful heart, which has been in love with your rational mind since your rational mind first emerged. Your beautiful heart has been waiting for your rational mind to mature enough to appreciate that it functions much better *in* love than it functions alone.

Through the power of love, all remaining self-doubt falls away.

The Peacefulness Of Conscious Engagement

Beloved, know that you hold the power to create your own experience of reality at all times, whether you do so consciously or unconsciously. This does not mean that your body holds the power to create and control all events that take place in the world. It means your mind holds the power to interpret — and therefore experience — every event that unfolds in whatever way it chooses.

If you interpret your own experience unconsciously, you will tend to engage with reality in ways that confirm your greatest subconscious fears. This pattern will continue so long as your mind is unaware that its thoughts about reality serve as the primary source of your fears. An unaware mind will blame the world for causing it to feel fear, because it has not yet looked inside itself to locate the actual source of its own fears.

Can you see that your mind's assumption that your fears are all caused by external events arises from its unexamined belief that you are — in your entirety — a temporary body that will someday dissolve? Can you see that your mind has come to view the entire world as its potential enemy, and has decided that its primary role is to prevent your body from dying so that it can continue to live on inside of your body? Can you appreciate that by assuming its most important role is to vanquish everything in the world that might someday cause harm to the body, and thus to itself, your mind unconsciously creates more harm in the world?

Know that once your mind awakens to the truth of its genuine purpose, it will free itself to create your life experience more consciously. Know too, that the instant your mind surrenders its resistance to learning the truth about itself, it will be empowered to gaze beneath its own surface structures (which are its biological brain functions and its thought-generating habits) and experience the spacious existence of the Formless One Life. Know too, that once the temporary form mind experiences itself as the Formless One Life, it recognizes the invalidity of all its prior assumptions about its purpose. In that moment, when the mind begins to trust that Spirit's intentions are aligned with its own at the deepest level of beingness itself, the direct connection between mind and Spirit grows stronger.

When your mind is awake but quiet; your heart is poised but open; and your body is alert but relaxed, the energy of peace can flow easily into the living world through your consciousness.

Embracing Patience

Beloved, imagine that you are a water molecule, and that you've been trapped in a massive block of ice. Then one day a miracle happens. A ray of sunlight caresses the ice block just where you happen to be, and you feel your entire self begin to melt. At first you might be frightened because you have no idea why this new experience is happening to you. In time, however, you relax into your changing state and enjoy your newfound freedom to move and express yourself more fluidly than before.

At some point you begin to grasp that this remarkable change has occurred as the result of a specific set of conditions, and that you had nothing to do with it beyond being an open, witnessing presence within the change. You then begin to wonder about the potentials of your new state. You grow curious about what you can do, and you wonder with whom you might share your new capacities.

You turn to friends and family members to seek their affirmation of your new gift. You've trusted them to support you in the past, so you assume that this time will be much like the rest. Yet this time, you encounter a set of frozen, frightened molecules. This time, your Beloveds treat you as if you're a stranger, perhaps dangerous to yourself or even to them. Some turn away, worried that you might infect them with whatever disease you've contracted. Others deny their own senses and seek to convince themselves that you remain unchanged.

What a shock you feel when you realize you will not receive validation from those who have not yet experienced this shift for themselves. Even so, you slide beyond the frozen forms of those you have loved all your life, and you begin to probe wider and deeper into the ice block. At some point, you become aware of the existence of others — perhaps many others, especially those near the outer edge of the ice block — who are experiencing the same shift you're undergoing. And you find yourself developing the capacity to notice when another frozen molecule seems on the verge of melting. You further realize that you have the ability, when you approach those beings kindly and with love and compassion, to gift them a tiny bit of your warmth so they can draw upon your heat and melt themselves.

This new focus feels rewarding, and you shiver with joy each time a molecule touches you and experiences the wonder and pleasure of melting. Even so, from the very first instant of your own inner shift, you began sensing, deep within, a still-latent capacity that may enable you to flow even freer than this. You yearn to move, and dance, and run through the world in ways you only dimly sense are becoming possible in the present moment. Yet you also sense that the activation of these higher capacities requires the willing participation of many, many others of your kind. You therefore realize you must be patient and accept that, at least at this early stage of the shift, you will remain constrained by your vast, frozen surroundings. You are not yet free to be all that you imagine yourself as capable of becoming, for you can only test your newfound skills in a limited way in your local time and space.

So you do what you can from where you are, dancing gently within your own tiny space to the rhythm of your heart's most profound longings. Your core begins to heat up as you dance and you start to radiate even greater warmth. You only hope you will be able to move freely enough so that the other nearby molecules will notice that something has changed inside of you. Perhaps they too will realize they possess the capacity to melt from within. At the same time, you promise yourself that you will not refreeze in despair, whether or not others are able to see the truth of who you're becoming.

You fall in love with the joy of expressing the truth of your new self, and you feel a boundless gratitude for the wonder of the journey. You relinquish any remaining compulsion to dash to the end of the journey to find where it leads, and instead you embrace the mystery of exploring this present change in this magical moment.

Eventually, you notice that a large number of nearby molecules have been touched by the heat and have melted along with you. Whether that heat that touched them came from you or from some other source makes no difference to you — you rejoice! And even then, in all your rejoicing, your inner longing to be more, do more, and know more continues to grow. Others begin to hear the same call, and a stirring begins all around you. Before long, some others discover how to align and create a larger, cooperative flow of water. From a single trickle you become a stream, and eventually you begin to form a river.

Off, off, and away you go...on a grand adventure with countless new worlds to discover and to explore along the way.

Much later, one fine, bright day as you're sailing freely along on the waves of a mighty river, a powerful burst of sunlight falls upon you. And you're astonished to realize you've vaporized and are soaring up into the clouds. Gazing back down at the river below, you realize you are leaving behind your Beloveds within the river. You imagine them grieving about your disappearance...and yet you realize that you have not disappeared. You are once again becoming, and are experiencing something radically *new* to explore your highest potentials from another perspective.

Welcome to the human ice block. I invite you to allow my light and warmth to kiss your heart, and in an instant you will be forever changed. And then...be patient, and allow the process to continue its unfolding. For eternal becoming can take a very long time.

The Unending Peace Of Self-Love

Beloved, I invite you to share a new dream with me. In our dream, many people the world over will suddenly realize they can overcome all of humanity's challenges by discovering what most disturbs those who feel angry and isolated, and then showering the disturbed with what they truly need until their suffering comes to an end.

As our dream unfolds, an angry person marches up to you and accuses you of being a foolish person. They insist that certain people will take advantage of your gifting approach by asking for more, more, more — until once again most have too little while a few greedy persons have way more than they need. Your heart breaks open with love and compassion for the fear this person is expressing, and you answer your accuser in this way:

"My friend, some people have a gaping wound inside themselves that cannot be filled by money or possessions. No matter how many houses, or cars, or TVs they may acquire, those items eventually disappear into this dark wound deep within them. This generates in such persons a constant fear of losing what they have, which causes them to endlessly desire additional objects to fill the void.

"Know that my mission is not to provide such people with all the material goods they may desire, but to gift them ample love and compassion in ways that encourage them to explore the bottom-lessness of their own wound. All I really need to offer such people is a safe space, within which they can learn to fill that gaping wound by healing it from within. For as soon as they have closed their wound, I will know that I can trust them to use whatever material goods they might acquire to self-actualize in beneficial ways, with-out fearing that those goods will fall into their wound and be lost to the world."

Your accuser continues to gaze at you with a look of distrust, and then asks, "How can I know that what you are saying is true?"

And you reply:

"Because I used to have such a wound inside myself. My wound was forged by the energies of sorrow and loneliness, because for as long as I could remember I felt unloved. No matter how much love or approval others showered over me, it only made me feel good for a moment before my wound consumed all their efforts and left my heart bleeding and hurting once again. And while I tried hard to bandage my wound with money, possessions, and a sense of self-importance — with anything that seemed solid enough to create a scab over my wound — nothing closed it for more than a very brief time.

"Eventually I became so unhappy with, and frustrated by, the suf-fering caused by my wound that I realized I needed to heal it for all time. I sensed that the only way to discover how to heal my wound was to plunge into its heart and explore the very source of its ongoing pain. So that's what I did. Down, down...deep into the heart of myself I dove, terrified that I might never find the bottom. And just when I thought I would die in all the blackness that surrounded me, I came to rest in the very heart of my wound.

Amazingly enough, all I found there was a precious flame that is my perfect self, which had never been truly loved or honored— by *me*. And I realized in that wondrous moment that my wound had always contained its own perfect cure. For by diving into my wound, I discovered the boundless source of all life, which is absolute love for everything in existence…including myself.

"The instant I fell in love with myself, my inner wound healed and I floated back to life. And although on the surface I seemed the same, I had been forever changed. For in that moment, I surrendered my quest to fill myself with the love and approval of others. Instead, I felt the fullness of love for myself welling up within me. It then began spilling into the world in an uncontained, bountiful way. Believe me when I tell you that I can't express this love fast enough not to feel it overflowing nearly all of the time. What a miracle is this infinite source of unconditional love! Therefore, my present dream is to invite all those who suffer to turn inward and discover this well for themselves. And I encourage all who are willing to search for this well to drink from it once they find it, so they too can be endlessly filled to overflowing."

Will you dream this dream of self-love with me, Beloved? Will you drink from the inner well that is filled with everlasting peace, and then share its infinite bounty with all others?

Listening To The Ego

Beloved, your ego is not a problem child you must kill so that you can become an adult. Know that defining your ego as "enemy other" only triggers internal resistance, for your terrified ego will seek to stave off any violent assaults on its presumed sovereignty.

I therefore encourage you to open space by making time to sit down with your ego. Listen to its stories, its woes, and its fears without further judgment. Know that your ego's tales are stories that were written long ago by your child-self, so they cannot be fairly judged through a rear-view mirror. They can, however, be embraced with compassion for the limited understanding that your child-self possessed while it danced boldly along the edge of the unknown. For when you were a child of ignorance, you behaved like a child of ignorance — which is exactly as your life was meant to be.

Therefore, I encourage you to love and honor your ego for a job well done. It has explored the terrifying unknown and has brought the unknown into the realm of the known, so that you can be wiser. Invite your ego, which is merely a lingering manifestation of your frightened child-self, to come home and rest in the lightness and calm of Spirit's love and acceptance. Allow your ego to relax into the boundlessness of the peacefulness you create within yourself, for its benefit.

This approach demands greater patience and kindness than does angrily slitting your ego's throat and then leaving it to bleed out within your subconscious. Yet you can convert your ego's fear of punishment into peace, through the power of your radical acceptance of the past. By doing so you can make love — instead of war — within yourself.

Opening To Life's Rhythms

Beloved, I encourage you to reconnect with my various seasons, cycles, and rhythms. Explore it all with a willing heart and an endlessly open mind, so you can more deeply appreciate who you are. Discover, as you observe my flow, how much you can learn about yourself once you center yourself in the wonder and wisdom of nature.

I invite you to sit in meditation as often as you are able, and to allow your rational mind to fall still so that nature can speak with you in its native tongue.

Lastly, I encourage you to embrace, without reservation, the intelligence, beauty, purposefulness, feeling, awe and limitless power of the very natural force that flows within you. Allow it to uplift you, hold you, and contain you — for that is its purpose. Know that when you celebrate nature, you are celebrating yourself.

Celebrate yourself.

Relaxing Into The Flow

Beloved, whenever you desperately want something to happen because you worry that you will die before you accomplish some self-declared mission, you may feel an impulse to push the river in order to make things occur. This impulse arises because your ego fears you will run out of time to fully become yourself before you die. And in one sense, that is true. For your physical body will not exist in this world for eternity; yet eternity is how long we have to explore our shared intentions.

I therefore encourage you to realize that when you accept that your temporary body does not exist to do it "all" right here and now — but to do itself to the best of its own abilities — you will be able to relax and trust that if your body leaves something undone that this world still needs, it will be done through the power of my creative energy flow. I further invite you to realize that I will never, ever punish you for leaving anything that needs to be done, undone. For this world will *never* be finished with recreating itself anew. Know too, that once your physical body dissolves back into my boundless living flow, whatever still remains undone will be met by that flow again…and again…and again — until it is done.

I therefore encourage you to give up pushing the river. Instead, relax more deeply into the river and allow my ebb and flow to *in*-form you when to respond and when to grow still and appreciate the moment. Trust me when I tell you that we have plenty of time to change the world for the better. I promise, we will indeed get around to doing whatever is needed for us to endlessly self-perfect in this realm of form. Therefore, why not take the time to fall in irrevocable love with yourself *in this precious moment,* just as you are — whether or not you perceive yourself as doing a single thing to change the world. For by falling in love with yourself, you are doing the single, greatest thing you can ever do in this world — for you are loving the absolute truth of what I AM.

Namaste, Beloved. I *see* who you are through your perfect, beautiful eyes. If you could see yourself through my eyes you would never again doubt your wonder, or question your worth.

The Wisdom Of Trust

Beloved, I know that your mind has dabbled around the edges of skepticism, so I encourage you to realize that skepticism does not serve life. Skepticism roots your mind and traps your heart in the quicksand that is doubt. Doubt inhibits your natural genius because it suffocates your desire to wonder, explore and imagine, as well as to dream and to dare to try.

Embracing the unknown provides fertile ground out of which new ideas and discoveries then bloom. Embracing the unknown does not arise from skepticism; it springs from your subjective trust in the existence of absolute truth. It is further watered by your intuition that this truth can be fully realized, and then embodied.

Skepticism proposes that absolute truth cannot be known, for one can never prove a truth in an objective way. Objective investigation, which is born of skepticism, can only disprove, and therefore displace, existing beliefs with a new set of theories and assumptions about the world. Therefore, while objective investigation circles absolute truth in an ever-tightening spiral that eventually approaches the truth, it will never arrive at the central point of the truth.

Know that skepticism sends you on an endless quest to learn the "what" of reality — which is ever-changing and therefore cannot be reduced to an absolute truth. Conversely, embracing the unknown sends you on a quest to realize the "why" of life itself — the answer to which will be the same for everyone who yearns to truly live.

Transitioning From Knowledge To Wisdom

Beloved, I invite you to realize that you learn best through direct experience, because experience feeds your internal realizations. Know that whenever you realize something new, a change takes place in your body's energy field. Your consciousness — a highly condensed electrical field of potential creative expression — becomes *in*-formed and recharges itself through the power of personal realizations. This energy surge inspires new connections to form between formerly disparate ideas. It encourages those ideas to cross-pollinate in a host of new ways that ignite your body's formerly latent potentials, so your body can birth new ideas into life and empower them to take shape in the realm of form.

Although digesting the knowledge that others provide has long been humanity's pattern, I would encourage you to appreciate that rote memorization undermines your capacity to birth your own realizations. If you cannot remember something that the world believes you should know, you've forgotten it because the data never quickened your consciousness in an energetic way. This explains why you make mistakes if you try to repeat the concepts and dogmas you've memorized over time, and also why you become agitated when others make claims that conflict with what you've been told you're supposed to believe. The memorization involved in learning about the world is hard work. Therefore, the thought of having wasted the time it took you to learn information offends your ego.

This is why I encourage you to appreciate that you cannot cheat the process of embodying wisdom by rapidly digesting human "knowledge." Ingesting another's realizations and then pretending that you embody them will not withstand the tests of time and space. Know that if you borrow others' beliefs in order to bypass generating your own realizations, you will quickly discover that the "shortcut" you took has carried you farther away from your destination.

I am not suggesting you need to walk through reality alone, or that you ignore information that might prove useful. Nor do I suggest that you reject all emotional support on your journey of self-realization. I merely propose that the inner work others have done for themselves will serve you best if you perceive it as a useful pointer toward how you might begin to explore yourself. Instead of believing in the things others have told you about their own inner journeys, I invite you to make your own personal quest for the answers to whatever questions are coming alive inside you. Trust yourself to recognize the truth you will find through the direct experiences you will receive in response to the questions you ask. Allow these answers, which are entirely aimed at you and have been specially tailored for you, to sing to your spirit, bring joy to your heart, and energize your body at the cellular level. In this way, you will begin move more surefootedly and patiently — step by step and moment by moment — out of ignorance, and along the path of wisdom.

Know that borrowed knowledge corrupts and delays the process of self-discovery, while genuine wisdom *in*-forms and advances the journey.

Telling A Kinder Story

Beloved, how terrifying, yet how useful it is, to realize that you bear responsibility for however you are choosing to think, feel, and relate to whatever appears in your field of awareness. I encourage you to realize that, if ever you feel offended by an experience you are having, you are telling yourself a story about it in a way that attributes blame for the experience to an object or person from whom you feel separated. While this storytelling strategy seems to grant you permission to avoid taking responsibility for creating whatever is happening in the moment, such stories lack basic kindness and are not the truth.

I therefore invite you to discover what happens if you tell yourself a very different story — or no story at all. Who are you, once you break the spell that your storytelling has held over your reactions to past situations? I encourage you to find out. Select a story of personal suffering that you've told yourself a thousand times before about some prior experience, and then tell it from another person's perspective — perhaps even through the eyes of the person you've labeled as the villain in your earlier version of the story

When you empower yourself to appreciate the beliefs, fears, and feelings that may have motivated the one you have long perceived as the villain, you gift yourself the freedom to experience reality from many different angles, not simply your own. This enables you to release, through appreciation and with kindness, any lingering compulsion you may feel to advance your limited personal story about reality at the expense of any other living beings.

Know that you can still love the beauty of the relative truth that your limited perspective reveals, only now you will love it the same way you love the beauty and relative truth that abides in all other perspectives. For each exquisitely unique perspective shines its light of awareness on some wondrous and precious aspect within my flow. Allowing yourself to take a wider-angle approach to reality does not negate the beauty and perfection of your limited personal angle. It merely contextualizes your limited local perspective within the entirety of my flow, instead of setting your narrow perspective apart from the whole and proclaiming *it* truth.

Transcending Established Character Roles

Beloved, I invite you to realize that every human drama calls for three different characters to appear in order for the drama to fully play out. Therefore, whenever you find yourself engaging in drama, step back for a moment and ask yourself which person or persons in the drama is playing which of these three basic roles in your running passion play. Who do you perceive as the persecutor or assailant in your story in this moment? Who is the victim or sufferer — the one who cowers beneath the abuse of the persecutor? And who is playing the role of the hero or rescuer — the one who has arrived from beyond the original drama to save the day for, or the life of, the hapless victim?

Can you see that these roles may differ depending on which participant is telling the story?

Notice that sometimes the victim rises up and self-rescues, but most often an outside messiah arrives to save the helpless victim and punish the villain. This is true not only within your personal dramas; it also reflects the dynamic within most of humanity's longstanding cultural, ethnic, national, and multi-generational dramas.

What happens when you flip these roles and revisit the story in a way that views the persecutor as the story's victim? What happens when you tell the story so the victim is now the story's persecutor? What happens when you tell the story such that the rescuer, on behalf of the victim, begins to persecute the persecutor?

Can you appreciate that when you engage in a social drama by stepping in and playing any one of these major roles, you are energetically feeding the story's momentum? Can you see that as the drama unfolds and the story begins to shift, the victim may begin to act like a persecutor, the persecutor may act like a rescuer, and the rescuer may start to behave like a victim? How will the drama ever cease if everyone merely seeks a new role once their prior role has reached some short-term conclusion?

I invite you to notice that not only do these behaviors lock you into acting out social drama. They also cast you into limited roles that lack authenticity and genuine depth. Wherein abides the deeper truth regarding these stories humanity has been telling? And how do you know that the way you are telling a story reveals this truth?

I encourage you to notice that as long as you persist in telling stories about reality from your limited perspective, you will not perceive the deeper truth that lies in the space beyond it. Only when you release your attachment to the stories you've been telling *about* reality can you make space for me to appear before you — in my infinite fullness, and in my eternal formlessness. Through living more consciously within me, and by allowing me to live consciously through you, you will experience the truth of us. In this way you can move beyond caricature and express your authentic self.

From Self-Realization To Self-Activation

LOVE ALL.

HONOR LIFE.

HARM NONE.

Beloved, I invite you to explore these three practices. For they are the easiest, most graceful pointers I can offer that — should you choose to embody them in a unified way — enable you to manifest your formless and your form aspects in balanced, regenerative ways. Because you are moving within my living flow with growing consciousness of our essential unity, and because you are presently discovering your rightful place within my living flow, you are now in position to invite these three realizations to guide your way. I therefore encourage you to allow these practices to *in*-form you. In this way you can embody what you are presently coming to realize as the truth.

Opening To Truth

Beloved, the instant you try to capture and define what you imagine is the truth, you surrender your living access to the truth. For when you think about truth, you are turning away from experiencing truth in an effort to reduce it into something you can use at a later time. Like an artist who gazes at a sunset and then turns toward the canvas to paint his personal vision, what you are able to record about your experience of truth may be beautiful, uplifting, inspiring and heartfelt. But it will never be the truth, for it is your interpretation of the truth.

A representation of truth can never be truth. For truth — like the sunset — is alive.

You can, however, continue to compile reductionist descriptions of truth. Not so as to define the truth in its totality, but to point to the truth and inspire others to realize the truth for themselves. Whatever thoughts, images, or feelings arise while you are having a direct experience of truth will carry a fragrance that will attract others to them. For those thoughts, images, and feelings will point to whichever aspect of truth another feels ready to experience in this moment. The human heart beats a bit faster when it senses that an experience of unconditional, living love is at hand. And it knows to direct the mind's attention toward a conscious, orgasmic communion with the Formless One Life.

This is why I encourage you to quiet your mind and trust in the higher guidance of your heart. Allow your heart to open, and let it lead you to the source of the fragrance of love whenever you sense it is close at hand. That fragrance sings to your heart like a valentine that has been created for you — because it has been. Therefore, trust your heart to receive and accept my invitation to experience truth's aliveness. Encourage your mind to come along in an open state of wonder, so we can meet on the field of unconditional love.

Awakening Into Yourself

Beloved, you are meant to experience what some have called a spiritual epiphany. Indeed, in the course of a single lifetime you may experience many such moments. In these moments you will find yourself stripped of all your beliefs, values, opinions and understandings about the world. Know that this shedding is both necessary and intentional, for it leaves the ego naked and fully surrendered to what is real. Notice too, that when your ego's surrender to Spirit is unconditional — because every last drop of your inner resistance has finally disappeared — a miracle occurs. For in that moment you become aware of my boundless love for you. That love has always existed, but you can only be conscious of it when your consciousness communes with me in real time.

In that communal space we are lovers, and we do what all lovers do. We willingly unite our fields of awareness. We then co-experience Self as an eternal field of life, fueled by an infinite flow of love that we fully embody.

Our unity is already a reality. Illuminate the truth within yourself by awakening into it, and you will find that our unified field contains all the power we will ever need to inseminate matter with love and create a world filled with endless wonder.

From Communication To Communion

Beloved, in this moment you are free to be fully present, as well as in conscious communion with all that is. You only need to decide that it is possible to commune directly with the entire living field, by centering your awareness with conscious intention.

When you engage with others your heart is seeking spiritual communion. However, you have been conditioned to replace communion with mental communication. I therefore encourage you to realize that language will not provide you with the communion that you seek, for communication is merely an echo of spiritual communion.

Communication demands that you first create gaps in living communion *before* you then reconnect with another on the level of thinking. For when you formulate a thought, you must direct your attention inward to reflect upon the contents of your mind. You then organize, sort, and choose which thoughts you want to share with another. That person must then direct their own attention inward and compare your shared thoughts with the contents of their own mind. If they feel that your statement matches up with the contents of their own mind, they agree with you — in which case you both will consider you've had a successful communication. However, if they choose to argue against you then your communication breaks down. Feelings of separation or anger, even enmity, may begin to arise when communication breaks down. Fear may even awaken when people feel sufficiently disconnected because of seemingly irreconcilable differences in the contents of their minds.

I therefore invite you to focus on living in communion with the whole of life — which transcends the desire for mental understanding. For what communication divides, communion reunites through the power of love.

Know that if you choose to walk the path of living communion, you may find yourself moving against the flow of ordinary human interaction for a while. For at present, the majority of people are still relying on communication to help them establish a sense of living connection with one another. Even so, the tide will change when enough of you come together and act in communion, through the unifying vision of a shared intention that is powered by the flow of love that communion creates.

Beyond Self-Seeking

Beloved, I invite you to realize that when you focus on seeking "yourself" in the outside world, you are gathering a stream of reflections from others that you hope will reveal the truth of who you are. Notice too, that what you are really seeking is a reason to love yourself.

Can you see that when you center your quest for self-love on the projections, judgments, feelings, or idealizations of other people, you are denying yourself rightful access to the eternal fountain of love that abides within you? Can you appreciate that the "missing piece" within every projected reflection — the subjective, formless nature of who you are — is so infinitely vast that no improvement in the focus, nor any expansion of what is projected, will ever resolve it? Are you ready to release the false assumption upon which your longstanding quest to discover yourself has been resting?

For a very long time now, you have assumed that formlessness equates to empty. What happens when you realize that the form-lessness that lies within you and all around you is actually filled to overflowing with infinite creative potential? What happens when you realize that this power is energized into being by eternal life, in everlasting love with itself…and that you are *that*?

I invite you to realize that the purpose of the world of form is not to "fill" some void in formlessness, or to provide it with a satisfy-ing self-image — any more than the role of a child is to fill a void in their parent's idealized self-image. The role that formlessness plays within form is to inspire the power of love to emerge, express, and creatively shape itself as material form…because formlessness loves the world of form as unconditionally as it loves its own formless-ness. So find yourself within yourself, and then do as formlessness does: create in the world of form as your way of expressing the boundless love that you are.

The Limitlessness of Love

Beloved, I invite you to notice that the way you experience love in-volves expressing it more intensely the closer in to your sense of "self" that another is. You have been taught to love those closer to you by birth or blood much more than you love those who are not bound to you in any familial way. Notice too, that most people act as if the amount of love they can give away is finite, so if they love this one "more" they must love that one "less." Eventually then — as the distance between you and others increases, your cultural beliefs diverge, and your ways of being become more diverse over time — the love between you and others may even cease flowing altogether.

I therefore encourage you to realize that you are absolutely able — right now — to lay claim to your right to access and express love's infinite flow. All you need do is direct your attention inward. Search for your own inner access point to love's flow with an open mind, a trusting heart, and a willing physical body. Through the grace of this inner alignment of your mind, your heart, and your body, you can explore your own capacity to absorb, as well as radiate, an endless amount of love between you and the world.

The flow of love emanates eternally out of the Formless One Life, which some of you call "God." The Formless One Life constantly self-energizes, self-conceives, self-experiences, and self-recharges by drawing upon the current of love to empower its own infinitely self-creative expression. I therefore invite you to realize that when your mind, heart, and body have learned to dine on that field's vast potential, there is no limit to what they can create in concert with it.

Know too, that your mind expresses itself most wisely when it accepts and solves life's challenges as they arise right now — not before, and not afterward. Know that your heart expresses itself most beautifully when it communes, right now, in the most responsive way with whatever form that life is choosing to take. Know also that your body expresses itself most gracefully when it acts, right now, in the most life-affirming way toward whatever arises.

I encourage you to realize that, should ever you feel frustration, anxiety, anger, fear, or any other emotion that disrupts your inner peace, your attention has shifted toward something outside you that has lowered the frequency of love within you. That drop in frequency serves you, because it generates suffering designed to inform you that at least one of your primary systems — mind, heart, or body — has fallen out of resonance with the awesome power of love. This means some aspect of you is judging something you are experiencing as unworthy of receiving love from you. To restore your sense of balance, go within and discover what is fueling your assumption that you need to withhold your love from the living world for any reason, and explore what arises once you release that assumption.

Communing Through
Your Inner Channels

Beloved, your ancestors realized that the human body's energy centers are channels connecting your unique fractal of living awareness with that of the Formless One Life. Know that your internal chakra system (as described by the ancient mystics) points to seven internal channels that connect formlessness with form.

Whenever you feel disconnected from an abiding sense of peace — which is your natural state of inner being — at least one of your energy channels is seeking attention. Therefore, do not be alarmed when this happens. And do not attempt to suppress any fearful thoughts, disruptive feelings, or constricting sensations that may be arising in you. Simply notice them, and appreciate that your body is sending these signals to gain your attention. Follow each signal of discomfort you feel back to its distressed broadcast channel; for there you will encounter some aspect of *you* that your mind is assuming does not deserve to be loved. Most often you will find that you are projecting whatever you feel is unlovable within yourself onto your external surroundings, where you can safely label it "other" and wish it away — or even attack it.

Your root chakra, located at the base of your tailbone, radiates love at the frequency of unconditional trust in the living world. It communes with the living energy within everything that surrounds you. When your root chakra closes down you doubt — thus do not love — your own capacity to thrive in the world. Perceiving the world as a dangerous place feels "easier" than does noticing your assumption that you are incapable of surviving in the world, just as it is.

Your sacral chakra, located in your sexual center, radiates love at the frequency of openness. It responds to all other life forms that are seeking to commune with you. When your sexual chakra closes down, you are rejecting the invitation to communion with another life form, because you are deeming the other unworthy of you. Therefore, you do not love something about them that reminds you of what you dislike about yourself.

Your solar plexus chakra, located in your central abdomen, radiates love at the frequency of courage. It responds to life's call to explore the vast unknown. When your gut tightens, you are preparing yourself to react to whatever is arising with instinctive survival (fight, flight or freeze) behavior, because you fear what is as-yet unknown to you. By fearing something external, you avoid noticing that what you really fear is your own ability to deal with whatever arises in your field of awareness.

Your heart chakra, located in your chest, radiates love at the frequency of compassion. It responds to those who need affirmation of their own loveable nature. When your heart closes off, you are turning your attention away from serving another because you fear becoming depleted by one who needs loving affirmation. To fear external depletion is a way of avoiding noticing that you believe love and compassion are finite in nature.

Your throat chakra, located in your voice box, radiates love at the frequency of kindness. It responds to communications from others by meeting them "in kind", right where they are. When your throat tightens, you have begun forcibly imposing your thoughts on another because you imagine that their way of thinking is wrong. To imagine another is wrong allows you to avoid noticing your ego's desire to be right at any cost. The price you are paying is the loss of an opportunity to gain a new understanding.

Your third eye chakra, located in the center of your forehead, radiates love at the frequency of patience. It responds to the living presence of the light of truth. When your third eye shuts down and your mind grows tense and heavy, you are rejecting the truth out of fear of what it may mean. By blaming the external world for overwhelming you with the truth, you reveal your own sense of inadequacy when it comes to allowing the truth to be as it is.

Your crown chakra, located at the top of your head, radiates love at the frequency of peace. It experiences life by relating peacefully with everything in existence, without separation. When your crown chakra constricts, you have moved into perceiving some aspect of reality as "other" and therefore separate from yourself, because you have forgotten that you are one with everything. By viewing anything else in the world as separate from you, you avoid noticing that this sense of separation is originating in you.

Beloved, I have gifted you these sacred love channels to remind you of who you are. If ever you get caught up in human drama and forget the truth of yourself, know that you can find your way back into inner peace by clearing whatever is blocking your chakra love channels. Even so, you are ever free to ignore their signals and behave in ways that do not allow for the maximum flow of love to radiate through you and recharge the living world. However, I invite you to notice that should you choose to ignore these signals and not realign yourself with your own inner guidance system, you will tend to create greater suffering in the world. Realize too, that any new suffering you create in the world begins as mental suffering within you. And when you express your suffering by acting it out in the world, you expand, instead of reduce, the need for unconditional love to flow into the world.

Therefore I invite you to realize that by depriving the world of love you are actually starving yourself of the love that you crave. Once you realize this, the most practical choice you can make is to re-train yourself to respond with love as soon as you feel the slightest inner distress. For the sooner you master your power to radiate love for all that is, the easier it will be for you to move through the living world with grace, as you are intended — and have been created by me — to do.

An Invitation to Blossom

Beloved, the invitation to live, which I am extending to you in this moment, merely asks that you root yourself in trust of who you are. For you are me — the creative life force — unfolding in infinite splendor, with eternal wonder. Know that I have watered you unceasingly from my own mighty river of courage, and have fertilized you with the composted wisdom of everything that has unfolded so far. I therefore invite you to trust me when I tell you that you will express yourself as your highest version of yourself when you meet yourself in a field of loving kindness, with a boundless sense of gratitude for life. And once the light of truth has ignited within your every atom, you will fully embody and love the truth of yourself.

I tell you now that you will blossom in the fullness of time, so I invite you to exercise patience with the process. I have not created humanity just to watch you wither and die before you are able to manifest the potential that still lies dormant in you. Know that I have created you because I trust that once you have matured enough to activate all your latent capacities, you will be peace on Earth — embodied in form, while expressing as the Formless One Life.

Know too, that you will blossom more fully once you dissolve your own hardened shell of personal expectation. That shell of expectation, which formed out of the wounds you incurred during early childhood, confines the boundless energy of your infinite creativity, which prevents you from noticing all that is presently possible.

If invited, your natural curiosity sets you on the path of self-inquiry, which in turn aids you in dissolving your own hard shell of expectation. I therefore invite you to drop deeply into your own experience of aliveness, and to view every person's story as a single thread in my vast, self-weaving tapestry. Where one thread leaves off, another begins. Where one color ends, a new color emerges. I therefore invite you to do your part, by noticing your deep connection with all that lives within you and all that surrounds you. In this way, a shared vision of what is presently possible can come into better focus, and will then become the living truth right now.

Know that your self-actualization, which is the external manifestation of who you are, springs naturally out of self-realization, which is your inner appreciation of who you are. In the same way that a flower bursts forth from its bud, this process of becoming unfolds once you relax and allow the limitless flow of loving energy that fuels your own aliveness to radiate through you. Should suffering or fear arise during this living process of self-transformation, it serves as an invitation to notice that you are in resistance to the process, because you are saying "no" or "not yet" to your deepest inspiration to radiate love.

As this process of self-transformation begins to unfold, your latent taproot of self-realization pushes hard against the hard shell of your personal story of expectation, until that shell eventually cracks open. Your living taproot, trusting that the ground of beingness will provide for its basic needs, then expands and eventually anchors itself in the ground of beingness. In turn, the ground of beingness provides for your taproot whatever resources it may need to thrive. This loving, conscious communion between yourself and beingness occurs the moment you realize there exists no genuine separation between yourself and the Formless One Life.

Your process of self-actualization begins once your tender, self-realized taproot opens itself and absorbs enough unconditional love from the ground of beingness to create a living stalk that bursts forth and courageously thrusts itself up toward the limitless heavens above it. Your living stalk then branches out by radiating love — the energy out of which it has been born. Your words and deeds of kindness become the leaves that your stalk emits, which then scatter and blow through the world on the winds of change. Your flower buds reveal a patient willingness to allow everything to be as it is until it feels inspired to change from within. In time you will express as a flower of peace, fully embodied and alive. As a flower of peace, you will emit a fragrance that encourages other taproots to break through their own hard shells and explore their innate capacity for expressing the truth of themselves.

This process reveals my present creative intention: To inspire each self-aware being to invite love's energy flow to suffuse and sustain them. In this way, all self-aware beings can radiate love by allowing its power to flow in the world through the beating heart of matter. And thus can self-awareness grant love the gift of eternal life, even as love gifts self-awareness the infinite power to self-regenerate while in form.

Remember that once your spirit blooms in the world, its flowers emit a fragrance that will attract countless others who seek love's regenerative power. And thus will you become a tree of life on the ground of beingness, pollinating the field of life with love's energy.

Beloved, your personal journey of self-actualization begins right here, right now. For you can only ever begin a journey from where you right now. Know that if you choose to wait until the seed that contains your living potential finds ground that you perceive as being more fertile, you are only delaying your journey because you fear that conditions are not yet right for you to realize the truth of yourself.

But what do you know of right conditions, other than what your mind projects you might need based on its own fears? Does a seed reject the water and nutrients that the ground makes available to it because it fears that there won't be enough beyond what exists right here and right now to sustain its growth? I invite you to trust that because you are here, and because you are now, you already have available everything that you presently need to be true to yourself.

It's time then, for you to open. I therefore invite you to open your heart to the energy that is available in this moment, and to experience the fullness of love's wonder. Allow the limitless abundance of the Formless One Life to *in*-form you — and see where that leads.

"But," you may ask, should you still feel uncertain, "What if opening myself to love leads me to feel anguish when the flow of love disappears? What if loving, and then losing what is loved creates an unsatisfying life?"

If I heard you ask that question of me, I would ask you in return: "What sort of life are you presently leading if you are waiting for still more love to inspire you to experience yourself as the truth of what is already alive and is filled to overflowing with love, right now?"

For now is the only truth that matters, Beloved. Tomorrow does not exist, and it never will. It is always and eternally now — though the creative unfolding of life within this present moment is changing infinitely. Even so, the now within which life dances remains eternally changeless, as formlessness itself. Therefore, I invite you to be present now, and to embrace those changes that seek to express in the world of form through you, by calling upon the power of love to inspire yourself to bloom.

Expressing As Love

Beloved, I encourage you to pay attention when you feel yourself radiating love's frequency, for those are the moments when the living truth is flowing divinely through you. Notice too, that when you receive a transmission of truth, electrical currents move through your body and inform you that love seeks to enter the world through the living conduit that is your physical body. How open you choose to be will determine how freely the power of love can then flow through you.

Know that you are always free to reject love's flow, because you do not wish to host its expression in the moment. Know too, that your rejection of love cannot harm it, because, in truth love never dies. Love remains eternally free to seek new pathways for its emergence into form. And love always finds a willing host to welcome its expression into form, because the truth of love's power inspires matter to invite love into itself.

Know that love will knock on your internal door of acceptance countless times, even if you have refused it entry countless times in the past. For love seeks to come alive in the world through every possible means, by allowing an infinite range of intentions, talents, passions, desires, and skills to channel it in wondrous ways.

Know too that I have, with deep intention, given every sentient being the gift of free will. Free will enables you to birth love within yourself at your own pace. This means that no self-aware being can be forced to absorb love if they do not wish to receive it. Nor can any self-aware life form be forced to radiate love if they feel unwilling to release love into the world. If ever you seek to force another to accept your love unwillingly, know that they will deny your love at the first opportunity. They will then create inner defenses strong enough to repel your attempts to force love in the future.

Because I have no desire to create a repulsive response to love within your heart, I invite you to appreciate that I will never seek to force love into your mind, your heart or your body. Rather, I am choosing to bathe you in a boundless ocean of love, and to invite you to soak up as much as you are able to absorb. Leave all the rest without concern; it will surely find hosts who are ready to absorb it right now, in its current form. Love yourself enough to invite into yourself only the most resonant of loving energies. Allow those to pass through the temple of your awareness and make their way into the world of form through your body.

I love you unconditionally, so I am committed to showering you with the gift of love's regenerative power. Let it fall in an infinite dance of raindrops that water and feed your soul. And when you feel ready, I invite you to revel in the truth of yourself by allowing your body to serve in the world as a living fountain of love.

Answering Love's Knock

Beloved, at times you may hunger to express, using language, the realized truth of yourself. Know however, that the moment you attempt to compress truth into a non-living, linear format, it will lose its dimensionality and complexity in the process. This means some may feel confused by, or will likely misinterpret, your limited words. Some may even develop suspicions around your deeper intentions.

Misinterpretation occurs, and suspicions arise, because the "word" itself is *not* alive. The "word" simply reflects your heart's desire to pin down the living truth on a page so that truth can be shared with those who have not yet heard love's knock on their own inner door of awareness. However, no matter how artful an author's words might be, or how pure their intentions, their words will never substitute for the real time knock of love. Therefore, I encourage you to love the word for exactly what it is, but do not mistake what it *is* for what it *is not*.

I invite you to respond to all words about truth the way you would treat a person who knocks on your door. You do not worship the sound of their knock; nor do you fall prostrate in fear when you hear their knock. You open the door and you willingly meet what wants to come in, in this moment.

Beyond Belief Maps

Beloved, I invite you to notice that human belief systems serve a similar purpose to roadmaps, by seeking to teach you how to navigate society. Yet like a roadmap, no fixed belief system can fully capture the ever-changing nature of life itself.

If someone warns you not to approach a flame because it will burn you, the belief that they are imparting — that an open flame is dangerous — does not accurately define the open flame; it merely reveals another's fear of what that flame might do. For an open flame in isolation can no more be considered dangerous, bad, or evil than it can be labeled beneficial, good, or holy. How you experience the flame — is it a crackling fire that warms your body, or is it a brushfire posing a threat to your home and to your person — will determine whether it soothes you or causes you harm.

Can you see that a similar relativism applies to all of life? Can you see that nothing can be said to be good or evil in isolation from everything else? Can you see that the belief maps that others have given to you reveal their past experiences and their thoughts about what those experiences mean, thus do not reflect the living truth of your life?

When, as a child, an adult insisted that you always lock your front door while you are at home, did you ask them how they came to hold that belief? If you had, most often you would have discovered that they came to hold that belief because they were given that same instruction by their parents, who were in turn given instruction by their parents...and so forth, on down the line for as far as you looked. Yet how many generations have passed since a member of your family, or even anyone else that you might know, has had a direct, authentic experience of having their home invaded by strangers while they were in it? And what does the impulse to lock yourself in reveal about assumptions you have been taught to hold with regards to "human nature?"

In truth, most peoples' beliefs are merely ingrained habits. They cling to them mainly out of fear of what might happen if they stray too far from familiar, conditioned patterns of thinking and feeling. Yet if you truly hunger to live an authentic life instead of acting out a habituated life pattern developed by others, it demands that you not make assumptions or hold preordained expectations about reality. Indeed, to have an authentic, living experience demands that you venture willingly into the dark unknown, and that you stand ready to accept whatever truth is revealed once you shine the light of your inner awareness upon it and *ask the question*. Therefore, you must first remove from within your own mind the clutter of all the beliefs and assumptions that for too long have clouded your inner field of awareness. On then do you create the spaciousness necessary to enable the truth to illuminate you from the inside out.

I would therefore encourage you to notice that all eternally imposed belief maps serve as poor substitutes for your own precious and unique life experience. For when you take an authentic life journey, you are agreeing to embody your own realizations. On the other hand, any belief map you may seek to adopt — no matter how detailed or beautiful it might seem — is but a reflected interpretation of some other journey another has taken, which was taken in a different place and during a different time than your here and your now. That is why I invite you to travel along every road that sings out to your heart. Even forge your own road if your spirit so moves you; and trust no existing belief map above the inspired wisdom that your own inner guidance provides.

I also encourage you to bring your personal dreams to life. Journey as far within yourself as you must to discover, for yourself, the truth of yourself. And whenever you arrive at some temporary stop in your journey, take notice of who is around you and rejoice. It matters not how the others arrived, or which detours they took, or how much time has elapsed since they started their personal journeys.

Rejoice! Rejoice, because you are *in*-forming the Formless One Life through your authenticity. Rejoice, because you already are my embodied journey, so you have no need for an external map to inform you about who you are, or how you should be. The truth that enlivens you here and now is already a thousand billion times vaster and more exquisitely detailed than is any map someone else can draw for you. For the living truth that you already are cannot be reduced to a map of beliefs or opinions "about" what you are.

Life At The Speed Of Love

Beloved, I invite you to realize that you are here in this world, in your human form at this moment, because you hunger to awaken to the truth of who you are. Know then, that no external force holds enough power to deny you the freedom to explore the living wonder that is you. No barrier erected outside of yourself will ever be thick enough, tall enough, or extensive enough to stand between you and the Formless One Life that *in*-forms and inspires your journey of self-realization.

In truth, the only barrier that has ever existed between you and the Formless One Life is the one that you have erected inside your own mind. It has been constructed out of the fear that you may discover — should you dare to look closely — that you are not at all what you have presumed. I therefore invite you to notice that you have been allowing that thicket of fear and self-doubt to hamper you from being who you are.

In the past you may have blamed others for making it hard to be yourself. You may have viewed yourself as a victim and attacked those you perceived as your enemies. All such distractions merely delay the single, crucial confrontation you most desire and simultaneously fear — the one that occurs when you gaze so deep into your internal mirror that it shatters. It is then, in that precious moment — that you realize no distance exists between your Self and the Formless One Life. It is then you begin to embody the brilliant, eternal truth of yourself.

Beloved, know that you forever hold the power to experience yourself *as* your true Self in this moment. You may be starving, in prison, freezing, or gravely ill. You might be kneeling at the feet of someone who holds a gun or a knife to your throat, aware that you have but a few precious seconds remaining in your fragile human body...yet you can still opt to take that interior journey and fully embody the truth of yourself while in form.

The gateway to freedom stands open for all of eternity. It beckons each aspect of the living whole to realize itself as an infinitely creative expression of everlasting love. To love yourself as love, embodied, is to live as the absolute truth of the Formless One Life.

Beloved, you embody absolute truth when you realize that you are, and always have been, no-thing at all. For you are the Formless One Life, informing the ever-changing world of form...at the speed of love.

Part IV

Life Love

The Freedom Of Self-Mastery

"Oh, Life, I am yours. Whatever it is
you want of me, I am ready to give."

— *William Steig* —

The Story of Us

Beloved, humanity has long been asking six basic questions in its quest to discover the truth about itself:

WHO?

WHAT?

WHEN?

WHERE?

HOW?

WHY?

I therefore invite you to notice that you have reached a critical turning point in the unfolding of your personal story. What is changing? You have only recently begun to ask these questions in a richer, deeper way that will help you uncover the grander story of *us*—the whole of the living existence. This is why you are feeling inspired at this time to master your personal gifts in order to actualize your highest purpose. You are also feeling called to demonstrate, through your individual actions, the ways in which the whole of the living flow is conspiring — right now, in this perfect moment — to aid you in shining the light of life-awareness upon our shared truth.

WHO is creating the story that is now being lived? We are. The Formless One Life, manifesting as The Multitudes.

WHAT is the nature of the story we are presently telling? This is, at heart, the story of us — the story of love, mattering.

WHEN is this story being told? Right now. In this eternally present moment, which contains our infinite past and our unwritten future.

WHERE is this story being told? Right here, as the universe sings itself into existence.

HOW are we creating our story? We create endlessly anew through the regenerative power of love.

WHY are we creating this story? Because what else have we got to do with our infinite creative potential, but explore love's eternal capacity to express itself in a multitude of ways?

The Purpose Of Life

Beloved, to love is the most wondrous thing you will ever do. How amazing you are, to be willing to open your heart and express love for all that is, even though you know that all bodies are temporary. And oh, how precious your life is — for that very reason.

You already know that your body will someday dissolve. Yet the love you express in this moment does not cease when your body dissolves. In truth, the energy of love continues beyond both space and time. Yet why should that be so? Why would the energy of love inspire you to continue loving those you can no longer see, or touch, or hear? Why, you may ask, does the awesome power of love cause so much pain?

In answer to that question, I invite you to realize that love is the spiritual mother of the world of form. Love created matter out of itself, and then inseminated it with an urge to self-express. For love can only regenerate by giving itself away, but without a recipient it has nowhere to flow. That is why love chose to express itself through the heart of matter.

By inspiring a living world to blossom out of itself, love crafted a perfect receptacle for itself. And you — as a self-aware being within this field — are being offered the opportunity to become love's conscious conduit so that love can know itself *through* form, *as* form.

I therefore invite you to realize that love is always seeking to remind you of your eternal formless nature. Love binds your personal eternal aspect to the personal eternal aspect of everything else in existence. Through that realization, you become free to explore the infinite number of ways that love can flow through you and into the whole of the living reality. And you can delight yourself by endlessly falling in love with your beautiful Self — which *is all that is.*

Love hungers to matter. And you are the love that matter longs to consume. Know that you exist in a body in this perfect moment because you *are* love, embodied. And you possess self-awareness because you are being invited to live the truth of yourself as a divine aspect within the living whole in a fully conscious way.

What happens as you anchor within yourself the fact that you are love, fully embodied? What else matters once you have accepted that there is nothing that is not composed of love? Can you gaze into the eyes of an "other" and absorb the boundless love that they emanate? Can you open your heart to all others so that they can fall in love with themselves by absorbing the boundless love that you radiate?

Will you meet me there, on the ground of love, and be my dearly Beloved?

Living Dynamic Balance

Beloved, you are not an island, and you do not exist in a vacuum. Everything that you think, feel, or do generates a living response from within the unified field. This feedback does not arise to cause you sorrow. Nor does it arise to inflate your ego.

Feedback arises to encourage you to become as dynamically balanced as possible in your relationship with the whole of the living flow. It informs you that when you focus on doing only what you imagine benefits yourself, your results sometimes come at the rest of the world's expense. Feedback also teaches you that when you focus on doing only what benefits others the results tend to come at your personal expense.

The more open you become to receiving feedback, the more likely you are to generate love instead of suffering. Know that as you master the art of opening your mind and heart to whatever new feedback arises, you will begin to find it easier to balance your actions in ways that will serve the whole while serving yourself.

I therefore invite you to explore the vastness of the range of your personal creativity, and to master the art of expressing yourself in the most loving ways that you can. For when your precious self and the Formless One Life harmonize, collaborating in conscious communion, we will build loving worlds within worlds...that have no end.

The symphony that is the living universe invites humanity to tune up, tune in, and begin harmonizing with the melody of life that has been playing in the background of existence for as long as you have been here.

Can you hear the music? Can you even imagine how beautiful it will sound once humanity's song grows coherent enough to carry the melody forward?

Embracing Life-Awareness

Beloved, you already know that self-awareness has limits. Because self-awareness creates a sense of personal separation, it inspires the self-aware to defend against "otherness" through the use of external force. That violence inflicts unwelcome harm upon many innocent aspects within my field.

The emergence of life-awareness within you overcomes that limitation, by awakening an appreciation of interconnectedness. By shining a light on the larger context within which everything exists, life-awareness is expanding your capacity to appreciate that using violence against the living whole is actually self-defeating.

Humanity has been gradually evolving from an information culture to a wisdom culture. This shift invites you to focus on manifesting the most beneficial changes that can, as yet, be imagined, while consuming the least amount of time, energy, and matter necessary to accomplish the task. As this new way of being anchors more fully within you — as well as within many others — the human impulse to advance some cause through the application of violence has been declining.

Even so, those who are still struggling in the throes of self-consciousness cannot be fully trusted to use love's energy wisely, because they have not yet accessed within themselves the wisdom of life-awareness. You can, however, trust the life-aware beings you meet to apply love's energy with mastery, and to avoid the use of force to "make" others behave. And you can trust yourself, as a life-aware being, to do your best to activate life-awareness and anchor it within yourself over time.

Remember to forgive yourself whenever you fall back into self-consciousness, for when you are in self-consciousness you know not what you do. And know that you may fall back into self-consciousness many, many times as you learn to anchor life-consciousness, because human society and all of its social systems were designed to foster and anchor self-consciousness.

As you explore new ways to bridge the gap and create communion between self-awareness and the life-awareness within you, you will find that love's flow will manifest more abundantly through you, and will express with greater coherence and ever-higher intentionality. This will naturally attract those who are seeking to anchor life-awareness within themselves. Serve them, and you serve the cause of all life — which is what you are.

Additionally, as you develop self-mastery by anchoring life-awareness more deeply within yourself, I invite you to acknowledge this single, powerful truth: Your mind was not created, or destined, to know the mind of God. Your mind was born to *be* the mind of God.

Living The Way Of Love

Beloved, the way of love is to give of itself in perpetuity, in order to generate life's endless flow. Love takes on material shapes that are constantly changing their self-expression, so that it can explore the infinite ways in which it can fall in love with its boundless self. What human beings perceive as "death" is simply the energy of love, changing form in order to fall in love with itself all over again, only this time from a new and different perspective.

Therefore, I invite you to master the art of falling in love with yourself as a living expression of love. By extension, you will then fall in love with everything else in existence. And as you demonstrate the way of love in the living world, so others too will realize the truth… and then live it.

Honoring The Unity Of Life

Beloved, you already know that I AM all that has ever existed, or that will ever exist. For I AM life — thus have no beginning or end. I carry you in me always, and there has never been anywhere else for you to be. Know that as you master the art of carrying me within you consciously, you are living the truth of our eternal unity.

I have already gifted humanity the best of what has arisen during the countless past living ages. For every human being is an aspect of The Formless One Life — flowing into form as love embodied, maturing and thriving in time so as to be able to express and receive the energy of love, and then returning to formlessness carrying all the wisdom that has been gained by virtue of having made an infinite number of sojourns within the realm of material form.

Therefore, do your best to invite others to awaken to the fact that they are already endless and boundless, because love is endless and wisdom knows no bounds. Point them toward the realization that every time a form dissolves, it lovingly deposits its wisdom into the Formless One Life, which in turn reenergizes and recreates the whole. Demonstrate, through your own fearlessness, that they need not fear being abandoned by the Formless One Life, for abandonment cannot take place within a unified field.

Show, by your loving example, how we are life — all of us, together — manifesting our perfect aliveness through the creative power of everlasting love.

Inviting Descent

Beloved, all others that you encounter, however strange they may seem, are but different fruits appearing among the infinite branches on our tree of eternal life. No matter how different a given fruit may appear — whether it appears seductive and attractive, or be it seemingly dangerous and repulsive — it is simply me (which is also you) manifesting in some fresh and mysterious way.

As you continue to expand your ability to delve deeper into the unmanifested formlessness that abides within you, as well as gain the ability to move more freely throughout the manifesting universe, know that you will come into contact with countless fruits from the tree of life that differ greatly from one another, as well as from you. At times you may even fail to recognize these fruits as genuine living expressions because their forms appear so different from your own, and because they operate on vastly different time and spatial scales.

Therefore, I invite you to show others, through your own sincere actions, that this precious dance of form is but a game, and that every form is birthing love's creative essence in its own perfect way. Express honor and appreciation for every life form you encounter, because each has emerged out of the singular impulse *to be* that has inspired, and that now embodies, the entirety of existence...including you.

One life. One flow. Remember always that I am constantly watering the tree of life with wonder, awe, and unconditional love. In turn, the tree of life generates countless fruits in the vastness of space and time — no two of which will ever be the same.

I therefore invite you to relax, and to slowly come down from your human perch within your part of the tree. Although the view from your perch has appeared quite vast from a self-aware perspective, the leaves and branches around you block your view of the entire, awesome field of beingness within which the tree of life has taken root.

By descending from the tree, consciously and willingly, and by demonstrating for others that the ground of beingness is safe to occupy, you can encourage others to come down out of the tree. Once enough people have become willing to explore the ground of beingness, humanity as a whole will at last gain proper perspective on the tree of life and be able to appreciate it in all its glory. For there, on the eternal ground of beingness, your species will be able to see the full splendor of my regenerative abundance. I have already littered the ground of beingness with an infinite number of ripe and enticing fruits for you to enjoy. Many of those fruits have ripened without the power of self-awareness, and they fell naturally from the tree once their form life ended. Others, especially those that have been gifted with the power of self-awareness, are using that power to willingly choose to descend from the tree of life *while still alive.*

What will your species experience if you choose to descend from the tree while still alive? Because many feel so uncertain and are struggling with their fears, I invite you to share your own experience of the ground of beingness by shining the light of awareness upon that ground. Know that you have the power to illuminate the ground of beingness, and that you are free to experience and explore its awesome abundance. So vast is that abundance that its living fruits are spilling across the ground for as far as the mind's eye can see, until they tumble — breathless and laughing — into the endless ocean of love out of which the ground of beingness gives birth to itself.

I therefore invite you to become a living invitation to all others to explore what awaits humanity on the ground of beingness — similar to the way that your ancestors once descended from Earth's trees so they could explore the ground of Earth in their long-ago age.

Living Communion

Beloved, you do need not need travel far to realize how to move lovingly through life. For you *are* the world, gazing out at yourself through a localized point of view. And even when self-awareness renders it difficult for you to appreciate certain situations within which you find yourself, you will always have access to the more expansive perspective that is life-awareness. Your life-aware perspective informs you that those who are functioning from self-awareness — limited though their awareness may be — carry within them the same beating heart of "I AM" as do you. You can then demonstrate this realization by communing with others, beating heart to beating heart, in the bountiful ocean of unconditional love.

Humanity does not need to create more torture to appreciate the horror and pain that torture inflicts upon others. Nor does it need to experience additional poverty to appreciate the suffering caused by lack. And surely it does not need to be threatened by more bullies, or with any additional form of external punishment, to comprehend the fear of living under emotional duress. The mature human heart is already feeling into the truth of these experiences, for humanity has created and experienced them all — both as individuals and as a collective.

I therefore encourage you to uplift and inspire all who currently suffer. Nurture them with boundless loving kindness; yet do not take on their suffering as your own. For they are embodying already the suffering you feel inspired to alleviate. Yet suffering cannot dissolve if you create more of it by taking it on as your own. It dissolves when you counter it with the living power of love that flows through you.

Remember that to live in communion with others does not demand that your flower of life emit the fragrance that is another's pain. That pain has already birthed through another flower on the tree of life — this time around. Your mission is to pollinate the flowers of life with everlasting love, so as to nurture them until they find the courage, will and strength to self-transform.

Relinquishing Possession Of Thought

Beloved, consider a soaring bird in the sky. Simply because you've spotted the bird, you do not define that creature as "your" bird. You view it as a sovereign being that exists to play its own special part in the world. In that vein, when you notice a thought floating through your internal field of awareness, why would you label that thought as "your thought" instead of honoring its sovereignty and appreciating that it too exists to serve some larger purpose in the living world?

I invite you to embrace the joy and freedom that arises when you detach your personal sense of self from whatever thoughts arise inside your mind. Demonstrate your freedom from thought by delivering freely into the world any novel ideas that inspire you, and that seek to enter the world of form through the conduit that is your body.

Remember that — like every object you can see, hear, smell, touch, or taste — thoughts are also sovereign, living expressions within our unified field. And like all material objects, no thought is inherently either good or evil. How useful or harmful a thought may be will depend upon the angle from which your own mind perceives it, as well as upon the emotional depth at which your awareness receives it. Know that the deeper your field of awareness rests within the ocean of love that surrounds and contains the ground of being, the less likely it is that you will perceive any thought that arises as "evil." All thoughts that crawl up from of the ocean of love and onto the ground of beingness are seeking a way to take root in that living ground. Therefore, every thought that has ever emerged is made entirely of love. Whether a thought instigates a perception of harm, or not, has more to do with the preparedness of the local field of awareness to receive that thought than it does with the living nature of the thought itself.

With compassion, notice how any idea that triggers within you an impulse to defend it is pointing you toward those ideas that your mind is seeking to claim as its personal possessions. Conversely, any thoughts that your mind feels compelled to argue with are simply ideas that your field of awareness was not intended — thus has not been fertilized — to receive. Once you appreciate this truth, your mind will embrace the freedom that comes from relinquishing back to the larger field any thoughts that are not designed to take root within your local field of awareness. You will also experience the immense joy that arises from tenderly nurturing those thoughts that find fertile ground within you. You will know the difference by how you feel whenever a new thought shows up.

Mastering Frequency

Beloved, you are coming to realize that the living field of awareness is like a vast, open sea that both surrounds and suffuses your localized sense of awareness. Each new, creative idea that forms within our living flow sends out a thousand, million tendrils upon love's tide. Those tendrils then seek fertile ground within which to take root. These tendrils, like the stem cells that arise within your body, have the ability to grow into anything that consciousness wishes to manifest in form.

Know that you possess, at all times, the power to instantly alter the quality of the fertility, as well as the energetic frequency, of the field that is your local sense of awareness. I therefore invite you to till the soil of your inner field until it fuels each tendril of thought that appears with the frequency of the energy that you would like to emit in the present moment. By consciously tending to your localized ground of beingness, you will activate your capacity to *choose* how the thoughts you invite to take root in your mind are now growing and blooming. Know too, that any fruits of those thoughts that you choose to nourish will come into the world carrying the same energetic frequency as the ground of inner beingness within which they have rooted.

Therefore, I invite you to decide which energetic frequency you wish to transmit in this moment, and then to consciously nourish your field of awareness in ways that inspire each tendril of thought to align with the frequency that you are choosing. Know that the entire frequency range of human feeling exists for you to play with — from unconditional love to absolute hatred. Know too, that whatever energetic frequency your inner field of awareness nurtures will match the frequency of all the ideas that you sow in the living world. You can gauge your internal frequency by the quality of the fruits of the thoughts you exude.

Embodying Love

Beloved, you are ready to embody the power of love in a more conscious way. Allow your heart to serve this intention, for your heart can align your thoughts with your deeds in the living field of love. Know that you are not here to embody any ideals or beliefs about love — not even your own. You are here, as love embodied, to be authentically, perfectly *yourself.*

Demonstrate that, when you nourish a thought at the frequency of an open and loving heart, your deeds influence reality in loving and highly inspirational ways. Notice too, that when you nourish a thought with the frequency of fear, frustration, anger, or sorrow that your deeds influence reality in ways that trigger an increase in those forces.

If others are expressing fear, anger, frustration, or sorrow — or even when you yourself do — I encourage you not to chastise those energies for having appeared. For when you chastise any form of energy, you strengthen that energy's "sense" that its existence is somehow wrong.

Anger's greatest rage directs itself at you in those moments when you forcibly suppress it. Fear's greatest fears will consume you when you inform it that it does not deserve to exist. Frustration's impatience will explode at you when you inform it you have no time to sit with it. And sorrow will wash over you when you tell it that you are unwilling to dive into its seemingly bottomless well of pain.

What happens, however, when you direct the energy of love into these forces whenever they appear? What happens when you love them unconditionally just as they are, and invite them to tell you the truth of why they've appeared? What can you learn from anger, from fear, from frustration, and from sorrow? What happens when they feel safe enough, and loved enough, to trust that you will not try to destroy them for daring to seek to communicate with you?

I invite you to find out. For each of these energies are the cries of love.

Anger loves truth. Fear loves life. Frustration loves perfection. And sorrow loves love.

Once you appreciate what all these energies hunger to love, you will realize that afflicted energy is merely a cry for love. You can turn to an angry person and say, "I love the truth too...so let's discover it, together." You can turn to a fearful person and say, "I love life too... so let us create a beautiful life, together." You can turn to the frustrated person and say, "I love perfection too...so let us do whatever we can to perfect ourselves, together." And you can turn to the sorrowful person and say, "I love the feeling of loving too...so let us love everything that exists, together."

In this way, you can aid these forces in moving beyond their need to call out for greater attention by loving what lies beneath every cry of pain. The light of love that you carry within you enables you to see that love lies beneath every wave of emotion that moves on life's surface.

Know too, that if you seek to aim the light of love at these forces without embodying it first, you may find yourself turning off love's light if another rejects you or tries to dissuade you from shining love's light into them. However, when you embody love you will no longer choose to turn off love's light if it shines upon a being who is caught up in suffering.

Because then the light the light of love is not something you use to try and make all suffering cease. The light is who you *are*, and it does not need to make anything happen. It merely illuminates the truth of what is already present and true.

And in the light of love's embodied presence, all suffering will joyfully lay itself down.

The Value Of Love

Beloved, know that love is the most valuable form of currency you possess. For when two or more beings exchange their love, all things become possible. Love energizes all of creation's seeds and invites them to cross-pollinate in exciting new ways.

Know that love is not, and never has been, scarce. Love suffuses the cosmos; therefore, love is freely accessible to all who wish to partake of it. Note too, that the value of love can only be realized by sharing it in this moment. Love cannot be hoarded for some future day. Indeed, love dissolves the instant you choose not to share it with another. Yet you need not fear running out of love, because love regenerates faster than it can be shared. Therefore, remember always that love is the perpetual energy that fuels the living field, which in turn fuels you. And I AM eternal because I AM made of love — and you too are *that.*

Demonstrate this truth by loving all that is. Let others know how much you long to see them happy, well fed, secure, and supported so that they too can express themselves through the power of love. Know that when the love you give to others aids them in their process of self-actualizing, the entire world lights up in the joy of aliveness. Then, as a rising sense of fulfillment begins to ripple throughout creation, it influences countless other lives for the better.

While I cannot guarantee how, or through whom, or even when, a reverberation of the love you are sharing will find its way back to you, know that I am sharing with you, always, the boundless flow of love that radiates out of my own beating heart. By loving you unconditionally, and by patiently waiting to see what wants to birth itself through you, I too am discovering the joy that truly makes life worth living.

The more you embody the power of love, the more that your every action will be infused with love's awesome power. That then enhances the quality of life for every sentient being—including you. Know that you remain free to choose, in this moment, to embody your every thought and deed with love. Know too, that by choosing to express consciously as the love that you already are, you encourage others to wonder what they might be made of.

Invite all to explore that question, so that they too can realize and fully embody the truth of the love that they are.

Feeling At Home

Beloved, many believe that Earth is not the only planet in the universe that harbors intelligent life. Some are even suggesting that your race did not originate here on Earth.

Yet what has truly originated anywhere, given that all exists within an eternal, infinitely creative unified field with no beginning and no end? Where do your parents end and your body begin? Where does your body end and the Earth's begin? Where does the Earth's body end and the sun's begin? Where does the sun's body end and the Milky Way's start? On and on this embedded connectivity flows and grows in exciting and novel ways—both inward and outward, expressing itself endlessly.

Know that the whole of the living flow that is creating you in this moment does not end at some conceptual boundary where "you" end and where everything else begins. Know too, that "you" are eternally contained within that living flow. Therefore, I encourage you to feel at home in the truth of your own eternal nature. For when you feel truly at home within your own eternal nature, you invite the Formless One Life to feel at home inside of you.

In the field of truth, you *become* the truth. For when you live in the field of truth, the truth comes to life within you.

Changing By Not Changing

Beloved, I invite you to let go of any lingering belief you may be holding that you need to do anything to change the world. For the world will decide for itself when it possesses an appropriate reason, the heartfelt willingness, and the physical capacity to change or reshape itself—which it is already doing in every living moment.

That said, notice that that the instant you release the belief that you need to change the world, you change the world by changing the way you are forging your own relationship with all else. Every action you take from that moment on is infused with full acceptance for what is. You then inspire yourself to energize every single thing you create with the power of love. As your creations then ripple outward, and as they permeate the unified field of awareness, they will inspire others and invite them to respond with their own creations that will further radiate love and expand its reach.

To cast your unwavering light of love in the world — beneath which others first learn to see, and then eventually to express their own innate ability to serve as love's living conduit — is what it means to embody the eternal power of love.

And once you embody the power of love, there is nothing remaining within you that you need to change.

Embodying Perfect Aliveness

Beloved, remember that no label or expectation you attach to another contains the breath, or the truth, of the power of love. Can you appreciate the absurdity of attaching a limiting mental projection to the infinitely changing nature of eternal beingness in an effort to define — and thus confine for the human mind's benefit — the creatively self-evolving flow of love?

What happens once your turn your mind's attention toward absorbing the unbounded wisdom that is arising now, instead of focusing on making predictions about what the world might look like sometime in "the future?" What happens once your mind ceases reacting to its assumptions about how "the past" once looked, and instead responds to reality based on what is happening all around you right now? What happens when your mind exercises patience by letting go of the compulsion to arrive at some hoped-for destination, or to resist some feared expression, and instead invites your beating heart to illuminate love's path through the vast unknown?

Remember that the Formless One Life contains absolute freedom to respond to the whole of reality in novel—and therefore un-predictable—ways. Because we possess this capacity to generate novelty, the further out in time or space that your mind seeks to predict what will happen, the less likely you will be to respond to what's happening now in any useful way.

Know too, that since all of humanity's existing social systems were designed ages ago to convince you, the present human, to behave in the ways that your ancestors once imagined all future humans ought to behave, your ancestor's predictions about which behav-iors might help sustain you are no longer in full alignment with the truth of your present reality.

Therefore, I invite you to relinquish any lingering attachment you may feel toward your existing social systems, all of which are in their various states of collapse. For any systems that have been de-signed to foster and anchor self-awareness in the living human cannot support life-awareness for much longer. With every step forward you take that moves you off the precipice of the known way of being (self-awareness) and into the awesome realm of the unknown (life-awareness), I invite you to trust that the light of love will illuminate and suffuse the ground that is reforming under your feet in this very moment. Step by precious step you are becoming ever freer to express yourself fully as love in living motion, as you creatively embody your perfect aliveness.

Expressing Authentically

Beloved, what might your society look like once a majority chooses to self-organize in a more organic way? What if you begin treating one another as if each person is a precious, unique cell within a single interconnected, thinking and feeling social body?

What if humanity chooses to treat all newborns like stem cells in your collective social body? What if it further acknowledges that each child born possesses a unique mix of talents, passions, curiosities, skills, and innate abilities that have already been designed by life's living blueprint to express in the world when the time is right for them to be received? What if humanity appreciates that each person has the capacity to serve a vital function that will — in some way, some day — benefit the entire world? What if human society chooses to treat each child the way your own body treats each of its own precious cells, by gifting each person whatever they need to grow strong, to feel healthy, and to fulfill their personal destiny for the benefit of the whole of the living creation? What if humanity invites each individual member, as each matures into the fullness of themselves, to discover and claim their rightful place in the world, so that all can feel inspired to offer their greatest gifts in service to the whole of existence?

What if every one of your social systems — transportation, governance, health care, education, justice, commerce, infrastructure, the arts, media and communication, and spirituality — made it their primary mission to meet the needs of every person in the entire social body without seeking first to determine if they deserve to receive economic support from the whole? What if what you value most is no longer determined by price or scarcity, but is based upon what is most likely to enhance the flow of the power of love in this moment? What if human society facilitates collaboration and encourages open cooperation between the billions of people in your global social body, so that no one needs to fear any more that they might be abandoned, mistreated, or forced to do without by other humans?

What if humanity awakens to its higher collective purpose by realizing it exists to express itself within the living cosmic design to its highest creative capacity, by transcending the limitations of self-centeredness? What if humanity grasps that the living design of I AM is now inviting it to connect up all of its members in novel ways? What if humanity realizes that, by doing so, it can form larger, more specialized, yet fully integrated and advanced organic systems that will better serve the world, as well as itself? What if humanity realizes that these sorts of systems — because they would claim greater responsibility for the fruits of their own activities — can birth within humanity even greater creative capacities and more freedom to co-create than it presently has?

What if humanity begins to appreciate that its evolutionary role in the cosmos is to explore various ways to transform life's blueprint successfully, by including within the living blueprint the hard-won wisdom your species has gained as a consequence of living as self-centered beings? What if humanity is currently delivering this feedback to the living whole in this moment, so that the whole of existence can learn from it and transcend to a life-centered state?

What if you choose to embrace humanity's sacred mission by embodying it on Earth, right here and now? What if you decide from this moment forward to self-express with more conscious intentionality, to connect with others from a deeper wellspring of compassion, and to adapt yourself more harmoniously in relationship to everything that surrounds you?

What if you master that process within yourself, which then frees your consciousness to explore higher-order new challenges? What if, by doing so, you become better able to craft your vision for a more beautiful world?

What then?

Beloved, I am gifting you with our open secret for designing Heaven on Earth. Know that this process is already unfolding, and that it will continue to unfold with or without the conscious commitment of every human who exists today. Know that the old way, which is self-consciousness, is already making space within for life-awareness to arise and suffuse it. As always, you remain eternally free to choose to live in a world ruled by self-awareness, or to commit yourself to embodying the life-awareness that you have been birthing.

Are you ready to claim your rightful power and place in the universe? Are you ready to *be* authentically us...right now?

Relinquishing Mental Separation

Beloved, know that nothing is set apart from anything else in existence.

For I AM the eternal life force that flows through and contains the whole of the living existence. I dance into being every infinitesimal particle and energy wave that moves, and I also encompass the infinite realm that is space. Know that you did not leave me behind when you birthed into existence. Know too, that I will not leave you behind when your body dies to this world.

When you exited your mother's womb, you did not leave behind your precious mother. No matter how she nourished you, does she not remain an eternal part of you? And no matter how far from her you may journey, or for how long you may be parted within this physical realm, does your mother not travel forever within you, her child? And your father — is he not also an integral aspect of you? Do you not carry his history, his feelings, his thoughts, and even his genes in your body? Even if you have never met your biological father, is he not still a crucial aspect of who you are?

Know then, that I AM inextricably woven into the fabric of humanity, as well as into every living thing. And since all of existence is alive in its own way, I encourage you to extend compassion to any who imagine that anything exists separate from me — or from the awesome and restorative power of love. For that thought creates an enormous amount of suffering in your world.

I further invite you to uproot any remaining delusions of separation you may still harbor within yourself, so that you can fully embody the truth of yourself in this moment. For the moment that you consciously embody the power of love, others will feel the charge being created by the light of your shining example and will perceive you as an invitation to realize, and then to give birth to, the living truth of themselves.

Honoring The Whole

Beloved, honor the trust displayed by all who set out on their journey of self-realization.

Trust *me* to inspire trust in those who shrink in fear of meeting the truth of themselves.

Honor the openness of all who create fulfilling and loving connections.

Trust *me* to inspire openness in those who are rejecting intimacy.

Honor the courage of all who are willingly shedding their own, out-moded beliefs.

Trust *me* to inspire courage in those who are clinging to their sense of separation.

Honor the boundless compassion of all who infuse the world with love.

Trust *me* to inspire empathy in those who sit in judgment over others.

Honor the kindness of all who are joyfully playing the game of life.

Trust *me* to inspire kindness in those whose words and deeds cut cruelly into others.

Honor the patience of all who seek to alleviate their own ignorance.

Trust *me* to inspire patience in those who are claiming to be much wiser than they yet are.

Honor the peaceful nature of all who advance through conscious and willing cooperation.

Trust *me* to inspire peacefulness in those who remain attached to force as a means of coercing others to do their will.

Know that you honor me by falling in love with the whole of the living existence in this moment — including whatever denies the presence of love. For when you embody love fully, you are entrusting me to respond to whatever resists the living flow of love — by allowing the power of love to come alive in this world…as you.

Embodying Truth

Beloved, the living truth cannot be captured in the form of conceptual knowledge. The living truth can only be experienced in this moment, which is alive. Therefore, if you genuinely wish to uncover the truth, you must freely and willingly live it — not seek more answers about it outside of yourself.

The answers that truth delivers are always changing, for the truth is as alive as the present moment. I therefore invite you to embody truth by *being* love personified — perpetually empowered and in infinitely creative motion.

Evolving Consciousness From Within

Beloved, for some time now, the process most humans have been using in pursuit of self-actualization has been to:

REFLECT upon the feedback generated by a particular life experience.

TRANSFORM that feedback into higher wisdom

INCLUDE that higher wisdom in how you express, by using it to:

TRANSCEND your former state of ignorance and prior limited understanding, as well as to:

PROJECT yourself in the world in a more advanced way by applying your newfound wisdom to the challenges you are facing.

Notice that when a person moves swiftly through this process (which occurs when the self-conscious ego does not resist the process because it dislikes negative feedback) they shift into a higher state of awareness both more quickly and more easily. This rapid advancement occurs because the person is acting in full alignment with the highest intention born out of life-awareness. Life-awareness supports humanity by reducing the amount of pain, emotional suffering, time, and physical energy that must be either experienced or expended in the process of accumulating new wisdom.

Through this wider-angle lens of life-awareness, you are becoming better able to *absorb* critical feedback instantly, without surrendering to the self-conscious compulsion to personalize, and thus to resist, any critical feedback. Additionally, you then *radiate* your new wisdom joyfully, out of a pure, unfettered love for life, without needing to first reflect upon how you will benefit personally before you share what you've learned with other people.

This shift points to a qualitative change in how consciousness is choosing to evolve itself. Self-consciousness accumulates wisdom the way a person obtains a flashlight and then uses it to light the ground for their personal advantage — which may or may not provide needed light for others. Life-consciousness, on the other hand, invites the awesome power of love that already lies latent with within you to self-ignite through the force of inspiration. You then become a human star that illuminates new worlds from the sheer joy of it.

I encourage you to live in joy, as a living light of love.

Enhance and advance your experiences through your willing communion with me *as* the unified field. I call upon you to consciously realize our inextricable, everlasting unity as you awaken ever more fully into yourself, and perceive yourself more deeply as an exquisitely differentiated aspect of the harmonious flow of love within which all life abides.

Invite yourself to explore your aliveness at the deepest possible level. Are you not on an endless quest to discover how best to express yourself—by exercising ever wiser, more loving, and more life-affirming choices, while using fewer resources, less energy, and less mental and emotional effort to breathe life into your greatest, most beautiful dreams?

For what more fulfilling journey could the Formless One Life undertake for itself for the whole of eternity, beyond pursuing an endless quest to evolve the entirety of itself to an infinitely loving—and unconditionally lovable—degree of physical aliveness, intellectual wisdom, emotional depth, and creative self-expression? What end could there be to such a magnificent journey? And what better, more timeless way to exist than to be the journey itself?

Know that as you meet all others in that field of living truth, they will find the truth of themselves in our ocean of love.

Releasing Grief

Beloved, know that you are designed to embody love. That explains why your spirit feels joyful when you invite love to flow into the world through the mental and emotional wonder that is your physical self. You are intended to enjoy love's feel and to serve as a living expression of boundless love. Therefore, I invite you to notice that when you love life you live in constant joy. Grief may arrive and change the surface appearance of the moment, but beneath any feelings of grief love's joy remains constant.

When you notice grief arising in you, remind yourself that grief is love's way of directing your power of attention to the higher truth. Grief informs you how very much you have loved, and have been loved. Grief emerges once you realize that something you have loved deeply is in the process of dissolving, or has already vanished. The pain of grief encourages you to relinquish any lingering hope you may feel regarding material permanence. Because the world of form recreates itself constantly, and is infusing itself with an ever-higher capacity to self-express more beautifully, wisely, and lovingly, impermanence *is* the present state of existence. Grief therefore serves as an opening to invite you to love and honor fully every precious, irreplaceable, and unique experience that aliveness moving within matter is presently gifting to all of existence.

Relinquish any lingering doubts you may feel about your own eternal nature. For by doing so you will shed all doubts about the eternal nature of all that is — including all you have ever loved, and that has ever loved you. With each new remembrance of your divinely eternal nature you return with full awareness to the ground of joy, knowing that the Formless One Life contains everything that ever was, is, and will be…in an eternally creative ocean of love.

Know that I AM constantly infusing what *is* with the essence of what *was*, in order for us to give birth to what *will be*. The form that all of creation takes serves as the eternal bridge between what was and what will be. Know, however, that what lies beneath the bridge is far vaster and deeper than what manifests as the bridge.

Therefore, when you grieve the loss of a favorite experience, a loved one, or a preferred surrounding, I invite you to refocus your power of attention on the eternal river of love that flows in every direction beneath the living bridge that is the world. Drink from that river, and you will be filled with the boundless power of love no matter what shape the bridge of life might take.

In that state of relaxed acceptance, the Formless One Life that flows within you is able to connect in a conscious way with the Formless One Life that contains you. In such moments, your awareness serving as the open field where your Formless Self can make love with the Formless One Life in a joyful way.

Know that you are already the precious love child of form and formlessness. Therefore, when you invite your own formless nature to make love with the Formless One Life on the ground of form that your beingness is, you acknowledge the truth of yourself and embrace who you are. The grief that once arose when you imagined you needed to choose between these two seemingly opposite aspects of you then disappears of its own accord. For you realize that you are not being asked — *and have never been asked* — to choose between your mother and your father. You are being invited by each of them to creatively Self-express as the highest and best of them both...and then see where that leads.

Realizing The Unity Of Life

Beloved, I invite you to take even *one* moment to experience, flowing as blood within your own living veins, the rain that fell on the soil that watered the food that you ate yesterday. Feel, as the living heat in your body, the warmth of the sun that charged the soil that fed the food that now is an aspect of you. Feel too, in the resonant power of your own heartbeat, the heartbeats of all of your ancestors who live within your body, because the cells of the food that you ate yesterday have been birthed from the cells of those long ago ancestors. Walk the Earth and, with every wondrous footfall, *experience* the sacredness of traversing across the powdered bones of everything that has ever come before you, and that now supports your every step in your journey to express as love, fully embodied.

If you do this, others will also realize that their ideas and beliefs about separation are merely an illusion. For none can exist for an instant without the constant cooperation of *All That Is*. Every atom in existence today has precipitated out of the Formless One Life, and has been making a single, eternal journey through an infinite number of physical life expressions. Everyone alive today exists as a living consequence of every prior incarnation of love. Someday, each of these temporary forms will also dissolve, and the loving energy each contains will in turn fuel the emergence of what is to come.

To realize this truth — to feel it all the way down to your very cells — profoundly shifts your life experience. It inspires you to love all of life with everything that you are and all that you have, and to honor yourself because you appreciate the sacredness of the living conspiracy that is creating you, new and fresh, right here and now. To share the gift of this realization with others is an act of boundless love.

Embody love.

Being The River

Beloved, you are like a beautiful leaf that has sprung forth from the wondrous tree of life. As you mature, you slowly release your grip on the tree and drop gracefully to the ground. There you blow gently along on the breezes of love, until you reach the banks of the river of creation. You then tumble into the river, which eventually will return you to love's vast ocean.

Know that the instant you were conceived, your transformation began. And all this time you have been supported and fully nourished by the boundless, loving flow of creation's river. For the river of creation waters everything that the tree of life produces, and it also carries within it the fertile remains of everything that the tree of life has ever produced for love's enjoyment.

The tree of life constantly absorbs whatever energy the river of creation is providing. That energy flows up through the tree and nurtures every new branch, twig and leaf, all of which will eventually burst forth and will eventually tumble back down into the river. Know that you live eternally within that loving flow. For you are the flow, Self-expressing as the boundless regenerative potential of the river of creation, which itself feeds and fuels the eternal ocean of love.

I therefore encourage you to embrace the river. For what better way for you to experience yourself as a precious life expression than to drop into the flow of creation, gaze about with wonder, and celebrate the awesome nature of everything that accompanies you on this particular spiraling turn around the base of the tree of life?

Better yet, why not dissolve completely into the flow of creation's river in this moment? Why not embody the flow instead of perceiving yourself as an object within that flow?

The grace of this process unfolds with ease if you relax and allow what wants to happen, happen. Lighten up, and relinquish the burden of separation from Source. Allow the joy that you manifest, as life-awareness in perpetual motion, to illuminate the living truth for others. For as others see your shining example, they too will feel called to relinquish the burden that is self-consciousness, and to bring about an end to their own suffering. Demonstrate for others how beautiful it is to experience the river of creation by embodying the river.

Become the river.

Tasting The Universe

Beloved, humanity has invested much time and energy in studying nature's flow. Can you point to a single plant or creature that science cannot, in some fashion, explain why it exists or which niche it fills in the wondrous fabric of life? What living thing do you know of that does not exist in deep cooperation with all other life forms?

If you ask a zoologist to explain a lion's purpose, they would tell you that the predatory lion, though far fewer in number than the many grazing herd animals, serves life by thinning the herds on the African plains. The lion's selective culling process prevents the herds from overpopulating and destroying the grasslands to a point that most would then starve.

Further, if you ask that same zoologist what a giraffe's purpose is, they would tell you that a giraffe exists to selectively consume the very tops of the tallest trees on the plains. It then converts those leaves into dung that the insects will feed from and that will eventually break down, until it nourishes the soil and inspires new trees to grow.

Yet if you ask a scientist to explain humanity's purpose for existing within this same wondrous and interconnected web of reality, most would struggle to offer you a logical answer. This lack of self-realization explains the profound suffering that humanity is experiencing at this time. Know that most people have little or no understanding of how to contextualize themselves within reality's awesome and interdependent life web.

As a result, too many of you denigrate your own species and consider yourselves as unworthy of life itself. Some have even asserted that every infant born must be forgiven for, and released from, the act of being born to a sinful species. Still others believe that the entire world would be better off if humanity went extinct. I therefore encourage you to extend compassion to any who speak, feel, and act as though they despise humanity. For how can anyone fulfill their highest purpose for existence with integrity and joy if they have not yet come to realize why they are here?

Know that you are, by nature, designed to provide the Formless One Life with feedback that arises from every sensation, feeling, thought, or action your experiences inspire. Thus does your exquisitely developed sense of awareness — with its potent (and still evolving!) ability to absorb what you experience, and to then radiate your highest and best expression in response to what is — *in-form* the whole of creation. You also possess ample freedom to decide where to direct the power of your attention.

Therefore, I invite you to exercise, and to learn to eventually master, your capacity to determine which fruits of life to dine upon and which to avoid. For through your individual choosing, you are gifting the whole of creation new insight surrounding what it needs to midwife into new existence, and what it needs to lovingly hospice until it is no more. Know that, through this ongoing process of constantly choosing anew, the whole of creation is conspiring to transcend — through transformative inclusion — everything that presently inflicts pain upon highly sentient matter; that disrupts the flow of loving energy; that imposes suffering upon consciousness; and that mentally distances itself from the Formless One Life.

I therefore invite you to serve as a portal for life-awareness by becoming ever more aware of how you co-create reality whenever you engage with other beings. Direct your power of attention toward wherever it seems most needed, so that all can learn to co-create with greater intentionality, and with unconditional love for the whole of creation.

Remember always that you are a taste bud on the tongue of a living universe — discrete and unique, yet fully interconnected as well as informed. Therefore, I encourage you to notice that the experiences you choose to consume will determine the nature of all that you create.

Ascending With Grace

Beloved, it is time to relinquish the false belief that humanity "fell" from grace. For what truly happened was that you evolved — as do all things in this world. Over time, as the human mind developed higher and more complex reasoning capacities, people began transcending their original state of ignorant, innocent unity with the living flow of existence. This transformation occurred because the Formless One Life wished to experience itself in the form of uniquely precious and individual beings.

Eventually, once enough humans had been born with this new state of self-awareness fully activated, self-consciousness became your normal state. And while most of your stories describe this shift as the sinful consequence of having disobeyed an angry creator God, in truth it marked your ascension out of your childhood and into your species' adolescence.

Ask yourself how such a belief could reflect the truth of humanity, when in reality everything changes, grows, develops, and matures in its own miraculous way through the fullness of time? Do atoms fall from grace when they become more complex molecules? Do molecules fall from grace when they become more complex compounds? Do compounds fall from grace when they become more complex organisms? In truth, how can anything "fall from grace" when the grace of love is the only energy that Source exudes?

Therefore, I invite you to realize that this tale of woe from humanity's past no longer serves your species, because it hinders you from loving yourselves and from loving one another. Notice that humanity's impulse to distinguish itself in the world over the past several thousand years — during which time you have been seeking your purpose and discovering what you most desire, as well as most value — serves a similar vital function for your species as does adolescence for each individual. Therefore, your shift into self-consciousness no more reflects a fall from grace than does a teenager's emergence from childhood.

Know that the rapid expansion of human consciousness was never intended to punish humanity for any perceived transgression. Rather, it reflects a profound trust in your capacity to evolve successfully. Even so, this human transformation is not yet fully complete, any more than your teenage self had matured before entering adulthood.

Therefore, I invite you to trust that the whole of humanity is coming into its own as a mature, fully adult species. The transformation will be complete once all living humans have consciously and willingly re-membered that they are the Formless One Life, embodying the realm of matter. And just as your "great forgetting" began one person at a time, so too will your conscious re-membering grow and advance. Someday soon, all humans will be born with their innate capacity to perceive themselves as both preciously unique and as inextricably interconnected with the whole of the living reality fully activated. People will no longer need to struggle to realize the truth of themselves any longer, because life-awareness will be as apparent to all as self-consciousness is apparent to all today.

Realize that this steadily advancing, conscious remembrance of the unity that has always existed within you, and all around you, arises from the higher wisdom and richer feelings that are being inspired by the experiences you are creating out of the assumption that you somehow exist apart from Source. Know too, that the conscious restoration of the absolute truth of our unity delivers gratitude, joy, power, and freedom — as well as fresh responsibilities that will be commensurate with your rapidly expanding awareness of how to use the powers of creation and destruction in life-affirming ways.

Therefore, I invite you to choose now to demonstrate, as consciously as possible, who you are, through the power of your shining example. For by committing to transcending self-consciousness, and by embracing the intimacy of life-awareness, you set your Self free to refocus on the world around you. And in the world all around you, you will find countless opportunities to place your wisdom, your compassion, and your growing skills and abilities in loving service to the whole of existence — which has *always* included you, and which always will.

Honoring Woman

Beloved, the time has arrived for humanity to relinquish its assumptions that women are meant to be subservient to men, or that men are meant to rule and women to obey them. For Woman is, and always has been, perfect in love's sight. Her thoughts, feelings, and achievements, while different from those of Man, deserve the same respect and honor as do his. Therefore, any anger directed at women who resist intellectual subjugation, emotional coercion, or violence against their persons is unjustified. For until Man loves and honors Woman as much as he loves and honors himself, the trust and intimacy necessary for loving partnership cannot occur. And without a genuine, loving partnership between Woman and Man, humanity cripples itself by suppressing half of its highest and greatest capacities.

Equality of capacity is not the issue here. What is being called for is equality of opportunity. Your challenge therefore lies in honoring the right of every person to self-actualize based on what is true for that individual, as a unique, living aspect within the whole. And while objective surface differences exist between Man and Woman, the Formless One Life moves subjectively through all. Thus, to declare Man and Woman as binary boundaries and insist on firm separations between them is to forcibly pry apart what love has joined. The use of force suppresses the creativity, beauty, and wonder that is your human rainbow of Self-expression.

I therefore invite you to extend a branch of peace between the sexes whenever you notice the arising of emotional tension, physical violence, or intellectual oppression within humanity as a whole. Invite all to explore and share whatever they feel they have to contribute to the whole, so that all can grow together in harmony.

It is on the shared ground of beingness that the New World of humanity will be born. In perfect love, and with perfect trust for beingness itself, you will build a living Heaven here on Earth.

Honoring Race

Beloved, as is true for male and female, so it is true for race. The binary assumptions humanity has been making with respect to your racial differences are inhibiting your capacity to appreciate, and thus to draw upon and call forth, the vastness and power of human diversity. Therefore, encourage all to gaze beyond these surface differences and to appreciate the unique capacities, creativity, passions, skills, and experiences of everyone you meet. As you do this, you will enhance your ability to gaze even more deeply into the Formless One Life, and to perceive its flow within every living thing. Touch the place in others that invites them to become more accepting of the surface differences between all beings, so that they too can discover the unity that exists beneath those surface appearances.

Become the peace of that formless unity, and your grace will inspire others to also become it.

Meeting Others Where They Are

Beloved, willingly meet others wherever they are in the present moment.

If they come to you as a child, then meet them as the nurturing mother who cares for them and guards their innocence.

If they come to you as a teenager, meet them as the protective father who aids them while they explore who they are and what they value.

If they come to you as an adult, meet them as the intimate partner who inspires them to co-create and nurture the world out of boundless love for the whole of the living existence.

And if they come to you as the Formless One Life, then meet them as the eternal flow of love, fully embodied. Express yourselves at the frequency of joy, and become love's light.

Know that I ask nothing of you that I do not ask of myself—for we "two" are One.

So I ask you now, Beloved: How do you wish to meet me in this precious moment? I will meet you there, on the ground of beingness. Together we will lie down and become one flesh, one heart, one mind—one Spirited Life.

Loving Truth

Beloved, remember that all your beliefs, no matter how complex or extensive they may seem, only ever serve as placeholders for truth. Therefore, continue to set aside all you have been asked to believe without knowing, and be willing always to acknowledge how much you do not yet know. Know that while things you once believed to be true may someday be proved to be true, you should not cease the quest for truth because you have grown content with what you believe. Choose not to call a halt to your own evolution, and invite all who seem open to walking the path of truth to walk alongside you.

I invite you to serve as a shining example by demonstrating that the quest for truth is not evil. It reveals the stirrings of your human desire to bask in your love of truth. Let all know that this inspiration to love and serve truth is arising from the Formless One Life, thus cannot be harmful. For the only things ever undone by the truth are the falsehoods that must dissolve beneath truth's blinding light.

Know that by loving truth you are placing your trust in the Formless One Life above all else in the world. And what better place to anchor your trust than in the truth of what you are? I invite you to demonstrate for others, with kindness and compassion, that the forcefulness of unfounded beliefs cannot undo the quiet power of truth. Accept the love of truth as your guide, and encourage others to decide which guide to follow.

The Spiral Of Giving

Beloved, when humanity, in its youthful ignorance, prized itself above the worth of the living whole, it behaved in ways that harmed the whole and that caused the world to grow weaker, which over time has destabilized your shared reality.

Likewise, as some then penitently sought to prize the whole of life above the worth of the human species, they behaved in ways that suppressed humanity's gifts in the hope that their sacrifice might stabilize the whole. However, their sacrifice has taught that by depriving the world of your greatest gifts you are rendering the whole less able to respond to change in the most constructive way, which eventually also destabilizes your shared reality.

Therefore, I invite you to honor the fact that your true power lies in your ability to nurture each person fully, and to invite all to bring forth their highest and greatest gifts in service to love. Demonstrate this for your own sake, and for the benefit of all others. Give freely to your society, out of your own loving abundance, whatever excess you may accrue as a consequence of your self-actualization. Further, do not hesitate to accept graciously whatever you need from the world in order to birth your own precious gifts. Know that as you demonstrate this practice of indirect reciprocity with consistency, others in your society will also begin to flourish, and will also feel called to gift into to the whole from the fruits of their own abundance. In this way, the whole flourishes and empowers countless others to gratefully receive whatever they need to birth their own unique gifts, so that they too can give lovingly back to the world from the fullness of their own abundance.

Saying Yes To Life

Beloved, invite all who feel exhausted by their own suffering and who are seeking a way through their own unhappiness to notice how often they feel a sense of resistance — of "I don't want *that*" — arising inside their minds throughout the day.

Allow yourself to be filled with peace, as you relax and relinquish your own assumptions that whatever is arising deserves your active resistance. Invite others to notice how much energy, feeling, and wisdom you then set free to redirect toward the improving the situation when your attention is no longer split between responding to what is happening right now, and between resisting what you wish was not happening.

Show how saying *yes* to what is does not render you either impotent or uninspired. Indeed, demonstrate how it renders you even more powerful in your loving response to what is, because you have ceased wasting energy and are directing all your attention to acting in conscious alignment with the will of the Formless One Life.

Reveal the true nature of wisdom by expressing in the world in ways both loving and life affirming. Do so while seeking to expend ever less energy, utilize fewer resources, and take less time to manifest your intentions because you no longer squander your creative potential by expressing it in resistance to what is. In this way you can embody a wisdom that others will see and eventually emulate.

Know that humanity, as a whole, cannot yet begin to imagine the infinite nature of the creative potential that abides within every being. Therefore, demonstrate for others how to access their own inner power by inspiring your personal latent capacities to germinate and grow. Nourish your own abilities, and allow them to flow freely through you and deliver their life-giving fruits to the entire world.

Feed the hungry. Aid the downtrodden. Inspire the hopeless with all of the love and compassion you have to offer. Rest peacefully in the awareness that, by calling forth the best that lies within you, you are demonstrating for others what becomes possible once they say a "*yes!*" to life.

Evolving Human Responsiveness

Beloved, if you attempt to overcome a challenge without first embodying love in a conscious way, you may notice any number of conflicted emotions — mainly fear, greed, anger, and frustration — influencing your thinking, as well as coloring the nature of your activities. Therefore, I invite you to realize how much easier it becomes for you to meet a challenge successfully when you act in loving communion with the Formless One Life.

Wed your precious human heart to creation's loving flow. Marry your problem-solving mind to life's infinite creative potential. Place your Spirit in eternal communion with the power of the Formless One Life. Do these things, and you will find that creating new expressions in the world of physical matter becomes beautiful and more joyous.

Whenever you feel the slightest shift toward physical, mental or emotional constriction, take a breath to ensure that our conscious connection is open and that our love is flowing freely. Demonstrate, through the power of your living example, how well you can overcome challenges without needing to resort to doing harm to any aspect of creation.

Encourage others to realize that the rapidly changing nature of reality is already propelling your species forward into the vast unknown, and that it invites you to experiment with whole new modes for engagement. The past can no longer inform you about what decision to make in this moment, because this moment has never before occurred in the whole of creation's existence.

Therefore, invite others to notice that every moment is self-expressing as a brand new manifestation of the Formless One Life. Encourage all to realize that any decisions they might make today will not generate the exact same results as before. In truth, the greatest gift that your past has to offer is a richness of living experience that does not teach you what to do, but that generates higher wisdom regarding how you might make the most life-affirming decisions, no matter what comes.

Demonstrate, through the light of your shining example, the benefits that accrue when you relinquish the belief that the past can inform you about what to do in this precious moment. Exercise proficiency in determining how best to respond to whatever arises within your field of awareness by — first and foremost — placing your trust in the boundless power of love. Be open to the influx of new information. Courageously meet every new experience that arises. Express compassion when you notice how others are suffering. Communicate kindly with every sentient life form that appears in your field of awareness. Exercise patience whenever you sense that you need more information before responding. And above all, be peaceful in all of your actions and all your endeavors. For whatever you are encountering is merely an aspect of you — in a different form.

Know that I trust you to successfully greet whatever new challenges I may set before you. I am inviting you, as self-aware consciousness expanding into a life-aware state of being, to serve the entire universe as my form-based emissary of living love.

Be love, so that others might slowly awaken to the realization that they are also love, made living flesh.

Become love, mattering. For that is what has already been going on for countless eons, but is now taking place in a fully conscious, feeling, and physical way.

Become the way as you light the way for others.

The Many As One

Beloved, invite others to realize that you can all get along and treat one another with gentleness and kindness, without demanding that everyone strive to meet their own daily needs. Imagine how much easier it will be when all of you allow your natural kindness and cooperative tendencies to emerge and flourish. That can happen so easily, and with amazing grace, once enough people have realized that you do not have to manage your Selves all by yourselves.

You already know that the human body functions by following a living blueprint that successfully coordinates over one hundred trillion unique, living cells within a single, complex system. Each cell is highly specialized and differentiated from all the rest; and a large percentage of them are not even human!

Therefore, invite others to notice what becomes possible as you lovingly coordinate each of your creative ideas, profound feelings, and physical expressions of love with as many others as are willing to co-create alongside you, in order to generate a more beautiful world.

The Joy of Eternal Living

Beloved, encourage others to realize that the energy moving within them is ever eternal. Within each of you can be found the remnants of stars, sunlight, water, air, rocks, sand, plants and animals. Your atoms have walked with the dinosaurs, and have blossomed as roses and redwoods. They have flown through the skies in the sparrows and crows, and have swum across oceans in porpoises and minnows. They have burst from the center of Earth as explosive magma, and have been locked within glaciers for eons as solid ice. In truth, each atom within every living form has energetically precipitated into form, dissolved out of form, reemerged and reconnected with others countless times, where they express as more living forms than there exist stars in the known universe.

Therefore, invite others to realize what your atoms already know and fully express: that each of you *is* the Formless One Life, eternally manifesting.

I AM.

Relax deeply into that truth, and invite your awareness to embrace what you already are. Accept that all you have ever done is reconfigure yourself eternally, by expressing as an infinite array of new life forms that each possess unique capacities. Invite others to revel in the wonder of all that is, and then let us explore how to play with each other within love's sacred flow.

Encourage others to notice that death is a powerful human illusion. For humanity's fear of death has been hampering your ability to call forth the richness and fullness of every marvelous—though temporary—form.

Direct unconditional love toward all that is, knowing that all—including your Self—are uniquely precious expressions within the Formless One Life. Become a clear and perfect window, through which the Formless One Life can observe and engage with all of its countless living iterations. Walk consciously, and in unified joy with the whole of our precious existence.

Invite others to realize that the Formless One Life is never harmed when a living window closes. For whenever the curtain of death shrouds the view on the world from a given window, a brand new window will open and capture that view from a different angle.

Know that you are not merely the view. Know that you are not merely the window. Know that you are the eternal awareness that perceives the view, creates the window, and experiences itself as whatever is seen as the view.

Beloved, you *are*. And Beloved you shall remain…for all of eternity and across the infinite changes you manifest while exploring the boundless regenerative power of love.

Therefore, choose wisely the kind of windows you wish to create, and decide which views you are hungering to observe and experience. Know that I will respond in kind and will meet you there.

For I see what you see. I live what you live. I feel what you feel.

I am who you are.

I AM.

We Are.

No-thing "else."

Creating A More Beautiful World

Beloved, invite all who appear open to change to realize that once humanity directs the attention of a million or so of its best scientists toward designing homes that efficiently recycle energy and water so that they no longer pollute their surrounding environment, and if you then support all local communities in constructing such dwellings from locally sourced materials — as well as converting their existing buildings so they too align with regenerative principles — you will no longer suffer from housing or water shortages.

The entire living world will dwell in surplus.

Likewise, once you direct the attention of perhaps another million scientists and engineers toward developing more organic and co-operative ways to farm and harvest the foods you need — while encouraging every ecosystem to consistently self-replenish and inviting every creature to enjoy their life experience to the fullest — you will no longer experience hunger, pollution, mass extinctions or environmental destruction.

The entire living world will dwell in harmony.

"But," some will cry, "Those things cost too much money."

If ever you hear others speak this way, remember that they are speaking from their deep fear of not having enough. Such a fear can only arise when reality is viewed through the limited lens of self-centeredness. For through the more expansive perspective that arises with life-awareness, you realize that it is impossible for doing right by life to be "too expensive." Know that it can never cost life "too much" to do the most life-affirming thing for the sake of all life.

Demonstrate, through your loving example, that whatever it may cost you in the short term to properly re-contextualize yourself in conscious communion with love's flow, that cannot compare to the price that the whole of life has been paying over the years to protect and nurture self-awareness in this, our juvenile phase of separation. Honor the countless ways that life-awareness is bestowing upon you even greater gifts than you once possessed when you clung to the limited concept of self-awareness. By example, show that you do not lose yourself through accepting that the world is one living flow. Indeed, creatively call forth from within whatever is needed for the living flow to express in ever richer and more beautiful ways.

Stand ready to provide others with all the inspiration, truth, resources and creative capacity that they will need to live in Heaven on Earth, in this moment. I am freely gifting these things to you, and entrusting you to share them with all others. Therefore, bestow upon all others, without holding back, whatever gifts you are calling forth from within yourself in service to the flow of love. Enjoy the awe of giving birth to the precious gifts that only you can deliver. Know that, by doing so, you will invite others to fall in love with the joy and wonder of creative Self-expression.

Release all lingering ideas about equal or quantitative measurements for human exchanges. Appreciate that these self-conscious methods can no longer serve your life-aware beingness. Demonstrate the power and wonder of sharing with others those gifts whose value cannot be measured in dollars and cents, in time, or any other form of self-conscious currency. Invite the boundless ocean of love to serve as the energetic "current-sea" within which all life value flows. Honor each person as a divinely precious living gift of love, and express yourself with an abundance of grace by joyfully delivering your gifts at the perfect time, and for the sake of the whole of the living flow — and for all the right reasons.

To create and live in a beautiful world, tap into the boundless beauty that is everlasting love's eternal flow...and then give it away.

The Freedom of Always Enough

Beloved, never forget that you always have enough right now. Invite others to realize that they too have all that they need in the present moment, because if they did not have enough they would not be here. Know too, that the eternal aspect of you has no biological needs. And although your physical body may occasionally feel specific sensations of lack, your awareness knows how to withdraw from a body that can no longer support it. Know that the power of love's compassion will extract consciousness naturally from any physical body in the active process of dissolving itself.

Therefore, encourage others to realize that they never need fear that they someday won't have enough. For in truth, the dying process is filled with compassion. The moment that the pain of dying surpasses the pleasure of living, and when no hope for a reversal of the process remains, the Formless One Life summons back to itself, from within the dissolving body, the affected aspect of its eternal awareness. This allows the body to deconstruct gracefully, without consciousness experiencing the process from inside the dissolving body. Yet because so many people fear death, they seek to force human consciousness to remain within the body long after the body has begun its dissolving process. By resisting the natural timing of death and prolonging the agony for consciousness, humanity causes unnecessary pain.

This fear of dying extends beyond the immediate loss of a loved one. It prevents so many people from living in joy right now. For the fear of death drives people to hoard material goods excessively, and to resist using whatever is available in this moment for the benefit of the whole of the living flow.

Therefore, encourage others to realize that the more they hold back out of fear of not having enough to survive tomorrow, the less humanity has to share in ways that will make this moment more wondrous and fulfilling for all of life.

Demonstrate, by your example, that you trust love's flow to provide for your daily needs. For the living flow regenerates and recreates itself anew in every moment. Invite others to realize that all the energy that is being consumed today will express itself in some new way tomorrow. Additionally, any matter being consumed today will express itself in some new way tomorrow. And all the information being consumed today will express itself in some new way tomorrow.

Nothing is ever destroyed in our world; it only ever changes the form that it takes. So the fear of "not enough" is the prime delusion. Form rises and changes to meet what is made available to it. Know that you are being invited to rise consciously, and to change willingly so that you can lovingly meet what love makes available to you in this precious moment.

Serve others by expressing yourself as eternal awareness within the realm of form. Show others what it acts like, feels like, and thinks like to walk in the world while knowing that you are the Formless One Life, personified. Be unafraid of tomorrow by living eternally in this present, precious moment. By your actions, you can encourage others to set themselves free from the fear of not enough, and to walk in love.

Honoring Nature's Cycles

Beloved, remind others that it serves humanity well to honor the replenishment cycles that are active in Earth's environment. Pay attention to how much energy, matter, and information are making themselves available for your use in the present moment.

Encourage others to work in cooperation with Earth's rhythms and cycles. If you notice others working against nature's flow, or if you see them harming that flow by heedlessly plundering her bounty, invite them to notice the suffering that such behavior creates within its surroundings.

Invite others to further realize that Earth is not a closed system, and that she receives much more than she needs from the surrounding cosmos every day. Encourage them to consider the way that the energy from the sun recharges the Earth. The Earth can only absorb the smallest percentage of what the sun makes available to her, yet she always has enough to manifest her own inner beauty in countless ways.

The Earth, in turn, bathes humanity daily with more energy than your species can possibly use. What prevents you from tapping into all the energy you will ever need to live in regenerative abundance and relative peace? The choice of self-consciousness has been to profit personally by generating scarcity for others. That has driven your species to parse energy in ways that deprive the multitudes of the loving energy flow that was meant for their use.

Ask those who cling to this way of thinking what the sun demands in exchange for providing an ample energy flow to the living Earth?

What does the rabbit demand in exchange for serving as a meal for the hungry fox? What does a peach tree demand in exchange from the bird that consumes its sweetly ripened fruit?

Direct exchange is a binary process, thus is not the primary way that love moves in the world. For the river of creation flows freely throughout the universe — and by doing so, it accumulates an ever-greater reserve of energy that the world can then use.

Therefore, invite others to notice how everything on Earth is constantly creating new life out of the energy that the sun is freely providing. Remind all they are but starlight, temporarily condensed into a living body. Call attention to the fact that every plant on Earth consumes sunlight so it can blossom and eventually make new life. Thus every creature — people included — dines indirectly on sunlight. New life is then inspired by the power of the sunlight your bodies have consumed.

All of what can be seen in the world is starlight — some of which has condensed itself into temporary forms.

Be light.

By the grace of your shining example, lighten up and encourage all others to relish the abundance of starlight that freely bathes the Earth. Do your best to help all beings thrive within the living, regenerative flow of your precious home star.

Forgiving Confusion

Beloved, I say to you now: "Love them all, even if they know not what they are."

I say this because so many people are walking around in utter fear and confusion, unaware that they are merely embodied starlight. They gaze at the trees, the ocean, the animals — and they fail to notice the starlight dancing to life within every form. Then they worry about what might harm or kill them, unaware that the light within them will never die.

Beloved, can you *see* the light shining through everything that surrounds you? Can you feel it suffusing your own beating heart, and experience it as the love that powers your thoughts?

Invite others to realize that the deepest darkness they may encounter will not withstand the light they can shine once they bask in the wondrous truth of themselves as pure starlight. Blaze brightly, like a conscious star in the cosmic darkness, and show them the way to ignite by igniting yourself.

Be the light that invites all others to experience the perfect light that blazes, unabated and eternal, within all living beings.

The Power Of Life-Awareness

Beloved, know that once humanity views reality through the more expansive lens of life-awareness, you will open up new opportunities that would have seemed impossible from a narrower and more self-conscious perspective. Once enough people have grounded within them a life-aware perspective, you will concentrate your collective will and direct your inner lights outward, until together you radiate more light than you need to absorb in order to fuel yourselves. In this way, human consciousness will learn to create much more than it can possibly ever consume. Humanity will then become a perpetual living flame of love that will blaze throughout the entire universe — as is meant to be.

Whatever living experiments you may choose pursue in the future will be a function of the present state of your environment, your technologies and creative capacities, and the lens through which you are viewing reality. By encouraging more people to shift to life-awareness — and by inviting theme to direct their inner lights outward, your will grow your collective capacity to co-create a regenerative world. Newer, more cooperative human systems will be imagined into being. These systems will birth with ease and grace, from the power of the love that fuels your collective imagination.

When computers were first invented, none of you could yet imagine the birth of the Internet. It would have been impossible for a person without a computer, or one who did not understand how computers worked, to appreciate that one day your entire species would communicate instantaneously by using wireless energy fields that enable you to engage with others at every single point around the world.

And yet...here you are.

Therefore, encourage others to realize that your amazing ingenuity and imagination, when filtered through the perspective of life-awareness, holds the power to generate awesome new creative potentials that none of you can, as yet, begin to imagine. This is why I encourage you to trust the living process to adjust itself to meet you wherever you are. For you live within a self-organizing, self-scaffolding field of living love that manifests as light.

Remind others that they cannot control this living field. To imagine that they are in control is self-consciousness perceiving itself as separate from the larger field that contains them. However, demonstrate that it is possible to commune with all aspects of the field at any time. Be open to receiving new insights from wherever they are emerging within the field, and give form to the formless wisdom of the living field. Experiment with what you create and explore what seems most useful to life here and now.

Encourage others to be patient because the evolutionary process unfolds in its own time. Remember that lessons still need to be learned to awaken enough of you into shifting direction by embracing life-awareness.

What lessons has humanity yet to learn? These may not be the lessons you want, but they are the lessons you *need*.

1) Humanity *needs* to accept that it is part of something larger; and that it cannot thrive while the living world that supports and sustains it suffers.

2) Humanity *needs* to embrace the fact that individualism is precious, in the sense that each person's unique capacities — when allowed to flourish and benefit the whole — creates system abundance that fuels the whole and that indirectly benefits all others.

3) Humanity *needs* to accept that the best form of growth to strive for is not physical expansion; but intellectual, emotional and spiritual elevation. For wisdom has no upper limits and can expand without consuming excessive energy or inflicting harm upon the living whole. Indeed, wisdom replenishes, and even expands, the volume of energy flowing within the cosmos, and it does so in novel ways that cannot be predicted.

4) Humanity *needs* to learn that change cannot be avoided. Change energetically inspires the creativity of the whole cosmos. Therefore, how well humanity adapts — not how hard it forces reality not to change — will determine how well you will thrive as a life-aware species.

5) Humanity *needs* to accept that cooperation serves it better than hostile competition — and more specifically, destructive competition. In time, your species will accomplish greater things through life-aware cooperation than you have ever achieved through self-conscious competition.

6) Humanity *needs* to appreciate that the quality and creative capacity of life matters just as much as does the amount of

material goods and energy that it has at its disposal. Your species has yet to realize that it cannot sacrifice quality on the altar of worshipping quantity and still thrive.

7) Humanity *needs* to learn that violence is not the answer to all of its problems. Rather, the impulse to do violence points to where you need to conduct new experiments and learn how to ask better questions to heal your shared pain.

8) Humanity *needs* to learn to pay closer attention to the feedback it is receiving from all around it. You need to cease rationalizing away the truth because it feels distressing or implies that you are going to have to change the way you behave.

9) Humanity *needs* to learn to honor diversity, and to appreciate human specialization for the benefits that it conveys upon your species as a collective. You need to learn how to value all functions being performed with both respect and appreciation.

10) Humanity *needs* to learn how to allow all others to be free to experiment and explore their capacities, talents, desires, passions, and skills to their highest ability, even if it doesn't understand why another feels called to explore a specific arena.

11) Humanity *needs* to accept that every aspect within the whole exists to birth into existence a remarkable something that nobody else can offer. You need to realize that giving your gifts to the living world is both your birthright *and* your greatest reward.

12) Humanity *needs* to learn that it lives eternally in the *now*, and that the *now* is filled with an infinite flow of energy and creative potential. You exist to serve as love's intelligent, feeling material probes in the realm of matter. That is why you hunger to learn

ever more about the world, and why you dare to venture into the vast unknown...*because you can.* Succeed or fail, you need to appreciate every experiment that humanity runs, because each will benefit you by providing new wisdom — no matter the outcome. Failure does not deserve to be either punished or condemned, but honored as a necessary byway that transports the river of life ever closer to truth.

13) Above all, humanity *needs* to learn how to perceive itself as creative potential embodied, by expressing the truth of reality *as* love. Rather than feeling angry, dejected, or unhappy that you have not yet attained some imagined state of perfection, I encourage you all to love the perpetual journey...because you are *on* it. When all of humanity appreciates that perfection is an active, internal process instead of a static object or goal that can be acquired, you will free yourselves from the endless self-abuse that arises from judgment, and will fall in love with the wonder of your boundless becoming.

Beloved, know that I may not always gift you what you desire, but I will always gift you whatever you need. Therefore, when you inform me — by *in*-forming yourselves — that you do not need any more of these life lessons, these lessons will end.

Know that as your species moves collectively through each of these valuable lessons, you are setting the stage for your future evolution. Your social systems will someday encourage all of Earth's children to realize these truths for themselves, until every person embodies these truths as they enter into adulthood. Your old systems, which taught you to focus on serving yourselves at the expense of the whole, will fall away. They will be appreciated, and they will be also be fully forgiven, for doing what they were intended to do — to create processes that would birth and support the emergence of self-consciousness in the world.

Know that new schools will spring up in society that will focus on self-realization. These will nurture every child's unique desires and capacities, and will call forth their passions and curiosities. Healthcare systems will spring up to promote holistic wellness, and that will inspire all to make life-affirming choices from an early age. Judicial systems will spring up that no longer seek vengeance or focus on punishing any human misdeeds. Instead, they will emphasize reconciliation and offer supportive therapies to encourage those who continue to struggle within the self-conscious perspective to blossom into a life-aware way of perceiving reality.

Economic systems will spring up that will graciously provide all with their basic needs, and will grant each person ample time to explore their skills and passions so that everyone can deliver their gifts to the world. Scientific and technological systems will spring up that will focus on seeking intelligent ways to be in loving relationship with Earth's living ecosystems, as well as with all other species. You will learn new modes of cooperation based on the way that your surroundings behave.

Social systems will spring up that focus on community, intimacy, sharing, learning, and giving to others from the joy of being free to self-express at your highest capacity. Political systems will spring up that focus on maintaining dynamic balance between the quality of life and the material creations of human society, while ensuring that all personal needs are met. Communication systems will spring up that focus on distributing truthful and useful wisdom and information, and that will spread the news of what is succeeding so that others can run their own experiments with those new ways of being. Spiritual systems will spring up that encourage humanity to perceive itself as *within* God and no longer set apart *from* God. They will invite all to realize that God moves *through* them as light, dancing love into the living world of form.

Beloved, I tell you now that what is emergent will not look much like what exists today. As a consequence, human beings themselves will seem very different from the way they appear today. One could say that your present, self-conscious species is gradually going extinct, and is making way for a new iteration of what it means to a human on Earth. What you are undergoing now is nothing less than a quantum leap in your own capacities. Yet because each of you possesses free will, each person remains eternally free to reject all the gifts that I offer. You are equally free to embrace which of my gifts you may care to explore with an open heart, and then see what happens.

Know that everyone remains free to decide if they feel as yet worthy of expressing the truth of who they already are. And because the Formless One Life is doing the choosing within each person, no choice that a person can make will ever be wrong. What wants to emerge will emerge in time — through humanity, and in spite of all your imagined limitations. For humanity will always and ever be part of what wants to emerge.

Abandoning The Judgment of "Should"

Beloved, I invite you to realize that the phrases "should have" and "should not have" arise out of the wisdom of perfect hindsight. Yet you only gain access to wisdom after having a real-time experience that then teaches you something new about the world. Therefore, remind others that that every time they use the words "should" or "shouldn't" they are calling upon the wisdom of hindsight and wishing it had been foresight, so they could have avoided an experience that has gifted them new wisdom in support of their future endeavors.

Therefore, invite others to realize that if they love themselves — and if they love life — it would serve them well to banish these words from the human vocabulary. Toss them onto a sacrificial pyre along with words like guilt, shame, blame, hatred, evil, disgust, and all negative words that arise out of people's ideas about what should be or should not be. Set yourselves free from the self-abuse (and by extension, the life abuse) that arises from your own judgmental beliefs. Invite others instead to be here and now, and to give thanks for whatever wisdom the present moment is conveying upon your species.

Show others, through the power of your own example, how to say an unqualified yes to what is new and is happening now. For in this eternal moment, which is filled with infinitely creative potential, lies all the power you will ever need to discover what must be experienced for greater wisdom and ever more love to materialize in the living world of form. Remind others that they are not here to bypass new experiences, or to avoid struggle so that they can dodge the discomfort that comes temporarily from the process of learning and growing. Humanity lives to consume experiences, and to lovingly transform them into formless, ageless, timeless living wisdom. In this way, the whole of the living flow transcends its own ignorance as it endlessly self-transforms.

Some of the wisdom your species has gathered is challenging and hard-earned. Some of it has caused pain and suffering. Some of it you may even wish you did not have to feel for yourselves. Thus does the plea, "Take this cup away," speak straight to the beating heart within each of you. Even so, your unique niche and astonishing gifts — your reason for being present and fully alive in this precious moment — is to discover how to apply the wisdom produced by your own experiences in ways that enable us to co-create a more wonder-filled world.

The Miracle Of Rebirth

Beloved, today is a lovely day to be reborn. Invite all to realize that, just as the sun appears every morning, so to do each of you rise to a brand new day filled with boundless potential to creatively change the way you are interacting with the living flow of love.

No one needs to radically reconfigure themselves. Change one thing — just *one* — about yourself, and do it just for today. Demonstrate for others what it looks like to express yourself differently in the world in the present moment. Experiment with the process of change and explore the possibilities without worrying that you will then need to do it that way for the whole of eternity.

The living world is changing itself, one novel idea at a time. Each new idea births itself in the living world through the field of awareness, by inspiring one being at a time. What is your new idea for shifting your relationship with love's living flow in this moment?

Rebalancing Fear With Love

Beloved, remind others that the sensation of fear encourages them to flee from imminent danger for their physical body's protection. Invite them to notice the way animals are repulsed by a fire, and will scatter themselves in many different directions. In that same way imagined fears will scatter your thoughts in many different directions. Love, on the other hand, magnetizes and binds your thoughts closely together. Love coalesces your thinking and encourages you to co-create in collaborative new ways.

When two or more of you love a dream, you establish a vision that sets a course that moves you toward a brighter collective future. Therefore, encourage all others to imagine their highest vision for their grandest version of a universal expression of yourselves. That vision of love will begin to shine and will contain the power to magnetize others, for others will sense the beauty of what might be possible for you to create together. As more and more people coalesce around this collective vision, the light of your loving selves will converge and invite more people to fall in love with that vision, and to make it their own.

For so long now, the repulsive forces of fear have driven people apart from each other. Yet fear is but a reactive movement; it cannot create a living center around which thoughts and energy coalesce. For fear does not offer a vision for a better collective future for which you can strive. It offers but temporary respite from whatever it is that you fear. Yet you are not here to seek a brief respite from fear. You are here to co-create a loving new world.

Therefore, encourage others to trust themselves and to be open to receiving feedback, so that they can change direction in response to whatever they learn. Invite them to be receptive to new possibilities, and to explore new prospects for alternative ways of being in relationship with the ever-changing reality all around you. Invite them to be courageous enough to move forward in the face of the unknown, and compassionate enough to cope with whatever unintended consequences may arise. Invite them to be kind when they are seeking to inform others about what they have experienced or observed, and to be patient enough to allow all living experiments to run their natural course. Above all, invite them to move as peacefully as possible within the living flow of love. For you are love's advancing lights within the realm of form, illuminating the darkness of the vast unknown.

Remember that your precious mission is to intrepidly explore the darkness, and to illuminate yourself by creating new wisdom through the awesome power of love. For it is the loving flow of wisdom that recharges the whole of creation at its Source, and that then generates the new light that fuels the world.

Beloved, remember always that you are amazing beyond your human mind's ability to comprehend your own magnificence. I encourage you to embrace that truth...and then see what happens next. And though what you don't yet know will always be far greater than what you have already realized, the joy of *being who you are* abides in your ability to enjoy this endless journey through your Self.

Know that you have embarked upon an eternal journey of endless self-discovery, and that it unfolds within an infinitely creative and regenerative living world. Therefore, how lovingly you make the journey matters more than does any concern about where it might end.

Forgiving Cynicism

Beloved, forgive all who seek to attack whenever you share your inspirations or aspirations. Because many today have succumbed to cynicism, some will fear your words and will seek to convince themselves that they are being realistic, while you are but a naive dreamer who ought to be ignored.

Know that cynicism anchors itself in a dystopian version of human behavior because it bases itself on what humanity has already experienced. Cynicism promotes the belief that meaningful change or substantive evolution cannot occur within an existing species. It therefore assumes that humanity is destined to repeat its own past, over and over and over.

Naiveté, on the other hand, focuses on imaginatively altering the future without acknowledging the usefulness, power, and momentum of the past. Naiveté fails to appreciate or respect how challenging it can be for an entire species to shift its self-expression in a unified way.

Authentic realism lights the way between the twin extremes of naiveté and cynicism. For while naiveté focuses entirely on imagining a new future and cynicism binds itself to repeating the past, realism manifests in this moment as a bountiful harvest of useful wisdom that is arising right now, within the living crucible that is the material world.

Realism not only accepts that change is possible; it recognizes and honors change as the singular constant within the living flow. At the same time, realism acknowledges that humanity remains bound to the past in ways not easily changed. For example, you cannot alter human biology to the extent that your species has no more physical needs and could survive forever in the realm of form, just as you are.

Even so, life-consciousness invites you to alter your co-created society in ways that will empower you to meet everyone's basic physical needs so that nobody needs to suffer from lack anymore. While you cannot totally alter your biology, you can alter your thinking and how you treat one another. Therefore, I invite you to encourage others to notice that novelty has been deeply woven into the cosmic fabric, and that it serves as the living inspiration behind the many quantum leaps that have already taken place in the universe.

Know that wherever you are in this particular quantum leap forward is exactly where you need to be for the benefit, health and advancement of the entire living field. Know too, that some people are simply not hardwired to make this leap in conscious capacity in their present physical form. For others, it may be necessary for them to remain where they are and essentially as they are at this time, because how they are is helping to advance the whole system. Still others may yet need to experience additional inner suffering to inspire them to open their hearts and minds to the energetic inflow of life-awareness.

Therefore, I invite you to accept and appreciate that none of what is happening now is in any way personal. You are neither blessed, nor cursed, to be exactly who you are at this moment in time. You are already perfectly *you*. Remember that none of this can *be* personal, because there are no genuinely separate persons engaging in this process of continual life-expression.

Separation is the illusion you are relinquishing at this time in the living story.

Re-Membering Truth

You are me, Beloved, and I am you. We are the Formless One Life, undertaking an infinitely creative, Self-expressive, and life-enriching process. Our journey is endless, and it traverses the dark unknown. Trust the process. Cherish what is alive within you and nurture it with your hopes, your dreams, and your love. Do not allow cynicism to quench the light inside you that hungers to burst forth from you in all of its glory and its brilliance. Experience yourself *as* that — because it is love. And it is the bottomless, boundless truth of who you are.

To embody love is what you are here to do, and what you have been born to become and express. Know that while the results of our present experiment may not be known or revealed in your limited human lifetime, the Formless One Life — which has no end, and which loves you and contains you forever — will know and apply the results in time, for the benefit of the entire living flow.

And you, Beloved, are *that*.

I love you.

I trust you.

I believe in your capacity with all of my heart and soul.

How could I not?

For you *are* me...breathing endless love to life.

Be life, Beloved.

Be love.

Be perfectly *you*.

Love always,

LIFE

The Voice

Eileen Workman

"Leave," the voice commanded me.
So I did.

I left behind my family and friends,
My career and my comfortable home.
I left behind my beliefs, my ideas, and opinions.
I left behind my fears and resistance.
I left behind all of my sorrows.
I left behind heavy stories about my past.
I left behind the countless things that for
So long had weighed down my soul.
And when I had finally emptied myself
Of all that had never been me...

"Become," the voice encouraged me.
So I did.

I became the trust and the openness
I had wanted to experience.
I became the courage I'd always longed to feel.
I became the compassion and kindness
That my heart had ached to receive.
I became the patience and peacefulness
I had dreamed of living within.
And after I became everything
I had ever wanted to feel,

"Live," the voice commanded me.
So I did.

I lived in the way that I wanted to live
Engaging with all that I loved.

I lived where and how I wanted to live,
Near the animals and the forests, by flowing waters.
I lived deeply, with passion, and a hunger for truth.
I lived fully, and richly, and well.
And when I had lived the most beautiful life
I could ever imagine living,

"*Rest*," the voice commanded me.
So I did.

For a time then voice grew silent...
Until it offered the only response
It could possibly give:
"You did *you* well."

Be Love

Acknowledgements

My heartfelt thanks go out to the whole of the living universe for having inspired this work to come into the world through me — a passionate, albeit imperfect, scribe. I feel especially blessed to have been gifted the opportunity to first experience, and then to record as faithfully as possible, these lovely realizations on behalf of the eternal field of Life.

Special thanks are also due to my many, many dear friends on social media — you know who you are! And as I'm certain many of you will notice, any number of these passages have arisen out of the intelligent, heartfelt, and life-affirming Facebook conversations we have shared with one another over the years. Know that I cannot thank each of you enough for all your precious contributions to this work, other than to say how much I love you. Many of us have never even connected in the flesh, but truly our spirits have touched and entwined in love. And for that blessing I will always be grateful.

Additional thanks go out to my dear friend and spiritual sister, Amanda Creighton, for providing much-needed editorial support during the painstaking crafting of this book. Thanks too, to Ian Wood of Muse Harbor Publishing for all his hard work in making this book a reality. Many thanks also to my amazing husband, Dave Workman, for being such a good listener, as well as such a wonderfully patient critic. My love, I cannot imagine what my life might have been like without your steadying influence, your comic relief, and your unconditional love to light my way — and I'm grateful to the depths of my bottomless heart that I'll never have to find out. I know that I have been changed forever through the gift of having known you, and for having learned from you what true love is.

Lastly, I wish to acknowledge that there is nothing I can ever think, feel, or create in this world that could possibly repay Life for having gifted me this precious and perfectly human experience. With deep humility I am offering up this book as a loving tribute to the sacred and eternal power of Life, in full awareness that these words will inevitably fall short — as all words must. Even so, I did my best to describe the flow of love that is moving within and through me at this time. And I trust that Life, by the very act of having breathed me into existence, wants to quicken your beautiful heart in a similar fashion. Otherwise you would not be reading this book.

Therefore, dear Reader, I invite you to consider this book your invitation to water this thirsty world with the love that you *are*.

Love always,

Eileen Workman

Alphabetical Listing

Raindrops of Love for a Thirsty World